Dianna Menadeo
8-19-88

BERLITZ®

POR… E
fo…

By the staff of Berlitz Guides

How best to use this phrase book

● We suggest that you start with the **Guide to pronunciation** (pp. 6–10), then go on to **Some basic expressions** (pp. 11–16). This gives you not only a minimum vocabulary, but also helps you get used to pronouncing the language.

● Consult the **Contents** pages (3–5) for the section you need. In each chapter you'll find travel facts, hints and useful information. Simple phrases are followed by a list of words applicable to the situation.

● Separate, detailed contents lists are included at the beginning of the extensive **Eating out** and **Shopping guide** sections (Menus, p. 39, Shops and services, p. 97).

● If you want to find out how to say something in Portuguese, your fastest look-up is via the **Dictionary** section (pp. 164–189). This not only gives you the word, but is also cross-referenced to its use in a phrase on a specific page.

● If you wish to learn more about constructing sentences, check the **Basic grammar** (pp. 159–163).

● Note the **colour margins** are indexed in Portuguese and English to help both listener and speaker. And, in addition, there is also an **index in Portuguese** for the use of your listener.

● Throughout the book, this symbol ☛ suggests phrases your listener can use to answer you. If you still can't understand, hand this phrase book to the Portuguese-speaker to encourage pointing to an appropriate answer.

● Sometimes you will find alternatives for words given in brackets [ ]. These are the expressions used in Brazil.

Library of Congress Catalog Card No. 86-70987

Second revised edition – 2nd printing 1987 Printed in Hungary

Contents

Travelling around 65

Sightseeing 80

Relaxing 86

Making friends 93

Shopping guide 97

Acknowledgments
We are particularly grateful to Amélia Jeandrevin for her help in the preparation of this book, and to Dr. T.J.A. Bennett who devised the phonetic transcription.

Guide to pronunciation

The imitated pronunciation used in this book should be read as if it were English except for any special rules set out below. It is based on Standard British pronunciation, though we have tried to take account of General American pronunciation also. Of course, the sounds of any two languages are never exactly the same; but if you follow carefully the indications supplied here, you'll have no difficulty in reading our transcriptions in such a way as to make yourself understood. Letters written in **bold** should be read with more stress (louder) than the others.

Brazilian Portuguese differs from the Portuguese spoken in Portugal in several important respects. Brazilian speech is slower and the words are less linked together than in Portugal. Unstressed vowels sound clearer when spoken by Brazilians, while in Portugal they're rapidly slurred over; **s** and **z** at the end of a syllable tend to be pronounced like **s** in sit and **z** in razor (rather than like **sh** in **sh**ut or **s** in pleasure). Vowel groups or diphthongs are often simplified.

Consonants

Letter	Approximate pronunciation	Symbol	Example	
f, l, p, p, t, v	as in English			
b	as in English, but often less decisive, especially between vowels	b	**boca**	**boa**ker
c	1) before **a, o, u,** or a consonant, like **k** in **k**ill	k	**casa**	**kah**zer
	2) before **e** and **i**, like **s** in **s**it	s	**cedo**	**say**doo
ç	like **s** in **s**it	s	**começar**	koomer**ssah**r
ch	like **sh** in **sh**ut	sh	**chamar**	sher**mahr**

d	as in English, but often less decisive, especially between vowels	d	**dia**	**deeer**
g	1) before **a**, **o** and **u** or a consonant, like **g** in **go**, but often less decisive, especially between vowels	g/gh	**garfo** **guia**	**gahr**foo **gheeer**
	2) before **e** and **i**, like **s** in plea**s**ure	zh	**gelo**	**zhay**loo
h	always silent		**homem**	**om**mahng^y
j	like **s** in plea**s**ure	zh	**já**	**zhah**
lh	like **lli** in mi**lli**on	ly	**olho**	**oal**yoo
m	1) when initial or between vowels, like **m** in **m**et	m	**mais**	**mighsh**
	2) between a vowel and a consonant, or if the last letter of a word, it indicates that the vowel is nasalized, but the **m** is then generally silent*	ng ng^y	**tempo** **tem**	**tayng**poo **tayng^y**
n	1) when initial or between vowels, like **n** in **n**o	n	**novo**	**noa**voo
	2) in a consonant group and in plural endings it nasalizes the preceeding vowel, but the **n** is then generally silent*	ng ng^y	**branco** **homens**	**brahng**koo **om**mahng^{y}sh
nh	like **ni** in o**ni**on	ny	**vinho**	**vee**nyoo
q	like **k** in **k**ill	k	**querer**	ker**rayr**
r	strongly trilled as in Scottish speech	r	**rua**	**roo**er
s	1) when initial, after a consonant or written **ss**, like **s** in **s**it	s/ss	**saber**	ser**bayr**
	2) between vowels (not necessarily in the same word), like **z** in ra**z**or	z	**casa**	**kah**zer
	3) when final, or before **c**, **f**, **p**, **q**, **t**, like **sh** in **sh**ut	sh	**país**	per**eesh**
	4) elsewhere, like **s** in plea**s**ure	zh	**cisne**	**seezh**ner

* See "Nasal vowels" and "Semi-nasalized diphthongs".

x	1) generally like **sh** in **sh**ut	sh	**baixo**	**bigh**shoo
	2) in **ex**- before a vowel, like **z** in razor	z	**exacto**	iz**zah**too
	3) sometimes like **x** in exit	ks	**táxi**	**tah**ksi
z	1) when initial or between vowels like **z** in razor	z	**zero**	**zeh**roo
	2) when final or before **c, f, p, q, s** or **t**, like **sh** in **sh**ut	sh	**feliz**	fer**leesh**
	3) elsewhere like **s** in pleasure	zh	**luz da**	loozh der

Vowels

a	1) like a mixture of **u** in cut and **ar** in party	ah	**nado**	**nah**doo
	2) when unstressed or before **m, n** or **nh**, but not in the same syllable, like **a** in about	er*	**porta**	**por**ter
e	1) when stressed generally like **e** in get	eh	**perto**	**pehr**too
	2) when stressed sometimes like **a** in late**	ay	**cabelo**	ker**bay**loo
	3) when unstressed, like **er** in other	er*	**pesado**	per**zah**doo
	4) at the beginning of a word and in certain other cases, like **i** in hit	i	**exacto** **antes**	iz**zah**too **ahng**tish
é	like **e** in get	eh	**café**	ker**feh**
ê	like **a** in late**	ay	**mês**	maysh
i	1) when stressed like **ee** in seed	ee	**riso**	**ree**zoo
	2) when unstressed, like **i** in coming	i	**final**	fin**nahl**
o	1) when stressed, like **o** in rod	o	**fora**	**for**rer
	2) sometimes when stressed or unstressed, like **o** in note** (most common **o**-sound)	oa	**voltar** **Lisboa**	voal**tahr** lizh**boa**er
	3) when unstressed, usually like **oo** in foot	oo	**caso**	**kah**zoo

* The **r** should not be pronounced when reading this transcription.
** But a pure vowel, not a diphthong.

ô, ou	like **o** in **note**, but a pure vowel, not a diphthong	oa	**pôs**	poash
u	1) generally like **oo** in **soon** 2) silent in **gu** and **qu** before **e** or **i**	oo	**número** **querer**	**noo**merroo kerrayr

Diphthongs

A diphthong is two vowels pronounced as a single vowel sound, e.g., in English **boy** there is a diphthong consisting of **o** plus a weak **i** sound. In Portuguese diphthongs, **a, e** and **o** are strong vowels and **i** and **u** are weak vowels. In diphthongs the strong vowels are pronounced with more emphasis than the weak ones, e.g., **ai** is pronounced like **igh** in **sigh,** and **au** like **ow** in h**ow.** Sometimes the weak vowels can combine to make a diphthong. In the word **muito,** the diphthong **ui** is pronounced nasally (oong^{y}). This is the only example in the language of a semi-nasalized diphthong. Apart from these generalizations the exact pronunciation of Portuguese diphthongs is not easy to predict.

Nasal vowels

These are pronounced through the mouth and through the nose at the same time, just as in the French nasal vowels (e.g., in the French b**on**) and quite similar to the nasal twang heard in some areas of America and Britain.

ã, am, an	something like **ung** in l**ung**, or like **an** in French d**an**s	ahng	**maçã**	mer**ssahng**
em, en	something like **ing** in s**ing**, but recalling also the **a** in late	ayng	**cento**	**sayng**too
im, in	a nasalized version of the **ee** in f**ee**t	eeng	**cinco**	**seeng**koo
om, on	like **orn** in c**orn**cob or like **on** in French b**on**	awng	**bom**	bawng
um, un	a nasalized version of the **oo** in f**oo**t	oong	**um**	oong

Semi-nasalized diphthongs

In these, the first element is nasalized and combined with a weak **i** (pronounced like **y** in **yet**) or **u** (pronounced like **w** in **was**).

ãe, ãi, êm, final **en(s)**, usually final **em**				
	pronounced as **ã** followed by **y** in **yet**	ahng^{y}	**mãe** **sem**	mahng^{y} sahng^{y}
ão, final unstressed **am**				
	pronounced as **ã** followed by **w** in **was**	ahng^{w}	**mão**	mahng^{w}
õe	pronounced as **orn** in **corn-cob** or as **on** in French **bon,** followed by **y** in **yet**	awng^{y}	**põe**	pawng^{y}

Stress

1) If a word ends with **a, e** or **o,** the stress falls on the next to the last syllable, e.g., **rosa** (pronounced **ro**zzer). Plural endings **m** and **s** are generally disregarded.

2) All other words are stressed on the last syllable, e.g., **animal** (pronounced erni**mmahl**).

3) Words not stressed in accordance with these rules have an accent (´or `) over the vowel of the stressed syllable.

Pronunciation of the Portuguese alphabet

A	ah	**G**	zhay	**N**	ehn	**T**	tay
B	bay	**H**	ergah	**O**	oa	**U**	oo
C	say	**I**	ee	**P**	pay	**V**	vay
D	day	**J**	zhotter	**Q**	kay	**X**	sheesh
E	eh	**L**	ehl	**R**	ehr	**Z**	zay
F	ehf	**M**	ehm	**S**	ehss		

The letters **k, w, y** occur only in foreign names and their derivatives, as well as in certain abbreviations.

Some basic expressions

Yes.	**Sim.**	seeng
No.	**Não.**	nahng^{w}
Please.	**Por favor/Se faz favor.**	poor fervoar/ser fahsh fervoar
Thank you.	**Obrigado(a)*.**	oabriggahdoo(er)
Thank you very much.	**Muito obrigado(a)*.**	moong^{y}too oabriggahdoo(er)
You're welcome.	**De nada.**	der nahder
That's all right. (Don't mention it.)	**Não tem de quê.**	nahng^{w} tahng^{y} der kay

Greetings *Saudações*

Good morning.	**Bom dia.**	bawng deeer
Good afternoon.	**Boa tarde.**	boaer tahrder
Good evening.	**Boa noite.**	boaer noyter
Good night.	**Boa noite.**	boaer noyter
Good-bye.	**Adeus.**	erdehoosh
See you later.	**Até logo.**	erteh loggoo
This is Mr. ...	**Apresento-lhe o Senhor ...**	erprerzayngtoo lyer oo sinnyoar
This is Mrs./Miss ...	**Apresento-lhe a Senhora/Menina [Senhorita] ...**	erprerzayngtoo lyer er sinnyoarer/merneener [sinnyoareetah]
How do you do? (Pleased to meet you.)	**Muito prazer em conhecê-lo(la).**	moong^{y}too prerzayr ahng^{y} koonyerssay loo(ler)
How are you?	**Como está?**	koamoo ishtah
Very well, thanks. And you?	**Muito bem, obrigado(a). E você?**	moong^{y}too bahng^{y} oabriggadoo(er). ee vossay

*In the case where there are masculine and feminine forms of a word, we give the masculine first, with the feminine in parentheses afterwards; in this example, a woman would say **obrigada**.

How's life?	**Como vai isso?**	koamoo vigh **ee**ssoo
Fine.	**Bem.**	bahng^{y}
I beg your pardon?	**Como disse?**	koamoo **dee**sser
Excuse me. (May I get past?)	**Com licença.**	kawng li**ssayng**ser
Sorry!	**Desculpe!/Perdão!**	dish**kool**per/perr**dahng**^{w}

Questions *Perguntas*

Where?	**Onde?**	**awng**der
How?	**Como?**	**koa**moo
When?	**Quando?**	**kwahng**doo
What?	**O quê?**	oo kay
Why?	**Porquê?**	poor**kay**
Who?	**Quem?**	kahng^{y}
Which?	**Qual?**	kwahl
Where is ...?	**Onde é/fica ...?**	**awng**der eh/**fee**ker
Where are ...?	**Onde são/ficam ...?**	**awng**der sahng^{w}/ **fee**kahng^{w}
Where can I find/ get ...?	**Onde posso encon-trar/arranjar ...?**	**awng**der **po**ssoo ayng-kawng**trahr**/errahng**zhahr**
How far?	**A que distância?**	er ker dish**tahng**syer
How long?	**Quanto tempo?**	**kwahng**too **tayng**poo
How much?	**Quanto?**	**kwahng**too
How many?	**Quantos*?**	**kwahng**toosh
How much does this cost?	**Quanto custa isto?**	**kwahng**too **koosh**ter **eesh**too
When does ... open/ close?	**Quando abre/ fecha ...?**	**kwahng**doo **ah**brer/**fay**sher
What do you call this/that in Portuguese?	**Como se chama isto/ aquilo em português?**	koamoo ser **sher**mer **eesh**too/er**kee**loo ahng^{y} poortoo**gaysh**
What does this/that mean?	**O que quer dizer isto/aquilo?**	oo ker kehr diz**zayr** **eesh**too/er**kee**loo

* For feminine and plural forms, see grammar section page 160 (adjectives).

Do you speak ...? *Fala ...?*

Do you speak English?	**Fala inglês?**	fahler eeng**glaysh**
Does anyone here speak English?	**Há aqui alguém que fale inglês?**	ah erkee ahl**gahng**y ker **fah**ler eeng**glaysh**
I don't speak (much) Portuguese.	**Não falo (bem) português.**	nahngw **fah**loo (bahngy) poortoo**gaysh**
Could you speak more slowly, please?	**Pode falar mais devagar, por favor?**	**po**dder fer**lahr** mighsh derver**gahr** poor fer**voar**
Could you repeat that?	**Pode repetir?**	**po**dder rerper**teer**
Could you spell it?	**Pode soletrar?**	**po**dder sooler**trahr**
Please write it down.	**Escreva, por favor.**	ish**kray**ver poor fer**voar**
Can you translate this for me?	**Pode traduzir-me isto?**	**po**dder trerdoo**zeer** mer **eesh**too
Please point to the ... in the book.	**Por favor, mostre-me ... no livro.**	poor fer**voar mosh**trer mer ... noo **lee**vroo
word	**a palavra**	er per**lah**vrer
phrase	**a expressão**	er ishprer**ssahng**w
sentence	**a frase**	er **frah**zer
I understand.	**Compreendo*.**	kawng**pryayng**doo
I don't understand.	**Não compreendo*.**	nahngw kawng**pryayng**doo
Do you understand?	**Compreende?***	kawng**pryayng**der

Can/May ...? *Pode ...?*

Can I have ...?	**Pode dar-me ...?**	**po**dder dahr mer
Can we have ...?	**Pode dar-nos ...?**	**po**dder dahr noosh
Can you show me ...?	**Pode mostrar-me ...?**	**po**dder moosh**trahr** mer
I can't.	**Não posso.**	nahngw **po**ssoo
Can you tell me ...?	**Pode dizer-me ...?**	**po**dder di**zzayr** mer
Can you help me?	**Pode ajudar-me?**	**po**dder erzhoo**dahr** mer

* In Brazil: **Entendo/Não entendo/Entende** (ayng**tayng**doa/nawngw ayng**tayng**doa/ayng**tayng**di).

Can I help you?	**Posso ajudá-lo(la)?**	possoo erzhoodah loo(ler)
Can you direct me to ...?	**Pode indicar-me a direcção para ...?**	podder eengdikkahr mer er dirrehssahng perrer

Wanting ... *Desejos ...*

I'd like ...	**Queria ...**	kerreeer
We'd like ...	**Queríamos ...**	kerreeermoosh
What do you want?	**O que deseja?**	oo ker derzayzher
Give me ...	**Dê-me ...**	day mer
Give it to me.	**Dê-mo.**	day moo
Bring me ...	**Traga-me ...**	trahger mer
Bring it to me.	**Traga-mo.**	trahger moo
Show me ...	**Mostre-me ...**	moshtrer mer
Show it to me.	**Mostre-mo.**	moshtrer moo
I'm looking for ...	**Estou à procura de ...**	ishtoa ah prokkoorer der
I'm hungry.	**Tenho fome.**	taynyoo fommer
I'm thirsty.	**Tenho sede.**	taynyoo sayder
I'm tired.	**Estou cansado(a).**	ishtoa kahngsahdoo(er)
I'm lost.	**Perdi-me.**	perrdee mer
It's important.	**É importante.**	eh eengpoortahngter
It's urgent.	**É urgente.**	eh oorzhayngter

It is/There is ... *É/Está/Há ...*

It is ...	**É/Está* ...**	eh/ishtah
Is it ...?	**É/Está ...?**	eh/ishtah
It isn't ...	**Não é/Não está ...**	nahng^{w} eh/nahng^{w} ishtah
Here it is.	**Aqui está.**	erkee ishtah
Here they are.	**Aqui estão.**	erkee ishtahng^{w}
There it is.	**Aí está.**	eree ishtah
There they are.	**Aí estão.**	eree ishtahng^{w}

* See grammar section page 162 (verbs).

There is/are ...	**Há ...**	ah
Is/Are there ...?	**Há ...?**	ah
There isn't/aren't ...	**Não há ...**	nahng^{w} ah
There isn't any.	**Não há nenhum (nenhuma).**	nahng^{w} ah ni**nnyoong** (ni**nyoo**mer)
There aren't any.	**Não há nenhuns (nenhumas).**	nahng^{w} ah ni**nnyoongsh** (ninnyoomersh)

It's ... *É/Está ...*

big/small	**grande/pequeno***	**grahng**der/per**kay**noo
long/short	**comprido/curto**	kawng**pree**doo/**koor**too
quick/slow	**rápido/lento**	**rah**piddoo/**layng**too
hot/cold	**quente/frio**	**kayng**ter/**free**oo
full/empty	**cheio/vazio**	**shay**oo/ver**zee**oo
easy/difficult	**fácil/difícil**	**fah**ssil/dif**fee**ssil
heavy/light	**pesado/leve**	per**zah**doo/**leh**ver
open/shut	**aberto/fechado**	er**behr**too/fi**shah**doo
right/wrong	**certo/errado**	**sehr**too/i**rrah**doo
old/new	**velho/novo**	**veh**lyoo/**noa**voo
old/young	**idoso/jovem**	i**ddoa**zoo/**zho**vvahng^{y}
next/last	**próximo/último**	**pro**ssimmoo/**ool**timmoo
beautiful/ugly	**lindo/feio**	**leeng**doo/**fay**oo
free (vacant)/ occupied	**livre/ocupado**	**lee**vrer/okkoo**pah**doo
good/bad	**bom/mau**	bawng/mow
better/worse	**melhor/pior**	mi**llyor**/pyor
early/late	**cedo/tarde**	**say**doo/**tahr**der
cheap/expensive	**barato/caro**	ber**rah**too/**kah**roo
near/far	**perto/longe**	**pehr**too/**lawng**zher
here/there	**aqui/aí**	er**kee**/er**ee**

Quantities *Quantidades*

a little/a lot	**um pouco/muito**	oong **poa**koo/**moong^{y}**too
few/a few	**poucos/alguns (algumas)**	**poa**koosh/ahl**goongsh** (ahl**goo**mersh)
much/many	**muito/muitos**	**moong^{y}**too/**moong^{y}**toosh
more/less	**mais/menos**	mighsh/**may**noosh
more than/less than	**mais que/menos que**	mighsh ker/**may**noosh ker
enough/too	**bastante/demasiado**	bersh**tahng**ter/dermer**zyah**doo

* For feminine and plural forms, see grammar section page 160 (adjectives).

A few more useful words *Outras palavras úteis*

at	a, em	er, ahng^{Y}
on	sobre	soabrer
in	em	ahng^{Y}
to	a	er
after	depois (de)	derpo^{Y}sh (der)
before (time)	antes (de)	ahngtish (der)
before (place)	em frente (de)	ahng^{Y} frayngter (der)
for	por, para	poor, perrer
from	de	der
with	com	kawng
without	sem	sahng^{Y}
through	através (de)	ertrervehsh (der)
towards	para, cerca de	perrer, sayrker der
until	até	erteh
during	durante	doorahngter
next to	ao lado de	ow lahdoo der
near	perto de	pehrtoo der
behind	atrás (de)	ertrahsh (der)
between	entre	ayngtrer
since	desde	dayzhder
above	acima (de)	ersseemer (der)
below	abaixo (de)	erbighshoo (der)
under	debaixo (de)	derbighshoo (der)
inside	dentro	dayngtroo
outside	fora	forrer
up	para cima	perrer seemer
upstairs	em cima	ahng^{Y} seemer
down	para baixo	perrer bighshoo
downstairs	em baixo	ahng^{Y} bighshoo
and	e	ee
or	ou	oa
but	mas	mersh
not	não	nahng^{W}
never	nunca	noongker
nothing	nada	nahder
none	nenhum, nenhuma	ninnyoong, ninnyoomer
very	muito	moong^{Y}too
too (also)	também	tahngbahng^{Y}
yet	ainda	ereengder
only	só	saw
soon	em breve	ahng^{Y} brehver
now	agora	ergorrer
then	então	ayngtahng^{W}
perhaps	talvez	tahlvaysh

Arrival

Passport control *Controle de passaportes*

Here's my passport.	**Aqui está o meu passaporte.**	erkee ishtah oo mehoo persserporrter
I'll be staying ...	**Fico ...**	feekoo
a few days	**alguns dias**	ahlgoongsh deeersh
a week	**uma semana**	oomer sermerner
a month	**um mês**	oong maysh
I don't know yet.	**Ainda não sei.**	ereengder nahng^{w} say
I'm here on holiday.	**Estou aqui de férias.**	ishtoa erkee der fehryersh
I'm here on business.	**Estou aqui em [a] negócios.**	ishtoa erkee ahng^{y} [ah] nergossyoosh
I'm just passing through.	**Estou de passagem.**	ishtoa der perssahzhahng^{y}

ALFÂNDEGA
CUSTOMS

After collecting your baggage at the airport (*o aeroporto*—ow erehro**ppoar**too) you have a choice: use the green exit if you have nothing to declare. Or leave via the red exit if you have items to declare (in excess of those allowed).

artigos a declarar
goods to declare

nada a declarar
nothing to declare

I've nothing to declare.	**Não tenho nada a declarar.**	nahng^{w} taynyoo nahder er derklerrahr
I've ...	**Tenho ...**	taynyoo
a carton of cigarettes	**um pacote de cigarros**	oong perkotter der siggahrroosh
a bottle of ...	**uma garrafa de ...**	oomer gherrahfer der
It's for my personal use.	**É para uso pessoal.**	eh perrer oozoo persswahl

O seu passaporte, por favor.	Your passport, please.
Tem alguma coisa a declarar?	Do you have anything to declare?
É favor abrir este saco.	Please open this bag.
Tem de pagar direitos por isto.	You'll have to pay duty on this.
Tem mais bagagem?	Do you have any more luggage?

Baggage—Porter *Bagagem—Carregador*

Porter!	**Carregador!**	kerrerger**doar**
Please take this luggage.	**Por favor, leve esta bagagem.**	poor fer**voar leh**ver **ehsh**ter ber**gah**zhahng^{y}
That's mine.	**Essa é a minha.**	**eh**sser eh er **mee**nyer
That's my bag/ suitcase.	**Esse é o meu saco/ Essa é a minha mala.**	**ay**sser eh oo **meh**oo **sah**koo/ **eh**sser eh er **mee**nyer **mah**ler
One piece is missing.	**Falta um volume.**	**fahl**ter oong voo**loo**mer
Please take this/my luggage to the ...	**Por favor, leve esta/ a minha bagagem até ...**	poor fer**voar leh**ver **ehsh**ter/er **mee**nyer ber**gah**zhahng^{y} er**teh**
bus	**ao autocarro [ônibus]**	ow owto**kkah**rroo [**oa**nibbooss]
taxi	**ao táxi**	ow **tah**ksi
Where are the luggage trolleys (carts)?	**Onde estão os carrinhos da bagagem?**	**awng**der ish**tahng**^{w} oosh ker**ree**nyoosh der ber**gah**zhahng^{y}

Changing money *Câmbio*

Where's the currency exchange office?	**Onde fica a agência de câmbio?**	**awng**der **fee**ker er er**zhayng**syer der **kahng**byoo
Can you change these traveller's cheques (checks)?	**Pode trocar estes cheques de viagem?**	**po**dder troo**kahr aysh**tersh **sheh**kersh der **vyah**zhahng^{y}
I want to change some dollars/pounds.	**Quero trocar dólares/libras.**	**keh**roo troo**kahr** **do**llersh/**lee**brersh

BANK—CURRENCY, see page 129

| Can you change this into escudos/cruzados? | **Pode trocar isto em escudos/cruzados?** | podder trookahr eeshtoo ahng⁽ʸ⁾ ishkoodoosh/kroozahdoass |
| What's the exchange rate? | **Qual é o câmbio?** | kwahl eh oo kahngbyoo |

Where is ...? *Onde é ...?*

Where is the ...?	**Onde é ...?**	awngder eh
booking office	**a marcação de lugares**	er merrkerssahng⁽ʷ⁾ der loogahrersh
duty-free shop	**a free shop**	er "free shop"
newsstand	**o quiosque [a banca] de jornais**	oo kyoshker [ah bahngkah] der zhoornighsh
restaurant	**o restaurante**	oo rishtowrahngter
How do I get to ...?	**Como posso ir para ...?**	koamoo possoo eer perrer
Is there a bus into town?	**Há um autocarro [ônibus] para o centro da cidade?**	ah oong owtokkahrroo [oanibbooss] perrer oo sayngtroo der siddahder
Where can I get a taxi?	**Onde posso apanhar [pegar] um táxi?**	awngder possoo erpernyahr [paygahr] oong tahksi
Where can I hire a car?	**Onde posso alugar um automóvel?**	awngder possoo erloogahr oong owtoomovvehl

Hotel reservation *Reserva de hotel*

Do you have a hotel guide?	**Tem um guia de hotéis?**	tahng⁽ʸ⁾ oong gheeer der ottehish
Could you reserve a room for me at a hotel?	**Podia reservar-me um quarto num hotel?**	poodeeer rerzerrvahr mer oong kwahrtoo noong ottehl
in the centre	**no centro**	noo sayngtroo
by the sea	**à beira-mar**	ah bayrer mahr
a double/single room	**um quarto duplo/individual**	oong kwahrtoo dooploo/eengdivviddwahl
not too expensive	**não muito caro**	nahng⁽ʷ⁾ moong⁽ʸ⁾too kahroo
Where is the hotel?	**Onde é o hotel?**	awngder eh oo ottehl
Do you have a street map?	**Tem uma planta da cidade?**	tahng⁽ʸ⁾ oomer plahngter der siddahder

HOTEL/ACCOMMODATION, see page 22

Car hire (rental) *Aluguer de automóveis*

To hire a car you must produce a valid driving licence (hel for at least one year). Some firms set the minimum age a 23, others at 25. Holders of major credit cards are normall exempt from deposit payments, otherwise you must leav a substantial (refundable) deposit for a car. Third-part insurance is usually automatically included.

I'd like to hire (rent) a ... car.	**Queria alugar um automóvel ...**	kerr**ee**er erloo**gahr** oong owtoo**mo**vvehl
small	**pequeno**	per**kay**noo
medium-sized	**de tamanho médio**	der ter**mer**nyoo **meh**dyoo
large	**grande**	**grahng**der
automatic	**automático**	owtoo**mah**tikkoo
I'd like it for a day/ a week.	**Queria-o por um dia/uma semana.**	kerr**ee**er oo poor oong **dee**er/**oo**mer ser**mer**ner
I want to leave it in ...	**Quero deixá-lo em ...**	**keh**roo day**shah** loo ahng^{y}
Are there any week-end arrangements?	**Há condições especiais de fim-de--semana?**	ah kawngdi**ssawng^{y}sh** ishper**ssyighsh** der feeng der ser**mer**ner
Do you have any special rates?	**Há tarifas especiais?**	ah ter**ree**fersh ishper**ssyighsh**
What's the charge per day/week?	**Qual é o preço por dia/semana?**	kwahl eh oo **pray**ssoo poor **dee**er/ser**mer**ner
Is mileage included?	**A quilometragem está incluída?**	er killoomer**trah**zhahng^{y} ish**tah** eeng**klwee**der
What's the charge per kilometre?	**Qual é o preço por quilómetro?**	kwahl eh oo **pray**ssoo poor ki**llo**mmertroo
I want full insurance.	**Quero um seguro contra todos os riscos.**	**keh**roo oong ser**goo**roo **kawng**trer **toa**doosh oosh **reesh**koosh
How much is the deposit?	**De quanto é o sinal?**	der **kwahng**too eh oo si**nnah**
I've a credit card.	**Tenho um cartão de crédito.**	**tay**nyoo oong kerr**tahng^{w}** der **kreh**dittoo
Here's my driving licence.	**Aqui está a minha carta de condução [carteira de motorista].**	er**kee** ish**tah** er **mee**nyer **kahr**ter de kawng-doo**ssahng^{w}** [kahr**tay**rah di moatoa**reest**ah]

CAR, see page 75

Taxi *Táxi*

In Portugal, taxis are usually found at taxi ranks. Rural taxis, marked "A" for *aluguer,* are not normally metered, but follow a standard-fare table based on mileage. All Brazilian taxis have meters.

Where can I get a taxi?	**Onde posso apanhar [pegar] um táxi?**	**awng**der **po**ssoo erper**nyahr** [pay**gahr**] oong **tah**ksi
Please get me a taxi.	**Chame-me um táxi, por favor.**	**sher**mer mer oong **tah**ksi poor fer**voar**
What's the fare to ...?	**Qual é o preço do percurso [da corrida] para ...?**	kwahl eh oo **pray**ssoo doo perr**koor**soo [dah koar**ree**dah] **per**rer
How far is it to ...?	**A que distância fica ...?**	er ker dish**tahng**syer **fee**ker
Take me to ...	**Leve-me ...**	**leh**ver mer
this address	**a este endereço**	er **aysh**ter ayngder**ray**ssoo
the airport	**ao aeroporto**	ow erehro**ppoar**too
the town centre	**ao centro da cidade**	ow **sayng**troo der si**ddah**der
the ... Hotel	**ao Hotel ...**	ow o**ttehl**
the railway station	**à estação dos caminhos de ferro [estação ferroviária]**	ah ishter**ssahng**^{w} doosh ker**mee**nyoosh der **feh**rroo [istah**ssahng**^{w} fehrro**vvyah**ryah]
Turn left/right at the next corner.	**Vire à esquerda/ à direita na próxima esquina.**	**vee**rer ah ish**kayr**der/ ah di**rray**ter ner **pro**ssimmer ish**kee**ner
Go straight ahead.	**Vá sempre em frente.**	vah **sayng**prer ahng^{y} **frayng**ter
Please stop here.	**Páre aqui, por favor.**	**pah**rer er**kee** poor fer**voar**
I'm in a hurry.	**Estou com pressa.**	ish**toa** kawng **preh**sser
Could you drive more slowly?	**Pode conduzir mais devagar?**	**po**dder kawngdoo**zeer** mighsh derver**gahr**
Could you help me carry my luggage?	**Pode ajudar-me a levar a bagagem?**	**po**dder erzhoo**dahr** mer er ler**vahr** er berga**hzh**ahng^{y}
Could you wait for me?	**Pode esperar por mim?**	**po**dder ishper**rahr** poor meeng
I'll be back in 10 minutes.	**Volto daqui a 10 minutos.**	**voll**too der**kee** er 10 min**noo**toosh

TIPPING, see inside back-cover

Hotel—Other accommodation

Early reservation and confirmation are essential in major tourist centres during the high season. But if you're stuck without a room, go to the tourist information office (*turismo*—too**reezh**moo). You'll find one in most towns.

Hotel (ot**tehl**)	There are five official categories for hotels in Portugal and Brazil; you may still find price variations within the same category, depending on the location and the facilities offered.
Pousada (poa**zah**dher)	A state-owned inn (Portugal) in the regional style, located near places of interest to tourists. It's comfortable and serves good food. You're allowed to stay for only 5 days during high season.
Estalagem (ershter**lah**zhayng)	Similar to the pousada, but more expensive; a privately-owned inn.
Motel (mot**tehl**)	Increasingly found, especially in Brazil.
Pensão (payng**sahng**[w])	Corresponds to a boarding house. Usually divided into three categories: luxury, first class and second class.
Pousada de juventude (poa**zah**der der zhoovayng**too**dher)	Youth hostel (Portugal). You'll find Y.M.C.A. *(Associações Cristãs de Moços)* accommodation in Lisbon, and a few youth hostels on the coast.

Furnished flats (apartments) or bungalows are available through specialized estate agents.

Can you recommend a hotel/a boarding house?	**Pode recomendar-me um hotel/uma pensão?**	podder rerkoomayng**dahr** mer oong ot**tehl**/**oo**mer payng**sahng**[w]
Are there any flats (apartments)/villas vacant?	**Tem apartamentos/ casas para alugar?**	tahng[y] erperrter**mayng**toosh/**kah**zersh perrer erloo**gahr**

Checking in—Reception *Recepção*

My name is ...	**O meu nome é...**	oo **mehoo noa**mer eh
I've a reservation.	**Mandei reservar.**	mahng**day** rerzerr**vahr**
We've reserved two rooms.	**Reservámos dois quartos.**	rerzerr**vah**moosh doysh **kwahr**toosh
Here's the confirmation.	**Aqui está a confirmação.**	er**kee** ish**tah** er kawngfirrmer**ssahng**w
Do you have any vacancies?	**Tem quartos vagos?**	tahngy **kwahr**toosh **vah**goosh
I'd like a ... room ...	**Queria um quarto ...**	ker**reeer** oong **kwahr**too
single	**individual**	eengdivvid**wahl**
double	**duplo**	**doo**ploo
with twin beds	**com duas camas**	kawng **doo**ersh **ker**mersh
with a double bed	**de casal**	der ker**zahl**
with a bath	**com banho**	kawng **ber**nyoo
with a shower	**com duche**	kawng **doo**sher
with a balcony	**com varanda**	kawng ver**rahng**der
with a view	**com vista**	kawng **veesh**ter
We'd like a room ...	**Queríamos um quarto ...**	ker**reeer**moosh oong **kwahr**too
in the front	**para a frente**	perrer er **frayng**ter
at the back	**para as traseiras [nos fundos]**	perrer ersh trer**zay**rersh [noass **foong**doass]
overlooking the sea	**com vista para o o mar**	kawng **veesh**ter **per**rer oo mahr
It must be quiet.	**Tem de ser tranquilo.**	tahngy der sayr trahng**kwee**loo
Is there ...?	**Há ...?**	ah
air conditioning	**ar condicionado**	ahr kawngdissyoo**nah**doo
heating	**aquecimento**	erkehssi**mmayng**too
a radio/television in the room	**rádio/televisão no quarto**	**rah**dyoo/terlervi**zzahng**w noo **kwahr**too
a laundry service	**serviço de lavandaria**	serr**vee**ssoo der lervahngder**reeer**
room service	**serviço de quartos**	serr**vee**ssoo der **kwahr**toosh
hot water	**água quente**	**ah**gwer **kayng**ter
running water	**água corrente**	**ah**gwer koo**rrayng**ter
a private toilet	**casa de banho [banheiro] particular**	**kah**zer der **ber**nyoo [bah**nyay**roa] perrtikkoo**lahr**

CHECKING OUT, see page 31

Could you put ... in the room?	**Podia pôr ... no quarto?**	poo**deeer** poar ... noo **kwahr**too
a cot	**uma cama de bebé [nenê]**	**oo**mer **ker**mer der beh**beh** [nay**nay**]
an extra bed	**mais uma cama**	mighsh **oo**mer **ker**mer

How much? *Quanto?*

What's the price ...?	**Qual é o preço?**	kwahl eh oo **pray**ssoo
per night/week	**por noite/semana**	poor **noy**ter/ser**mer**ner
for bed and breakfast	**da dormida e pequeno almoço***	der door**mee**der ee per**kay**noo ahl**moa**ssoo
excluding meals	**sem refeições**	sahng^y rerfay**ssahng^w**sh
for full board (A.P.)	**da pensão completa**	der payng**sahng^w** kawng**pleh**ter
for half board (M.A.P.)	**da meia-pensão**	der **may**er payng**sahng^w**
Does it include ...?	**O preço inclui ...?**	oo **pray**ssoo eeng**klooy**
breakfast	**o pequeno almoço [café da manhã]**	oo per**kay**noo ahl**moa**ssoo [kah**feh** dah mah**nyahng**]
service	**o serviço**	oo ser**vee**ssoo
value-added tax (VAT)	**o IVA**	oo **ee**ver
Is there any reduction for children?	**Há desconto para crianças?**	ah dish**kawng**too **per**rer **kryahng**sersh
Do you charge for the baby?	**O bebé [nenê] paga?**	oo beh**beh** [nay**nay**] **pah**ger
That's too expensive.	**É caro demais.**	eh **kah**roo der**mighsh**
Haven't you anything cheaper?	**Não tem nada mais barato?**	nahng^w tahng^y **nah**der mighsh ber**rah**too

How long? *Quanto tempo?*

We'll be staying ...	**Ficamos ...**	**fi**kker**moosh**
overnight only	**só esta noite**	saw **ehsh**ter **noy**ter
a few days	**alguns dias**	ahl**goongsh dee**ersh
a week (at least)	**uma semana (pelo menos)**	**oo**mer ser**mer**ner (**pay**loo **may**noosh)
I don't know yet.	**Ainda não sei.**	er**eeng**der nahng^w say

* In Brazil: **pernoite e café da manhã** (pehr**noy**ti ee kah**feh** dah mah**nyahng**).

NUMBERS, see page 147

Decision *Decisão*

May I see the room?	**Posso ver o quarto?**	possoo vayr oo **kwahr**too
That's fine. I'll take it.	**Está bem. Fico com ele.**	ish**tah** bahng^y. **fee**koo kawng **ay**ler
No. I don't like it.	**Não, não gosto dele.**	nahng^w nahng^w **gosh**too **day**ler
It's too ...	**É muito ...**	eh **moong^y**too
cold/hot	**frio/quente**	**free**oo/**kayng**ter
dark/small	**escuro/pequeno**	ish**koo**roo/per**kay**noo
noisy	**barulhento**	berroo**lyayng**too
I asked for a room with a bath.	**Pedi um quarto com banho.**	per**dee** oong **kwahr**too kawng **ber**nyoo
Do you have anything ...?	**Tem alguma coisa ...?**	tahng^y ahl**goo**mer **koy**zer
better	**melhor**	mi**llyor**
bigger	**maior**	may**or**
cheaper	**mais barata**	mighsh ber**rah**ter
quieter	**mais sossegada**	mighsh soosser**gah**der
Do you have a room with a better view?	**Tem um quarto com uma vista melhor?**	tahng^y oong **kwahr**too kawng **oo**mer **veesh**ter mi**llyor**

Registration *Registo*

Upon arrival at a hotel or boarding house you'll be asked to fill in a registration form (*uma ficha*—**oo**mer **fee**sher).

Apelido/Nomes próprios*	Name/First name(s)
Morada/Rua/Nº	Home address/Street/Number
Nacionalidade/Profissão	Nationality/Profession
Data/Lugar de nascimento	Date/Place of birth
Origem/Destino	Coming from .../Going to ...
Número do passaporte	Passport number
Lugar/Data	Place/Date
Assinatura	Signature

* In Brazil: **Sobrenome/Nomes.**

What does this mean?	**O que quer dizer isto?**	oo ker kehr di**zzayr eesh**too

Posso ver o seu passaporte?	May I see your passport?
Queira preencher esta ficha, se faz favor.	Would you mind filling in this registration form?
Assine aqui, por favor.	Please sign here.
Quanto tempo vai ficar?	How long will you be staying?

What's my room number?	**Qual é o número do meu quarto?**	kwahl eh oo **noo**merroo doo mehoo **kwahr**too
Will you have our luggage sent up?	**Pode mandar subir a nossa bagagem?**	**po**dder mahng**dahr** soo**beer** er **no**sser ber**gah**zhahng^{y}
Where can I park my car?	**Onde posso estacionar o carro?**	**awng**der **po**ssoo ishterssyoo**nahr** oo **kah**rroo
Does the hotel have a garage?	**O hotel tem garagem?**	oo o**tte**hl tahng^{y} ger**rah**zhahng^{y}
I'd like to leave this in your safe.	**Gostava de deixar isto no cofre do hotel.**	goosh**tah**ver der day**shahr** **eesh**too noo **ko**ffrer doo o**ttehl**

Hotel staff *Pessoal do hotel*

hall porter	**o porteiro**	oo poor**tay**roo
maid	**a criada de quarto [arrumadeira]**	er **kryah**der der **kwahr**too [ahrroomah**day**rah]
manager	**o gerente**	oo zher**rayng**ter
page (bellboy)	**o paquete/groom [boy de hotel]**	oo per**kay**ter/groom [boy di o**ttehl**]
porter	**o bagageiro**	oo berger**zhay**roo
receptionist	**o recepcionista**	oo rerssehssyoo**neesh**ter
switchboard operator	**a telefonista**	er terlerfoo**neesh**ter
waiter	**o criado de mesa [garçom]**	oo **kryah**doo der **may**zer [gahr**sawng**]
waitress	**a criada de mesa [garçonete]**	er **kryah**der der **may**zer [gahrso**nneh**ti]

Call the members of the staff *senhor* (si**nnyoar**), *senhora* (si**nnyoa**rer) or *menina [senhorita]* (mer**nee**ner [sinnyoa**ree**tah]).

TELLING THE TIME, see page 153

General requirements *Perguntas gerais*

The key to room ..., please.	**A chave do quarto ..., por favor.**	er **shah**ver doo **kwahr**too ... poor fer**voar**
Will you wake me at ..., please?	**Pode acordar-me às ...?**	**po**dder erkoor**dahr** mer ahsh
Is there a bathroom on this floor?	**Há uma casa de banho [um banheiro] neste andar?**	ah **oo**mer **kah**zer der **ber**nyoo [oong bah**nyay**-roa] **naysh**ter ahng**dahr**
What's the voltage?	**Qual é a voltagem?**	kwahl eh er voll**tah**zhahng^Y
Where's the socket (outlet) for the shaver?	**Onde está a tomada para a máquina de barbear [o barbeador]?**	**awng**der ish**tah** er too**mah**der **per**rer er **mah**kinner der berr**byahr** [oa bahrbyah**doar**]
Can you find me a ...?	**Pode arranjar-me [arrumar-me]?**	**po**dder errahng**zhahr** mer [ahrroo**mahr** mi]
baby-sitter	**uma babysitter**	**oo**mer "babysitter"
secretary	**uma secretária**	**oo**mer serkrer**tah**ryer
typewriter	**uma máquina de escrever**	**oo**mer **mah**kinner der ishkrer**vayr**
May I have a/an/some ...?	**Pode dar-me ...?**	**po**dder dahr mer
ashtray	**um cinzeiro**	oong seeng**zay**roo
bath towel	**uma toalha de banho**	**oo**mer **twah**lyer der **ber**nyoo
(extra) blanket	**(mais) um cobertor**	(mighsh) oong kooberr**toar**
envelopes	**uns envelopes**	oongsh ayngver**lo**ppish
(more) hangers	**(mais) cabides**	(mighsh) ker**bee**dish
hot-water bottle	**um saco de água quente**	oong **sah**koo der **ah**gwer **kayng**ter
ice cubes	**cubos de gelo**	**koo**boosh der **zhay**loo
needle and thread	**uma agulha e linha**	**oo**mer er**goo**lyer ee **lee**nyer
(extra) pillow	**(mais) uma almofada [um travesseiro]**	(mighsh) **oo**mer ahlmoo**fah**-der [oong trahvay**ssay**roa]
reading lamp	**um candeeiro [abajur]**	oong kahng**dyay**roo [ahbah**zhoor**]
soap	**um sabonete**	oong serboo**nay**ter
writing paper	**papel de carta**	per**pehl** der **kahr**ter
Where's the ...?	**Onde é ...?**	**awng**der eh
dining room	**a sala de jantar**	er **sah**ler der zhahng**tahr**
emergency exit	**a saída de emergência**	er ser**ee**der der immerr-**zhayng**syer
hairdresser's	**o cabeleireiro**	oo kerberlay**ray**roo
lift (elevator)	**o elevador**	oo illerver**doar**

BREAKFAST, see page 38

Telephone—Post (mail) *Telefone—Correio*

Can you get me Lisbon 12 34 56?	**Pode ligar-me para o 12 34 56 em Lisboa?**	podder li**ggahr** mer **per**rer oo 12 34 56 ahng^{y} lizh**boaer**
Do you have stamps?	**Tem selos?**	tahng^{y} **say**loosh
Would you post (mail) this for me, please?	**Pode pôr-me isto no correio, por favor?**	podder poar mer **eesh**too noo koor**ray**oo poor fer**voar**
Is there any post (mail) for me?	**Há correio para mim?**	ah koor**ray**oo **per**rer meeng
Are there any messages for me?	**Há algum recado para mim?**	ah ahl**goong** rer**kah**doo **per**rer meeng
How much is my telephone bill?	**Quanto devo pelas chamadas telefónicas?**	**kwahng**too **day**voo pay**lersh** sher**mah**dersh terler**fo**nnikkersh

Difficulties *Dificuldades*

The ... doesn't work.	**... não funciona.**	nahng^{w} foong**syo**nner
air conditioner	**o ar condicionado**	oo ahr kawngdissyoo**nahdo**
fan	**a ventoinha**	er vayng**twee**nyer
heating	**o aquecimento**	oo erkehssi**mmayng**too
light	**a luz**	er loosh
radio	**o rádio**	oo **rah**dyoo
television	**a televisão**	er terlervi**zzahng^{w}**
The tap (faucet) is dripping.	**A torneira da água verte.**	er toor**nay**rer der **ah**gwer **vehr**ter
There's no hot water.	**Não há água quente.**	nahng^{w} ah **ah**gwer **kayngte**
The washbasin is blocked.	**O lavatório está entupido [A pia está entupida].**	oo lerver**to**rryoo ish**tah** ayngtoo**pee**doo [ah **pee**er is**tah** ayngtoo**pee**dah]
The window/door is jammed.	**A janela/porta está empenada.**	er zher**neh**ler/**por**rter ish**tah** ayngper**nah**der
The curtains are stuck.	**Os cortinados estão perros.**	oosh koorti**nnah**doosh ish**tahng^{w}** **pay**rroosh
The bulb is burned out.	**A lâmpada está fundida.**	er **lahng**perder ish**tah** foong**dee**der
My room has not been made up.	**O meu quarto não foi arrumado.**	oo **meh**oo **kwahr**too nahng^{w} foy erroo**mah**doo

POST OFFICE AND TELEPHONE, see page 132

The ... is broken.	**... está partido(a) [quebrado(a)].**	ishtah perrteedoo(er) [kaybrahdoa(er)]
blind	**o estore**	oo ishtorrer
lamp	**o candeeiro [abajur]**	oo kahngdyayroo [ahbahzhoor]
plug	**a ficha**	er feesher
shutter	**a janela de madeira**	er zhernehler der merdayrer
switch	**o interruptor**	oo eengterrooptoar
Can you get it repaired?	**Pode mandar consertar?**	podder mahngdahr kawngserrtahr

Laundry—Dry cleaner's *Lavandaria—Lavandaria a seco*

I want these clothes ...	**Quero que esta roupa seja ...**	kehroo ker ehshter roaper sayzher
cleaned	**limpa**	leengper
ironed/pressed	**passada a ferro**	perssahder er fehrroo
washed	**lavada**	lervahder
When will they be ready?	**Quando estará pronta?**	kwahngdoo ishterrah prawngter
I need them ...	**Preciso dela ...**	prersseezoo dehler
today	**hoje**	oazher
tomorrow	**amanhã**	ahmernyahng
before Saturday	**antes de sábado**	ahngtish der sahberdoo
Can you ... this?	**Pode ... isto?**	podder ... eeshtoo
mend	**arranjar [consertar]**	errahngzhahr [kawngsayrtahr]
patch	**remendar**	rermayngdahr
stitch	**coser [costurar]**	koozayr [koastoorahr]
Can you sew on this button?	**Pode pregar este botão?**	podder prergahr ayshter bootahng^{w}
Can you get this stain out?	**Pode tirar esta nódoa [mancha]?**	podder tirrahr ehshter noddwer [mahngshah]
Is my laundry ready?	**A minha roupa está pronta?**	er meenyer roaper ishtah prawngter
This isn't mine.	**Isto não é meu.**	eeshtoo nahng^{w} eh mehoo
There's something missing.	**Falta qualquer coisa.**	fahlter kwahlkehr koyzer
There's a hole in this.	**Isto tem um buraco.**	eeshtoo tahng^{y} oong boorahkoo

Hairdresser—Barber *Cabeleireiro—Barbeiro*

Is there a hairdresser/ beauty salon in the hotel?	**Há um cabeleireiro/ instituto de beleza no hotel?**	ah oong kerberlayrayroo/ eengshtittootoo der berlayzer noo ottehl
Can I make an appointment for Thursday?	**Posso fazer uma marcação para quinta-feira?**	possoo ferzayr oomer merrkerssahng^{w} perrer keengter fayrer
I'd like it cut and shaped.	**Quero cortar e fazer mise.**	kehroo koortahr ee ferzayr meezer
I want a haircut, please.	**Quero cortar o cabelo, por favor.**	kehroo koortahr oo kerbayloo poor fervoar
bleach	**uma descoloração**	oomer dishkooloorerssahng^{w}
blow-dry	**um brushing**	oong "brushing"
colour rinse	**uma rinsage**	oomer rahngsahzher
dye	**uma pintura do cabelo**	oomer peengtoorer doo kerbayloo
face pack	**uma máscara de beleza**	oomer mahshkerrer der berlayzer
manicure	**uma manicura**	oomer mernikkoorer
permanent wave	**uma permanente**	oomer perrmernayngter
setting lotion	**um fixador**	oong fikserdoar
shampoo and set	**lavar e fazer mise**	lervahr ee ferzayr meezer
with a fringe (bangs)	**com franja**	kawng frahngzher
I'd like a shampoo for ... hair.	**Queria um shampoo [xampu] para cabelo ...**	kerreeer oong shahngpoa [shahngpoo] perrer kerbayloo
normal/dry/ greasy (oily)	**normal/seco/ oleoso**	norrmahl/saykoo/ ollyoazoo
Do you have a colour chart?	**Tem um mostruário de cores?**	tahng^{y} oong mooshtrwahryoo der koarersh
Don't cut it too short.	**Não corte muito curto.**	nahng^{w} korrter moong^{y}too koortoo
A little more off the ...	**Corte um pouco mais ...**	korrter oong poakoo mighsh
back	**atrás**	ertrahsh
neck	**na nuca**	ner nooker
sides	**dos lados**	doosh lahdoosh
top	**em cima**	ahng^{y} seemer
I don't want any hairspray.	**Não quero laca [laquê].**	nahng^{w} kehroo lahker [lahkay]

DAYS OF THE WEEK, see page 151

I'd like a shave.	**Queria fazer a barba.**	kerreeer ferzayr er **bahr**ber
Would you trim my ..., please?	**Pode aparar-me ...?**	podder erper**rahr** mer
beard	**a barba**	er **bahr**ber
moustache	**o bigode**	oo bigg**o**dder
sideboards (sideburns)	**as suíças [costeletas]**	ersh **swee**ssersh [coaster**lay**tahss]

Checking out *Partida*

May I have my bill, please?	**Pode dar-me a conta, por favor?**	**po**dder dahr mer er **kawng**ter poor fer**voar**
I'm leaving early in the morning. Please have my bill ready.	**Parto amanhã de manhã cedo. Por favor, prepare-me a conta.**	**pahr**too ahmer**nyahng** der mer**nyahng say**doo. poor fer**voar** prer**pah**rer mer er **kawng**ter
We'll be checking out around noon.	**Partiremos por volta do meio-dia.**	perrtir**ray**moosh poor **voll**ter doo **may**oo **dee**er
I must leave at once.	**Tenho de partir já.**	taynyoo der perr**teer** zhah
Is everything included?	**Está tudo incluído?**	ish**tah too**doo eengk**lwee**doo
Can I pay by credit card?	**Posso pagar com cartão de crédito?**	possoo per**gahr** kawng kerr**tahng**ʷ der **kreh**dittoo
I think there's a mistake in the bill.	**Creio que se enganou na conta.**	**kray**oo ker ser aynggerno**a** ner **kawng**ter
Can you get us a taxi?	**Pode chamar-nos um táxi?**	**po**dder sher**mahr** noosh oong **tah**ksi
Would you send someone to bring down our luggage?	**Pode mandar trazer para baixo a nossa bagagem?**	**po**dder mahng**dahr** trer**zayr** perrer **bigh**shoo er **no**sser ber**gah**zhahngʸ
Here's the forwarding address.	**Aqui está o meu próximo endereço.**	er**kee** ish**tah** oo **me**hoo **pro**ssimmoo ayngder**rays**soo
You have my home address.	**Já têm a minha morada.**	zhah **tahng**ʸahngʸ er **mee**nyer moo**rah**der
It's been a very enjoyable stay.	**Tivemos uma estadia muito agradável.**	tivv**eh**moosh **oo**mer ishter**deeer moong**ʸtoo ergrer**dah**vehl

TIPPING, see inside back-cover

Camping *Campismo*

Most Portuguese camp sites are within easy reach of a beach. They range from basic grounds to vast recreational centres with all amenities. You must register with your passport, certain sites require membership of a national or international camping association. In Brazil camping outside official sites is not recommended.

Is there a camp site near here?	**Há um parque de campismo aqui perto?**	ah oong **pahr**ker der kahng**peezh**moo er**kee pehr**too
Can we camp here?	**Podemos acampar aqui?**	poo**day**moosh erkahng**pahr** er**kee**
Have you room for a tent/caravan (trailer)?	**Tem lugar para uma tenda/rulote?**	tahng^{y} loo**gahr per**rer **oo**mer **tayng**der/roo**lo**tter
What's the charge ...?	**Qual é o preço ...?**	kwahl eh oo **pray**ssoo
per day/person	**por dia/pessoa**	poor **dee**er/per**ssoa**er
for a car	**por automóvel**	poor owtoo**mo**vvehl
for a tent	**por tenda**	poor **tayng**der
for a caravan (trailer)	**por rulote**	poor roo**lo**tter
Is the tourist tax included?	**A taxa de turismo está incluída?**	er **tah**sher der too**reezh**moo ish**tah** eeng**klwee**der
Is there/Are there (a) ...?	**Há ...?**	ah
drinking water	**água potável**	**ah**gwer poo**tah**vehl
electricity	**electricidade**	illehtrissi**ddah**der
playground	**um campo de jogos**	oong **kahng**poo der **zho**ggoosh
restaurant	**um restaurante**	oong rishtow**rahng**ter
shopping facilities	**lojas**	**lo**zhersh
swimming pool	**uma piscina**	**oo**mer pish**see**ner
Where are the showers/toilets?	**Onde são os duches/ as casas de banho [os banheiros]?**	**awng**der sahng^{w} oosh **doo**shersh/ersh **kah**zersh der **ber**nyoo [oass bah**nyay**roass]
Where can I get butane gas?	**Onde posso arranjar [arrumar] gás butano?**	**awng**der **po**ssoo errahng**zhahr** [ahrroo**mahr**] gahsh boo**ter**noo
Is there a youth hostel near here?	**Há uma pousada de juventude aqui perto?**	ah **oo**mer poa**zah**der der zhoovayng**too**der er**kee pehr**too

CAMPING EQUIPMENT, see page 106

Eating out

From snack bars to luxury restaurants, eating out can be one of the most interesting experiences of your trip. Here are some of the types of eating and drinking places you'll come across. In Portugal the most distinctive are the *pousadas* and the *casas de fados* or *adegas típicas*, the little restaurants where you eat or drink to the sound of the *fado*, the national folk song.

In Brazil, don't miss the *churrascarias*, restaurants specializing in excellent barbecues.

Café (ker**feh**)	Coffee shop and bar, where hot and cold drinks are served; you should be able to get a snack there.
Casa de fados (**kah**zer der **fah**doosh)	A typical Portuguese restaurant, where you can listen to the famous *fado* songs, accompanied by guitars.
Cervejaria (serrverzherre**eer**)	A large *café* where you can drink beer and eat seafood snacks.
Churrasqueira (shoorrersh**kay**rer)	Restaurant; specializes in chicken.
Churrascaria (shoorrahskah**ree**ah)	Restaurant; specializing in barbecue, a *churrascaria* offers a great variety of grilled meat, generally served with fried potatoes and a hot sauce of onions, tomatoes and green peppers (Brazil).
Confeitaria (kawngfayterre**eer**)	A cake shop, also serving coffee, tea and other drinks.
Estalagem (ishter**lah**zhayng^{y})	Privately-owned inn, serving regional specialities.
Lanchonete (lahngshoa**neh**ti)	Snack-bar (Brazil).
Pastelaria (pershterlerre**eer**)	The same as a *confeitaria*.
Pousada (poa**zah**der)	State-owned inn, specializing in local dishes; located near places of interest to tourists.

Restaurante (rishtow**rahng**ter)	According to the cuisine and standard of service: *de luxo* (luxury), *de primeira, de segunda* or *de terceira classe* (first, second or third class).
Salão de chá (ser**lahng**[w] der shah)	A smart tearoom.
Snack-Bar (snahk bahr)	The same as at home.

Meal times *Horas de comer*

Breakfast (*o pequeno almoço* – oo per**kay**noo ahl**moa**ssoo – in Portugal, *o café da manhã* – oa kah**feh** dah mah**nyahng** – in Brazil) is usually served from 7 to 10 a.m.

Lunch (*o almoço* – oo ahl**moa**ssoo) is generally served from 12.30 to 14.30 p.m. in both Portugal and Brazil.

Dinner (*o jantar* – oo zhahng**tahr**) is served from about 7.30 to 9.30 p.m., except in a Portuguese *casa de fados,* where the show is likely to start around 10 p.m., so dinner is served later. In Brazil dinner time is from 8 to 11 p.m.

Eating habits *Hábitos de comer*

Most Portuguese start the day with a light breakfast and save their appetite for lunch. The latter generally consists of soup, fish or meat, and a dessert. For those with a sweet tooth, the afternoon coffee or tea accompanied by all kinds of delicious pastries, is the peak of the day, and it's also the moment for an ice-cream. To round off the day, the Portuguese have another two or three-course meal. You'll have no problem satisfying your appetite, especially as the portions are simply gargantuan.

Brazilian eating habits more or less follow the Portuguese pattern. Breakfast is, however, a bit heartier, and salad might replace the soup at other meals. Brazilians like to linger over the meal, so don't be surprised if service is slow—you're expected to take your time.

Portuguese cuisine *Cozinha portuguesa*

Portuguese cuisine is not the most sophisticated in the world, but there is no shortage of freshly-picked vegetables and fruit, or fish and seafood straight from the sea. The *bacalhau,* dried cod, served with boiled potatoes, remains the favourite national dish, followed by custards and all kinds of pastries. Pork comes in many guises, as do chicken and veal. As for the wines, some of them are world famous and certainly worth trying.

Brazilian cuisine has adopted many elements from that of Portugal, refined it with the use of new spices and exotic fruit, and also added a great variety of barbecued meat.

O que deseja?	What would you like?
Recomendo-lhe isto.	I recommend this.
O que deseja beber?	What would you like to drink?
Não temos ...	We haven't got ...
Quer ...?	Do you want ...?

Hungry? *Tem fome?*

I'm hungry/thirsty.	**Tenho fome/sede.**	taynyoo **fo**mmer/**say**der
Can you recommend a good restaurant?	**Pode recomendar-me um bom restaurante?**	**po**dder rerkoomayng**dahr** mer oong bawng rishtow**rahng**ter
Are there any inexpensive restaurants around here?	**Há restaurantes baratos aqui perto?**	ah rishtow**rahng**tish ber**rah**toosh er**kee** **pehr**too
I'd like to reserve a table for 4.	**Queria reservar uma mesa para 4 pessoas.**	ker**ree**er rerzerr**vahr** **oo**mer **may**zer **per**rer 4 per**ssoa**ersh
We'll come at 8.	**Viremos às 8.**	vir**ray**moosh ahsh 8

If you want to be sure of getting a table in a well-known restaurant or a *casa de fados,* it may be better to telephone in advance.

Could we have a table ...?	**Pode dar-nos uma mesa ...?**	podder dahr noosh **oo**mer **may**zer
in the corner	**num canto**	noong **kahng**too
by the window	**perto da janela**	**pehr**too der zher**neh**ler
outside	**lá fora**	lah **for**rer
on the terrace	**na esplanada**	ner ishpler**nah**der
in a non-smoking area	**numa zona para não-fumadores**	**noo**mer **zoa**ner **per**rer nahng^{w} foomer**doa**rersh

Asking and ordering *Pedidos e encomendas*

Waiter/Waitress!	**Se faz favor!**	ser fash fer**voar**
I'd like something to eat/drink.	**Queria comer/beber alguma coisa.**	kerr**ee**er koo**mayr**/ber**bayr** ahl**goo**mer **koy**zer
May I have the menu, please?	**Pode trazer-me a ementa [o cardápio], por favor?**	**pod**der trer**zayr** mer er im**mayng**ter [oa kahr**dah**pyoa] poor fer**voar**
Do you have ...?	**Tem ...?**	tahng^{y}
a set menu	**uma refeição a preço fixo**	**oo**mer rerfay**ssahng^{w}** er **pray**ssoo **feek**soo
local dishes	**pratos regionais**	**prah**toosh rerzhyoo**nighsh**
What do you recommend?	**O que me recomenda?**	oo ker mer rerkoo**mayng**der
I'd like ...	**Queria ...**	kerr**ee**er
Could we have a/an ..., please?	**Podia trazer-nos ... por favor?**	poo**dee**er trer**zayr** noosh ... poor fer**voar**
ashtray	**um cinzeiro**	oong seeng**zay**roo
cup	**uma chávena [xícara]**	**oo**mer **shah**verner [**shee**kahrah]
fork	**um garfo**	oong **gahr**foo
glass	**um copo**	oong **kop**poo
knife	**uma faca**	**oo**mer **fah**ker
napkin (serviette)	**um guardanapo**	oong gwerrder**nah**poo
plate	**um prato**	oong **prah**too
spoon	**uma colher**	**oo**mer koo**lyehr**
May I have some ...?	**Pode trazer-me ...?**	**pod**der trer**zayr** mer
bread	**pão**	pahng^{w}
butter	**manteiga**	mahng**tay**ger
lemon	**limão**	lim**mahng^{w}**
mustard	**mostarda**	moosh**tahr**der
olive oil	**azeite**	er**zay**ter
pepper	**pimenta**	pim**mayng**ter

Restaurante

salt	**sal**	sahl
sugar	**açúcar**	erssookerr
vinegar	**vinagre**	vinnahgrer

Some useful expressions for dieters and special requirements:

I'm on a diet.	**Estou a dieta.**	ishtoa er dyehter
I don't drink alcohol.	**Não bebo bebidas alcoólicas.**	nahng^{w} bayboo berbeedersh ahlkwollikkersh
I mustn't eat food containing ...	**Não devo comer alimentos que contenham ...**	nahng^{w} dayvoo koomayr erlimmayngtoosh ker kawngtaynyahng^{w}
flour/fat	**farinha/gordura**	ferreenyer/goordoorer
salt/sugar	**sal/açúcar**	sahl/erssookerr
Do you have ... for diabetics?	**Tem ... para diabéticos?**	tahng^{y} ... perrer dyerbehtikkoosh
cakes	**bolos**	boaloosh
fruit juice	**sumo [suco] de fruta**	soomoo [sookoa] der frooter
a special menu	**uma ementa [um cardápio] especial**	oomer immayngter [oong kahrdahpyoa] ishperssyahl
Do you have vegetarian dishes?	**Tem pratos vegetarianos?**	tahng^{y} prahtoosh verzherterryernoosh
Could I have ... instead of the dessert?	**Pode dar-me ... em vez da sobremesa?**	podder dahr mer ... ahng^{y} vaysh der soobrermayzer
Can I have an artificial sweetener?	**Pode dar-me um edulcorante artificial?**	podder dahr mer oong iddoolkoorahngter errtiffissyahl

And ...

I'd like some more, please.	**Queria mais um pouco, se faz favor.**	kerreeer mighsh oong poakoo ser fash fervoar
Can I have more ...?	**Pode dar-me mais ...?**	podder dahr mer mighsh
Just a small portion.	**Só um bocado.**	saw oong bookahdoo
Nothing more, thanks.	**Mais nada, obrigado(a).**	mighsh nahder oabriggahdoo(ah)
Where are the toilets?	**Onde são as casas de banho [os banheiros]?**	awngder sahng^{w} ersh kahzersh der bernyoo [oass bahnyayroass]

Breakfast *Pequeno almoço [Café da manhã]*

The Portuguese breakfast consists of coffee (black or with milk), rolls, butter and jam. In Brazil, breakfast is usually hearty: fresh fruit juice, fruit, toast and rolls, cake, butter and jam, accompanied by coffee with hot milk.

I'd like breakfast, please.	**Queria tomar o pequeno almoço [café da manhã].**	ker**reeer** too**mahr** oo per**kay**noo ahl**moa**ssoo [kah**feh** dah mah**nyahng**]
I'll have a/an/some ...	**Queria ...**	ker**reeer**
bacon and eggs	**ovos estrelados com toucinho**	ovvoosh ishtrer**lah**doosh kawng toa**ssee**nyoo
boiled egg	**um ovo cozido**	oong **oa**voo koo**zee**doo
soft/hard	**quente/cozido**	**kayng**ter/koo**zee**doo
cereal	**cereais**	ser**ryighsh**
eggs	**ovos**	ovvoosh
fried eggs	**ovos estrelados**	ovvoosh ishtrer**lah**doosh
scrambled eggs	**ovos mexidos**	ovvoosh mer**shee**doosh
fruit juice	**sumo [suco] de fruta**	**soo**moo [**soo**koa] der **froo**ter
grapefruit	**toranja**	too**rahng**zher
orange	**laranja**	ler**rahng**zher
ham and eggs	**ovos estrelados com presunto**	ovvoosh ishtrer**lah**doosh kawng prer**zoong**too
jam	**doce de fruta [geléia]**	**doa**sser der **froo**ter [zhay**lay**ah]
marmalade	**doce [geléia] de laranja**	**doa**sser [zhay**lay**ah] der ler**rahng**zher
toast	**torradas**	too**rrah**dersh
May I have some ...?	**Pode trazer-me ...?**	**po**dder trer**zayr** mer
bread	**pão**	pahng^{w}
butter	**manteiga**	mahng**tay**ger
(hot) chocolate	**chocolate (quente)**	shookoo**lah**ter (**kayng**ter)
coffee	**café**	ker**feh**
decaffeinated	**sem cafeína**	sahng^{y} kerfe**hee**ner
black	**sem leite**	sahng^{y} **lay**ter
with milk	**com leite**	kawng **lay**ter
honey	**mel**	mehl
(cold/hot) milk	**leite (frio/quente)**	**lay**ter (**free**oo/**kayng**ter)
rolls	**papo-secos [pãezinhos]**	**pah**poo **say**koosh [pahng^{y}**zee**nyoass]
tea	**chá**	shah
with milk/lemon	**com leite/limão**	kawng **lay**ter/lim**mahng**^{w}
(hot) water	**água (quente)**	**ah**gwer (**kayng**ter)

What's on the menu? *O que há na ementa [cardápio]?*

Most Portuguese and Brazilian restaurants display a menu (*ementa* in Portugal, *cardápio* in Brazil); a set menu is rarely offered. *A prato do dia* (**prah**too doo **dee**er—dish of the day) usually offers you a good meal at a fair price. *Especialidade da casa* written next to a dish listed on the menu tells you that the dish is a speciality of the restaurant.

Under the headings below you'll find alphabetical lists of dishes that might be offered on a Portuguese menu with their English equivalent. You can simply show the book to the waiter. If you want some fruit, for instance, let *him* point to what's available on the appropriate list. Use pages 36 and 37 for ordering in general.

	page	
Starters (Appetizers)	41	**Acepipes [Salgadinhos]**
Salads	42	**Saladas**
Eggs	42	**Ovos**
Soups	43	**Sopas**
Fish and seafood	44	**Peixes e mariscos**
Meat	46	**Carnes**
Game and poultry	48	**Caça e criação**
Vegetables	49	**Legumes**
Potatoes, rice, noodles	50	**Batatas, arroz, massa**
Cheese	51	**Queijos**
Fruit	52	**Frutas**
Dessert—Pastries	53	**Sobremesas—Pastelaria**
Drinks	55	**Bebidas**
Wine	56	**Vinhos**
Nonalcoholic drinks	59	**Bebidas não alcoólicas**
Hot beverages	60	**Bebidas quentes**
Snacks—Picnic	63	**Refeições leves—Piquenique**

Reading the menu *Para ler a ementa [o cardápio]*

Especialidades da casa	Specialities of the house
Especialidades regionais	Local specialities
Prato do dia	Dish of the day
À .../À moda de ...	... style
Caseiro(a)	Home-made
À escolha	Of your choice
Só por encomenda	Made to order
Da época	In season

acepipes	ersser**pee**persh	starters (appetizers)
aperitivos	erperrit**tee**voosh	aperitifs
arroz	er**roash**	rice
bacalhau	berker**lyow**	cod
bebidas	ber**bee**dersh	drinks
caça	**kah**sser	game
carnes	**kahr**nersh	meat
crustáceos	kroosh**tah**ssyoosh	shellfish
doces	**doa**ssersh	desserts
frango	**frahng**goo	chicken
fruta	**froo**ter	fruit
gelados	zher**lah**doosh	ice-creams
legumes	ler**goo**mersh	vegetables
mariscos	mer**reesh**koosh	seafood
ovos	**ov**voosh	eggs
petiscos	per**teesh**koosh	starters (appetizers)
peixes	**pay**shersh	fish
primeiro prato	prim**may**roo **prah**too	first course
prato principal	**prah**too preengsi**ppahl**	main course
pratos frios	**prah**toosh **free**oosh	cold dishes
queijos	**kay**zhoosh	cheese
refrigerantes	rerfrizzher**rahng**tish	soft drinks
saladas	ser**lah**dersh	salads
salgadinhos	sahlgah**dee**nyoass	starters (appetizers) (Braz.)
sopas	**soa**persh	soups
sobremesas	soabrer**may**zersh	dessert
sorvetes	soar**veh**tiss	ice-creams (Braz.)
sucos	**soo**koass	fruit juice (Braz.)
sumos	**soo**moosh	fruit juice
vinhos	**vee**nyoosh	wine

Starters (Appetizers) *Acepipes [Salgadinhos]*

If you feel like something to whet your appetite, choose carefully, for the Portuguese appetizer can be filling. Starters may also be listed on the menu under *Petiscos.*

I'd like an appetizer.	**Queria uns acepipes [salgadinhos].**	kerreeer oongsh ersserpee-persh [sahlgahdeenyoass]
What do you recommend?	**O que me recomenda?**	oo ker mer rerkoomayngder
acepipes variados	ersserpeepersh verryahdoosh	assorted appetizers
anchovas	ahngshoaversh	anchovies
atum	ertoong	tuna (tunny)
azeitonas recheadas/pretas/ de Elvas	erzaytoanersh rershyahdersh/pray-tersh/der ehlversh	olives stuffed/black/green
camarões	kermerrawng^y^sh	shrimp
caracóis à Algarvia	kerrerkoysh ah ahlgerrveeer	snails flavoured with oregano
carnes frias	kahrnersh freeersh	assorted cold cuts
chocos com tinta	shokkoosh kawng teengter	cuttlefish cooked in their own ink
espargos	ishpahrgoosh	asparagus
melão com presunto	merlahng^w^ kawng prerzoongtoo	melon with ham
moelas	mwehlersh	spicy stew of chicken stomach
ostras do Algarve	oashtrersh doo ahlgahrver	oysters baked in butter and dry wine
paio	pighoo	smoked, rolled pork fillet
pikles	peeklersh	pickled vegetables
pipis	pippeesh	spicy giblet stew
presunto	prerzoongtoo	cured ham
requeijão	rerkayzhahng^w^	curd cheese
salgadinhos variados	sahlgahdeenyoass vahryahdoass	assorted appetizers (Braz.)
sardinhas	serrdeenyersh	sardines

amêijoas na cataplana (ermayzhwersh ner kerterplerner)
clams with smoked ham, *chouriço* and pimento steamed in a pan shaped like a big nutshell

chouriço (shoareessoo)
smoked pork sausage flavoured with paprika and garlic

linguíça frita (leengg**wee**sser **free**ter)	very thin *chouriço* cut in slices and deep-fried in butter
pimentos assados (pimm**ayng**toosh erss**ah**doosh)	sweet peppers, roasted and served cold with olive oil and vinegar
rissóis de camarão (riss**oy**sh der kermer**rahng**ʷ)	deep-fried pastry envelopes filled with shrimp
santola recheada (sahng**to**ller rer**shyah**der)	spider-crab stuffed with its own meat, generally seasoned with mustard, curry powder, lemon juice and white wine

Salads *Saladas*

A green or mixed salad is seldom served with meals. You'll have to order it separately. Other salads may be ordered as a first course.

What salads do you have?	**Que saladas tem?**	ker ser**lah**dersh tahngʸ
salada	ser**lah**der	salad
de alface	der ahl**fah**sser	green
de atum	der er**toong**	tuna (tunny) and potato
de feijão frade	der fay**zhahng**ʷ **frah**der	black-eyed bean
mista	**meesh**ter	tomato and lettuce
russa	**roo**sser	diced vegetable
de tomate	der too**mah**ter	tomato

Eggs *Ovos*

ovos	**ov**vossh	eggs
cozidos	koo**zee**doosh	boiled
escalfados	ishkahl**fah**doosh	poached
estrelados	ishtrer**lah**doosh	fried
mexidos	mer**shee**doosh	scrambled
verdes	**vayr**dersh	stuffed with boiled yolks, onions and parsley, and fried
omelete	ommer**leh**ter	omelet
de camarão	der kermer**rahng**ʷ	shrimp
de chouriço	der shoa**ree**ssoo	smoked sausage
de espargos	der ish**pahr**goosh	asparagus

Soups *Sopas*

Portuguese meals often start with soup, a fairly substantial dish based on potatoes.

I'd like some soup.	**Queria uma sopa.**	ker**ree**er oomer **soa**per
açorda à Alentejana	er**ssoar**der ah erlayngter**zher**ner	bread soup with garlic and herbs
canja	**kahng**zher	chicken soup with rice
sopa	**soa**per	soup
à pescador	ah pishker**doar**	fish soup
de abóbora	der er**bob**boorer	pumpkin soup
de agriões	der er**gryawng^{y}sh**	potato and watercress soup
de camarão	der kermer**rahng^{w}**	shrimp soup
de cenoura	der ser**noa**rer	carrot soup
de ervilhas	der irr**vee**lyersh	green pea soup
de favas	der **fah**versh	broad bean soup
de feijão	der fay**zhahng^{w}**	red kidney bean and cabbage soup
de feijão frade	der fay**zhahng^{w} frah**der	black-eyed bean soup
de feijão verde	der fay**zhahng^{w} vayr**der	potato and runner bean soup
de grão	der grahng^{w}	chick-pea soup
de grelos	der **gray**loosh	turnip sprout soup
de hortaliça	der orrter**lee**sser	vegetable soup
de rabo de boi	der **rah**boo der boy	oxtail
transmontana	trahngshmawng**ter**ner	vegetable soup with bacon and bread

caldo verde (**kahl**doo **vayr**der) thick potato and kale soup with smoked sausage

gaspacho (gersh**pah**shoo) chilled soup with diced tomatoes, sweet peppers, onions, cucumber and croutons

migas de bacalhau (**mee**gersh der berker**lyow**) dried cod soup flavoured with garlic and thickened with bread

sopa de cozido (soaper der koozeedoo) meat broth with vegetables and macaroni

sopa de tomate (soaper der too**mah**ter) tomato soup with poached eggs and bread

sopa seca (soaper sayker) thick soup with beef, chicken, ham, smoked sausage, cabbage and bread

Fish and seafood *Peixes e mariscos*

While touring in coastal areas, don't miss the opportunity to sample some of the wide variety of fresh fish and seafood. The Portuguese are fond of boiled fish dishes served with cabbage and boiled potatoes—doused with oil and vinegar.

I'd like some fish.	**Queria peixe.**	keerr**eeer pay**sher
What kind of seafood do you have?	**Que espécies de mariscos tem?**	ker ish**peh**ssish der merr**eesh**koosh tahng^{y}
amêijoas	ermayzhwersh	clams
atum	er**toong**	tuna (tunny)
bacalhau	berker**lyow**	cod, usually dried
berbigão	berrbi**ggahng**^{w}	type of cockle
besugo	ber**zoo**goo	sunfish
camarões	kermer**rawng**^{y}**sh**	shrimp
camarões grandes	kermer**rawng**^{y}**ss grahng**diss	king prawns (Braz.)
caranguejo	kerrahng**gay**zhoo	crab
carapau	kerrer**pow**	horse mackerel
cavala	ker**vah**ler	mackerel
chocos	**shok**koosh	cuttlefish
congro	**kawng**groo	conger eel
eiró	ay**raw**	eel
enguia	ayng**gheeer**	eel
espadarte	ishper**dahr**ter	swordfish
gambas	**gahng**bersh	king prawns
lagosta	ler**goash**ter	spiny lobster
lagostins	lergoosh**teengsh**	Norway lobster
lampreia	lahng**pray**er	lamprey
lavagante	lerver**gahng**ter	lobster
linguado	leeng**gwah**doo	sole
lulas	**loo**lersh	squid
mexilhões	mershi**llyawng**^{y}**sh**	mussels
ostras	**oash**trersh	oysters
pargo	**pahr**goo	bream
peixe-agulha	**pay**sher er**goo**lyer	garfish
peixe-espada	**pay**sher ish**pah**der	cutlass fish
pescada	pish**kah**der	whiting
polvo	**poal**voo	octopus
robalo	roo**bah**loo	sea bass
salmão (fumado)	sahl**mahng**^{w} (foo**mah**doo)	(smoked) salmon
santola	sahng**toll**er	spider-crab
sardinhas	serr**dee**nyersh	sardines
truta	**troo**ter	trout

Here are some of the ways you may want the fish served:

baked	**no forno**	noo **foar**noo
fried	**frito**	**free**too
grilled (broiled)	**grelhado**	gri**lyah**dhoo
marinated	**marinado**	merrin**nah**doo
poached	**escaldado**	ishkahl**dah**doo
smoked	**fumado [defumado]**	foo**mah**doo [dayfoo**mah**doa]
steamed	**cozido ao vapor**	koo**zee**doo ow ver**poar**

Bacalhau (dried, salted cod) dishes are among the most famous Portuguese specialities. Here are the names of a few of the more common preparations you're likely to find:

bacalhau à Brás (berker**lyow** ah brahsh) — strips of dried cod fried with onions and potatoes, cooked in beaten eggs

bacalhau à Gomes de Sá (berker**lyow** ah **goa**mersh der sah) — dried cod with olives, garlic, onions, parsley and hard-boiled eggs

bacalhau podre (berker**lyow poa**drer) — a baked dish, in which layers of cod, fried in butter, alternate with layers of sliced, fried potatoes; topped with breadcrumbs and grated cheese

bacalhau com leite de coco (bahkah**lyow** kawng **lay**ti dee **koa**koa) — cod stewed in coconut milk (Braz.)

And try some of these specialities:

caldeirada (kahldayr**ah**der) — several kinds of fish simmered with onions, tomatoes, potatoes, and olive oil

lulas recheadas (**loo**lersh rershy**ah**dersh) — squid cooked with a stuffing of egg yolk, minced ham, onion and tomato sauce

moqueca de peixe (mok**kay**kah dee **pay**shi) — stew made of fish, shellfish or shrimp with coconut milk, *dendê* oil (yellow palm oil) and other seasonings (Braz.)

vatapá (vahtah**pah**) — fish and shrimp (dried and fresh) in a paste made of rice flour or breadcrumbs, coconut milk, *dendê* oil, peanuts, cashew nuts and other seasonings (Braz.)

Meat *Carnes*

In Portugal, *bife* (from the English word beef) turns out to be the word for steak even when referring to veal, pork or fish. Veal and pork *bifes* taste better than beef *bifes* most of the time. And you may try some lamb *costeletas* (chops) which are delicious. While in Brazil, don't miss the barbecue specialities.

I'd like some ...	**Queria ...**	kerreeer
beef	**carne de vaca**	kahrner der vahker
lamb	**borrego**	boorraygoo
pork	**carne de porco**	kahrner der poarkoo
veal	**vitela**	vittehler

bife	"beef"	steak
cabrito	kerbreetoo	kid
carneiro	kernayroo	mutton
carnes frias	kahrnersh freeersh	assorted cold cuts
chispe	sheeshper	pig's trotter (foot)
chouriço	shoareessoo	smoked sausage
costeleta	kooshterlayter	chop, cutlet
fígado	feegerdoo	liver
filé	filleh	steak (Braz.)
leitão	laytahng^w	suck(l)ing pig
língua	leenggwer	tongue
medalhão	merderlyahng^w	a tenderloin steak
presunto	prerzoongtoo	cured ham
presunto cru	prerzoongtoo kroo	dried ham
rins	reengsh	kidneys
salsicha	sahlseesher	sausage
toucinho	toasseenyoo	bacon

bife na frigideira
(beefer ner frizhiddayrer)
beefsteak fried in butter, white wine and garlic, served with ham and fried bread

carne de porco à Alentejana
(kahrner der poarkoo ah erlayngterzherner)
chopped pork cooked with clams, tomatoes and onions

carne de sol com feijão verde
(kahrni di soll kawng fayzhahng^w vayrdi)
meat dried in the sun (jerky) with green beans (Braz.)

cozido à Portuguesa (koozeedoo ah poortoogayzer)	boiled beef, bacon, smoked sausage and vegetables, served with rice
churrasco misto (shoorrahskoa meestoa)	mixed barbecue (beef, sausage and pork) (Braz.)
ensopado de cabrito (ayngsoopahdoo der kerbreetoo)	stew made of kid and vegetables, served on slices of bread
feijoada (fayzhwahder)	Brazil's national dish. Black beans cooked with bacon, dried and salted pork, jerky and sausage. You eat it with rice, slices of orange and *farofa,* manioc flour roasted in butter or oil
iscas à Portuguesa (eeshkersh ah poortoogayzer)	sliced liver marinated in white wine with garlic and herbs and then fried
rojões à moda do Minho (roozhawng[y]sh ah modder doo meenyoo)	chopped pork, marinated in dry white wine with onions and herbs and then fried
sarapatel (sahrahpahtehl)	porc or mutton stew, thickened with blood (Braz.)
tripas à moda do Porto (treepersh ah modder doo poartoo)	tripe cooked with assorted pork products, navy beans and chicken, served with rice

baked	**no forno**	noo foarnoo
barbecued	**na brasa**	ner brahzer
boiled	**cozido**	koozeedoo
braised	**estufado**	ishtoofahdoo
breaded	**panado**	pernahdoo
fried	**frito**	freetoo
grilled (broiled)	**grelhado**	grillyahdoo
minced	**picado**	pikkahdoo
roasted	**assado**	erssahdoo
stewed	**guisado**	gizzahdoo
stuffed	**recheado**	rershyahdoo
underdone (rare)	**mal passado**	mahl perssahdoo
medium	**meio passado**	mayoo perssahdoo
well-done	**bem passado**	bahng[y] perssahdoo

Game and poultry *Caça e criação*

In both Portugal and Brazil, chicken is a favourite dish prepared in dozens of ways. The Portuguese may surprise you with the great choice of game and poultry dishes available in various regions.

I'd like some game.	**Queria caça.**	kerreeer kahsser
borracho	boorrahshoo	squab
capão	kerpahngʷ	capon
codorna	koddoarnah	quail (Braz.)
codorniz	koodoorneesh	quail
coelho	kwaylyoo	rabbit
faisão	fighzahngʷ	pheasant
frango assado	frahnggoo erssahdoo	roast chicken
galinha	gerleenyer	stewing chicken
peito de galinha	paytoo der gerleenyer	chicken breast
perna de galinha	pehrner der gerleenyer	chicken leg
galinhola	gerlinyoller	woodcock
ganso	gahngsoo	goose
javali	zherverlee	wild boar
lebre	lehbrer	hare
pato	pahtoo	duck
perdiz	perrdeesh	partridge
peru	perroo	turkey
pombo	pawngboo	pigeon
veado	vyahdoo	venison

arroz de frango (erroash der frahnggoo) — fried chicken with white wine, ham and rice in a casserole

coelho assado (kwaylyoo erssahdoo) — roast rabbit with onions, white wine and seasoning

galeto com polenta (gahlaytoa kawng pollayngtah) — fried chicken with polenta (Braz.)

frango na púcara (frahnggoo ner pookerrer) — chicken stewed in Port wine and cognac, then fried with almonds cooked in wine sauce

pato no tucupi (pahtoa noa tookoopee) — roast duck with *tucupi*, a manioc juice (Braz.)

xinxim de galinha (sheengsheeng di gahleenyah) — chicken cooked in a sauce of dried shrimp, peanuts and parsley (Braz.)

Vegetables *Legumes*

aspargos	ah**spahr**goass	asparagus (Braz.)
abóbora	er**bobb**oorer	pumpkin
agriões	er**gryawng^{y}sh**	watercress
aipo	**igh**poo	celery
alcachofra	ahlker**shoff**rer	artichoke
alface	ahl**fahss**er	lettuce
alho porro	ahlyoo **poarr**oo	leek
batatas	ber**tah**tersh	potatoes
batata doce	ber**tah**ter **doass**er	sweet potato
berinjela	berreeng**zhehl**er	aubergine (eggplant)
brócolos	**brokk**ooloosh	broccoli
beterraba	berter**rahb**er	beetroot
cebolas	ser**boal**ersh	onions
cenouras	ser**noar**ersh	carrots
chicória	shik**korr**yer	endive (Am. chicory)
chuchu	shoo**shoo**	type of rutabaga (Braz.)
cogumelos	koogoo**meh**loosh	mushrooms
couve-flor	**koa**ver floar	cauliflower
couve lombarda	**koa**ver lawng**bahr**der	savoy cabbage
couve portuguesa	**koa**ver poortoo**gay**zer	kale
couve roxa	**koa**ver **roash**er	red cabbage
ervilhas	irr**veel**yersh	peas
espargos	ish**pahr**goosh	asparagus
espinafres	ishpin**nah**frersh	spinach
favas	**fah**versh	broad beans
feijão	fay**zhahng^w**	kidney beans
feijão verde	fay**zhahng^w vayr**der	runner (green) beans
grão	grahng^w	chick peas
grelos	**gray**loosh	turnip sprouts
lentilhas	layng**teel**yersh	lentils
milho	**meel**yoo	sweet corn (corn)
nabiças	ner**bees**sersh	turnip greens
nabos	**nah**boosh	turnips
palmito	pahl**mee**toa	palm hearts (Braz.)
pepino	per**pee**noo	cucumber
pepinos de conserva	per**pee**noosh der kawng**sehr**ver	gherkins (pickles)
pimentos	pim**mayng**toosh	sweet peppers
quiabo	**kyah**boa	okra (Braz.)
rabanetes	rerber**nay**tish	radishes
repolho	rer**poal**yoo	white cabbage
tomates	too**mah**tish	tomatoes
túberas	**too**berrersh	truffles
vagens	**vah**zhahng^{y}sh	runner (green) beans

And if you're touring in Brazil, try one of these delicious vegetable dishes:

acarajé (ahkahrah**zheh**)	grated beans fried in *dendê* (palm) oil, served with pepper sauce, onions and shrimp
tutu à mineira (**tootoo** ah min**nay**rah)	a dish made of beans, manioc flour, pork, cabbage, fried eggs and browned rashers of streaky bacon

Potatoes, rice and noodles *Batatas, arroz e massa*

In Portugal many dishes are served with both rice and potatoes.

arroz	er**roash**	rice
de alhos	**der ahl**yoosh	with garlic
de cabidela	der kerbi**ddeh**ler	with chicken blood
de cenoura	der ser**noa**rer	with carrots
de cozido	der koo**zee**doo	cooked in a meat stock
de feijão	der fay**zhahng**[w]	with red or white beans
de grelos	der **gray**loosh	with turnip sprouts
de manteiga	der mahng**tay**ger	with butter
de tomate	der too**mah**ter	with tomato
batatas	ber**tah**tersh	potatoes
cozidas (com pele)	koo**zee**dersh (kawng **peh**ler)	boiled (in their jackets)
fritas	**free**tersh	chips (french fries)
palha	**pah**lyer	matchsticks
massa	**mah**sser	pasta
esparguete [espaguete]	ishpahr**geh**ter [ispah**geh**ti]	spaghetti
macarrão	merker**rahng**[w]	macaroni

As for the seasoning ...

açafrão	ersser**frahng**[w]	saffron
alcaparras	ahlker**pah**rrersh	capers
alho	**ah**lyoo	garlic
azeite	er**zay**ter	olive oil
baunilha	bow**nee**lyer	vanilla
canela	ker**neh**ler	cinnamon
caril	ker**reel**	curry powder
coentros	**kwayng**troosh	coriander

colorau	kooloo**row**	paprika
cominhos	koo**mee**nyoosh	caraway
condimentos	kawngdi**mmayng**toosh	seasoning
cravinhos	krer**vee**nyoosh	cloves
erva-doce	**eh**rver **doa**sser	aniseed
gengibre	zhayng**zhee**brer	ginger
hortelã	orrter**lahng**	mint
louro	**loa**roo	bay leaf
manjericão	mahngzherri**kkahng**^{w}	basil
mostarda	**mooshtahr**der	mustard
noz-moscada	nosh moosh**kah**der	nutmeg
orégão	o**rreh**gahng^{w}	oregano
pimenta	**pi**mmayngter	pepper
piri-piri	**pi**rri **pi**rri	pimiento
rosmaninho	roozhmer**nee**nyoo	rosemary
sal	sahl	salt
salsa	**sahl**ser	parsley
tomilho	too**mee**lyoo	thyme
vinagre	vi**nnah**grer	vinegar

Cheese *Queijos*

Portuguese cheeses are usually a mixture of sheep's and goat's milk, or cow's and goat's milk. Brazil also produces some cheese, which you're expected to eat as a dessert, accompanied by preserves or sweets—*goiabada,* a paste made of guava, for instance. A cheeseboard is seldom served in Portuguese or Brazilian restaurants.

I'd like some cheese.	**Queria queijo.**	kerr**eeer kay**zhoo

creamy	Queijo da Serra, Azeitão, Évora, Castelo Branco, Serpa, Requeijão (a Brazilian cheese produced in Minas Gerais)
goat's milk cheese	Cabreiro (must be eaten fresh), Queijo de Minas (Brazilian, delicious with *goiabada*)
cow's milk cheese	São João, São Jorge, Ilha (from the Azores Islands), Queijo do Sertão (Brazilian)

Fruit *Frutas*

Do you have fresh fruit?	**Tem fruta fresca?**	tayng **frooter frayshker**
I'd like a (fresh) fruit cocktail.	**Queria uma salada de fruta (fresca).**	kerr**eeer oo**mer ser**lah**dher der **froo**ter (**fraysh**ker)
abacaxi	ahbahkah**shee**	pineapple (Braz.)
alperces	ahl**pehr**sersh	apricots
ameixas	er**may**shersh	plums
ameixas secas	er**may**shersh **say**kersh	prunes
amêndoas	er**mayng**dwersh	almonds
amendoins	ermayng**dweengsh**	peanuts
amoras	er**mo**rrersh	blackberries
ananás	erner**nahsh**	pineapple
avelãs	erver**lahngsh**	hazelnuts
banana	ber**ner**ner	banana
caqui	kah**kee**	persimmon (Braz.)
castanhas	kersh**ter**nyersh	chestnuts
cerejas	ser**ray**zhersh	cherries
coco	**koa**koa	coconut (Braz.)
caju	kah**zhoo**	cashew nut (Braz.)
damascos	dah**mahs**koass	apricots (Braz.)
figos	**fee**goosh	figs
framboesas	frahng**bway**zersh	raspberries
goiaba	goy**ah**bah	guava (Braz.)
laranja	ler**rahng**zher	orange
lima	**lee**mer	lime
limão	lim**mahng**^{w}	lemon
limão verde	lim**mahng**^{w} **vayr**di	lime (Braz.)
maçã	mer**ssahng**	apple
mamão	mah**mahng**^{w}	papaya (Braz.)
manga	**mahng**gah	mango (Braz.)
maracujá	mahrahkoo**zhah**	passion fruit (Braz.)
melancia	merlahng**seeer**	watermelon
melão	mer**lahng**^{w}	melon
morangos	moo**rahng**goosh	strawberries
nêsperas	**naysh**perrersh	crab apple
nozes	**no**zzersh	walnuts
passas (de uvas)	**pah**ssersh (der **oo**versh)	sultanas/raisins
pêra	**pay**rer	pear
pêssego	**pay**ssergoo	peach
tâmaras	**ter**merrersh	dates
tangerinas	tahngzherr**ee**nersh	tangerines
toranja	too**rahng**zher	grapefruit
uvas	**oo**versh	grapes
umbu	oong**boo**	a tropical fruit (Braz.)

Desserts—Pastries *Sobremesas—Pastelaria*

Cakes, custards and sweets—usually made of egg yolks (Portugal) or grated coconut (Brazil)—are part of every meal. You'll probably find them a bit too sweet. You can also try some ice-cream (*gelado*—zher**lah**doo—in Portugal, called *sorvete*—sor**veh**ti—in Brazil).

I'd like a dessert, please.	**Queria uma sobremesa, se faz favor.**	kerreeer oomer soobrer**may**zer ser fash fer**voar**
What do you recommend?	**O que me recomenda?**	oo ker mer rerkoo**mayng**der
Something light, please.	**Uma coisa leve, por favor.**	oomer **koy**zer **leh**ver poor fer**voar**
Just a small portion.	**Só um bocado.**	saw oong boo**kah**doo
aletria	erler**tree**er	vermicelli pudding
arroz doce	er**roash doa**sser	rice pudding
goiabada	goyah**bah**dah	thick paste made of guavas (Braz.)
leite-creme	layter **kreh**mer	custard, often with caramel topping
marmelada	merrmer**lah**der	thick paste made of quinces
mousse de chocolate	**moo**sser der shookoo**lah**ter	chocolate pudding
ovos moles de Aveiro	**ovv**oosh **moll**ersh der ah**vay**roo	beaten egg yolks cooked in syrup
pudim flan	poo**deeng** **flahng**	caramel custard

baba-de-moça (bahbah di **moa**ssah) dessert made of egg yolk, coconut milk and syrup (Braz.)

barriga-de-freira (ber**ree**ger der **fray**rer) dessert made of egg yolk, bread and syrup

canjica (kahng**zhee**kah) dessert made of grated sweet corn and coconut milk (Braz.)

farófias (fer**roff**yersh) beaten egg white poached in milk, topped with cinnamon and egg custard

fios de ovos (**fee**oosh der **ovv**oosh) fine golden strands of egg yolk cooked in syrup

pudim Molotov (poo**deeng** moll**ot**off) fluffy eggwhite mousse immersed in caramel sauce

And here are some pastries and biscuits (cookies) you can have with your coffee or tea:

arrufada de Coimbra	erroo**fah**der der **kweeng**brer	raised dough cake flavoured with cinnamon
bolinhos de amêndoa	boo**lee**nyoosh der er**mayng**dwer	almond biscuits
bolinhos de canela	boo**lee**nyoosh der ker**neh**ler	cinnamon biscuits
bolo de arroz	**boa**loo der er**roash**	rice cake
bolo inglês	**boa**loo eeng**glaysh**	cake with candied fruit
bolo podre	**boa**loo **poa**drer	cake flavoured with honey and cinnamon
broas castelares	**broa**ersh kershter**lah**rersh	sweet-potato biscuits
broas de mel	**broa**ersh der mehl	cornflour and honey biscuits
cavacas	ker**vah**kersh	glazed biscuits
cocadas	koa**kah**dahss	coconut macaroons (Braz.)
massapães	mahsser**pahng^{y}sh**	almond macaroons
mil-folhas	meel **foa**lyersh	cream slice (napoleon)
pão-de-ló	pahng^{w} der law	tea bread
papos-de-anjo	**pah**poosh der **ahng**zhoo	egg yolk macaroons
pastel de coco	persh**tehl** der **koa**koo	coconut pastry
pastel de feijão	persh**tehl** der fay**zhahng^{w}**	bean pastry
pastel de nata/ de Belém	persh**tehl** der **nah**ter/ der ber**lahng^{y}**	small cream tart
queijada	kay**zhah**der	small cottage-cheese tart
tarte de amêndoa	**tahr**ter der er**mayng**dwer	almond tart

bolo de chila do Algarve (**boa**loo der **shee**ler doo ahl**gahr**ver)	cake made of pumpkin jam, grated almonds, egg yolks and sugar
pastel de Tentúgal (persh**tehl** der tayng**too**gerl)	very thin flaky pastry filled with beaten egg yolks cooked in syrup
torta de laranja (**tor**ter der ler**rahng**zher)	swiss roll made of eggs, sugar and orange juice

Aperitifs *Aperitivos*

The Portuguese like to sip an aperitif before dinner, some drink vermouth while others prefer a dry Port or Madeira, or a *Moscatel de Setúbal* served chilled. Brazilians are likely to drink a *batida,* a blend of spirit distilled from sugar-cane, ice, sugar and fruit juice, or a *caipirinha* (see page 59).

I'd like a dry Madeira, please.	**Queria um vinho da Madeira seco, se faz favor.**	kerreeer oong **vee**nyoo der mer**day**rer **say**koo ser fash fer**voar**
Please bring me a vermouth.	**Por favor, traga-me um vermute.**	por fer**voar trah**ger mer oong vehr**moo**ter

À SUA SAÚDE!
(ah sooer serooder)
YOUR HEALTH!/CHEERS!

Beer *Cerveja*

Beer is a popular drink in Portugal and in Brazil. It is good and always served very cold. You may like to sample some of the local brews, for instance Sagres in Portugal and *Antártica* in Brazil. In Portugal beer is often served with *tremoços* (trer**mo**ssoosh—salted lupine seeds) or *amendoins* (ermayng**dweengsh**—peanuts).

I'd like a beer, please.	**Queria uma cerveja, se faz favor.**	kerreeer oomer serrvayzher ser fash fer**voar**
a dark beer	**uma cerveja preta**	oomer serr**vay**zher **pray**ter
a draught beer	**uma imperial [um chope]**	oomer eengperr**ryahl** [oong **shop**pi]
a lager	**uma cerveja (branca)**	oomer serr**vay**zher (**brahng**ker)
Please bring me a ... of beer.	**Por favor, traga-me ... de cerveja.**	poor fer**voar trah**ger mer ... der serr**vay**zher
bottle	**uma garrafa**	oomer ger**rah**fer
glass	**um copo**	oong **kop**poo
mug (a quart)	**uma caneca**	oomer ker**neh**ker
Waiter! Another beer!	**Se faz favor! Outra cerveja!**	ser fash fer**voar. oa**trer serr**vay**zher

Wine *Vinhos*

Climatic conditions in Portugal account for the variety in the nature and quality of the wine. Some wine-producing regions are classified and controlled by law, because of the distinguishing characteristics of their wines. This goes for the Douro Valley in northern Portugal (Port wine), and the districts of Dão, Bairrada, Bucelas, Carcavelos, Algarve and Madeira.

Wine production in the Douro Valley dates back to the Crusades. However the wine which we call Port originated later. In 1678, two Englishmen, having just bought the output of a monastery's vineyard, puzzled over how to ship it back to Britain in order that it might arrive in good condition. They hit upon the idea of adding a little brandy to each of the casks. Thus the famous Port wine was born.

To ensure the integrity of the wine, the Portuguese Port Wine Institute closely oversees production and shipment. Not only is the growing area for Port wine strictly limited, but constant checks are made on the wine leaving the country to monitor colour, bouquet and quality.

The Portuguese seem to prefer the drier, lighter types as aperitifs or dessert wines. You'll notice that a much more popular wine than Port is the light, white *Moscatel* from the Setúbal area, south of Lisbon. It's often drunk before meals.

The *vinhos verdes* (red or white) are called *verdes* (green) because the grapes, slightly underripe, are sour and contain little sugar. They have a low percentage of alcohol and originate from the Minho region, northwest of Portugal.

Brazilian wines are produced in the southern part of the country. This region turns out some good red wines, and white wines too. Brazilians, however—probably because of the hot climate—prefer beer or an exotic and refreshing long drink.

The chart below will help to identify some of the good regional wines. Fine provincial cooking is well accompanied by good local wine whereas exquisite cuisine calls for a noble wine.

Type of wine	Examples	Accompanies
dry, light white	Most of the white *vinhos verdes; Porca de Murça* and *Pérola* from the Douro region; *Bucelas; Óbidos* and *Alcobaça* from the Estremadura region	fish, seafood, appetizers, cheese
dry white	Madeira wines such as *Sercial* and medium-dry *Verdelho*	desserts, sometimes served as an aperitif
sweet white	*Moscatel* from the Setúbal region; wines from the Carcavelos and Favaios regions. Look also for bottles labelled *Grandjó,* from the Douro region	all kinds of desserts *Moscatel de Setúbal* is often taken before meals
rosé	Wines from the Pinhel region, the *Mateus rosé* from the district of Trás-os-Montes	poultry, cold dishes
light-bodied red	Douro *Clarete,* wines from the Lafões region and all red *vinhos verdes*	poultry, meat
full-bodied red	Wines from Colares, Dão, Lagoa and Bairrada regions	meat and game
sweet red	Madeira wines such as *Malmsey* and drier Bual. Port wine from the Douro region	desserts. Can also be used in sauces to impart a delicious flavour to meat
sparkling	Bairrada, especially the *vinhos espumantes naturais* from the Caves da Raposeira	desserts, or as an aperitif

May I have the wine list, please?	**Pode trazer-me a lista dos vinhos, se faz favor?**	**po**dder trer**zayr** mer er **leesh**ter doosh **vee**nyoosh ser fash fer**voar**
I'd like a bottle of white/red wine.	**Queria uma garrafa de vinho branco/ tinto.**	kerr**ee**er **oo**mer gerr**ah**fer der **vee**nyoo **brahng**koo/ **teeng**too
half a bottle	**meia-garrafa**	**may**er gerr**ah**fer
a carafe	**um jarro**	oong **zhah**rroo
half a litre	**meio-litro**	**may**oo **lee**troo
a glass	**um copo**	oong **ko**ppoo
Please bring me another bottle.	**Por favor, traga-me outra garrafa.**	poor fer**voar trah**ger mer **oa**trer gerr**ah**fer
Where does this wine come from?	**Donde é este vinho?**	**dawng**der eh **aysh**ter **vee**nyoo

red	**tinto**	**teeng**too
white	**branco**	**brahng**koo
rosé	**rosé**	ro**zzay**
sparkling	**espumante**	ishpoo**mahng**ter
dry	**seco**	**say**koo
full-bodied	**encorpado**	ayngkoor**pah**doo
light	**ligeiro**	li**zhay**roo
sweet	**doce**	**doa**sser
very dry	**extra-seco**	**aysh**trer **say**koo

Other alcoholic drinks *Outras bebidas alcoólicas*

I'd like to try a/an ...	**Queria provar ...**	kerr**ee**er proo**vahr**
anise liqueur	**um anis**	oong er**neesh**
cognac	**um conhaque**	oong ko**nnyah**ker
gin and tonic	**um gim tónico**	oong zheeng **to**nnikkoo
liqueur	**um licor**	oong li**kkoar**
Madeira wine	**um vinho da Madeira**	oong **vee**nyoo der mer**day**rer
port	**um vinho do Porto**	oong **vee**nyoo doo **poar**too
rum	**um rum**	oong roong
sherry	**um Xerez**	oong sher**raysh**
vermouth	**um vermute**	oong vehr**moo**ter
(double) whisky	**um uísque (duplo)**	oong **weesh**ker (**doo**ploo)
neat (straight)	**puro**	**poo**roo
on the rocks	**com gelo**	kawng **zhay**loo
with water/soda	**com água/soda**	kawng **ah**gwer/**so**dder

If you'd like to sip a brandy after dinner, try a Portuguese *aguardente velha* like *Borges* or *Constantino*. You may also sample a local *bagaço* (ber**gah**ssoo—spirit made from grape husks), as explosive as the Brazilian *cachaça* (kah**shah**ssah—spirit distilled from sugar-cane). But watch out for the effects!

Here are some other typical Portuguese and Brazilian drinks:

aguardente	ahgwerr**dayng**ter	spirits
de figo	der **fee**goo	fig
de medronho	der mer**droa**nyoo	arbutus berry
batida	bah**tee**dah	*cachaça,* fruit juice, sugar, ice (Braz.)
de caju	di kah**zhoo**	cashew nut
de coco	di **koa**koa	coconut
de maracujá	di mahrahkoo**zhah**	passion-fruit
caipirinha	kighpir**ree**nyah	*cachaça,* lime, sugar and ice (Braz.)
Cuba libre	**koo**bah **lee**bri	rum and Coke
ginjinha	zheeng**zhee**nyer	spirit distilled from morello cherries

Nonalcoholic drinks *Bebidas não alcoólicas*

I'd like a/an ...	**Queria ...**	ker**ree**er
fruit juice	**um sumo* de fruta**	oong **soo**moo der **froo**ter
grape juice	**um sumo* de uva**	oong **soo**moo der **oo**ver
iced coffee/tea	**um refresco de café/chá**	oong rer**fraysh**koo der ker**feh**/shah
lemon juice	**uma limonada**	**oo**mer limmoo**nah**der
lemonade	**uma gasosa**	**oo**mer gerzozzer
(glass of) milk	**(um copo de) leite**	(oong **kop**poo der) **lay**ter
milk shake	**um batido [milkshake]**	oong ber**tee**doo [milk**shay**ki]
mineral water	**uma água mineral**	**oo**mer **ah**gwer minne**rrahl**
fizzy (carbonated)	**com gás**	kawng gash
still	**sem gás**	sahng^{y} gash
orange juice	**um sumo* de laranja**	oong **soo**moo der le**rrahng**zher
orangeade	**uma laranjada**	**oo**mer lerrahng**zhah**der
pineapple juice	**um sumo* de ananás**	oong **soo**moo der erner**nash**
tonic water	**uma água tónica**	**oo**mer **ah**gwer **ton**nikker

* In Brazil: **suco** (**soo**koa)

Brazilians are very fond of refreshing drinks (*refrescos*—ray-**fray**skoas). Look for the bars advertising *sucos* (juices) with lots of fresh fruit on display. They serve as many as 20 different fruits, squeezed as you watch. Some are very exotic, some quite sweet. Try one!

água de coco	ahgwah di **koa**koa	coconut juice
caldo de cana	**kahl**doa di **kah**nah	sugar-cane juice
guaraná	gwahrah**nah**	a tropical fruit drink
leite de coco	**lay**ti di **koa**koa	coconut milk
mate	**mah**ti	ice-cold Paraguay tea
milkshake	milk**shay**ki	milk shake
de café	di kah**feh**	coffee-flavoured
de limão	di **limmahng**^{w}	lemon-flavoured
suco de abacaxi	**soo**koa di ahbahkah**shee**	pineapple juice
suco de mamão	**soo**koa di mah**mahng**^{w}	papaya juice
suco de manga	**soo**koa di **mahng**gah	mango juice
suco de tamarindo	**soo**koa di tahmah**reeng**doa	tamarind juice

Hot beverages *Bebidas quentes*

Drunk anytime of the day—or night—Brazilian *cafezinho* (kahfeh**zee**nyoa), a strong, espresso-type coffee, is served black with a lot of sugar to make it less bitter-tasting.

In Portugal, at the end of lunch or dinner most people order a *bica* (**bee**ker), similar to Brazilian *cafezinho*. With a few drops of milk in it, a *bica* is called a *garoto* (ger**roa**too); and a *galão* (ger**lahng**^{w}) is a white coffee in a tall glass. A diluted black coffee is called a *carioca* (ker**ryo**kker). But you also can ask for:

(hot) chocolate	**um chocolate (quente)**	oong shookoo**lah**ter (**kayng**ter)
(double) coffee	**um café (duplo)**	oong ker**feh** (**doo**ploo)
with milk	**com leite**	kawng **lay**ter
decaffeinated	**sem cafeína**	sahng^{y} kerfeh**ee**ner
tea	**um chá**	oong shah
cup of tea	**uma chávena [xícara] de chá**	**oo**mer **shah**verner [**shee**kahrah] der shah
with milk/lemon	**com leite/limão**	kawng **lay**ter/**limmahng**^{w}

Complaints *Reclamações*

There's a plate/glass missing.	**Falta um prato/ um copo.**	**fahl**ter oong **prah**too/ oong **kop**poo
I have no knife/ fork/spoon.	**Não tenho faca/ garfo/colher.**	nahng^{w} **tay**nyoo **fah**ker/ **gahr**foo/kool**yehr**
That's not what I ordered.	**Não é o que eu encomendei.**	nahng^{w} eh oo ker **eh**oo ayngkoomayng**day**
I asked for ...	**Pedi ...**	per**dee**
There must be some mistake.	**Deve haver um engano.**	**deh**ver er**vayr** oong ayng**ger**noo
May I change it?	**Não pode trocar?**	nahng^{w} **pod**der troo**kahr**
I asked for a small portion (for the child).	**Pedi uma dose pequena (para esta criança).**	per**dee** oomer **doz**zer per**kay**ner (**per**rer **ehsh**ter **kryahng**ser)
The meat is ...	**A carne está ...**	er **kahr**ner ish**tah**
overdone	**passada demais**	pers**sah**der der**mighsh**
underdone	**mal passada**	mahl pers**sah**der
too rare	**mal passada demais**	mahl pers**sah**der der**mighsh**
too tough	**dura demais**	**door**er der**mighsh**
This is too ...	**Isto está ... demais.**	**eesh**too ish**tah** ... der**mighsh**
bitter/salty/sweet	**amargo/salgado/ doce**	er**mahr**goo/sahl**gah**doo/ **doas**ser
I don't like this.	**Não gosto disto.**	nahng^{w} **gosh**too **deesh**too
The food is cold.	**A comida está fria.**	er koo**mee**der ish**tah** **free**er
This isn't fresh.	**Isto não está fresco.**	**eesh**too nahng^{w} ish**tah** **fraysh**koo
What's taking you so long?	**Porque demora tanto?**	**poor**ker der**mor**rer **tahng**too
Have you forgotten our drinks?	**Esqueceu-se das nossas bebidas?**	ishkeh**sseh**oo ser dersh **nos**sersh ber**bee**dersh
The wine tastes of cork.	**O vinho sabe a rolha.**	oo **veen**yoo **sah**ber er **roal**yer
This isn't clean.	**Isto não está limpo.**	**eesh**too nahng^{w} ish**tah** **leeng**poo
Would you ask the head waiter to come over?	**Pode mandar chamar o chefe de mesa?**	**pod**der mahng**dahr** sher**mahr** oo **sheh**fer der **may**zer

The bill (check) *A conta*

A service charge is generally included automatically in restaurant bills, but if service has been especially good, an extra tip is appropriate and appreciated. Credit cards may be used in an increasing number of restaurants. Signs are posted indicating which cards are accepted.

I'd like to pay.	**Queria pagar.**	kerreeer pergahr
We'd like to pay separately.	**Queríamos pagar separadamente.**	kerreeermoosh pergahr serperrahdermayngter
I think there is a mistake in this bill.	**Creio que se enganou na conta.**	krayoo ker ser aynggernoa ner kawngter
What is this amount for?	**A que corresponde esta importância?**	er ker koorrershpawngder ehshter eengpoortahngsyer
Is service included?	**O serviço está incluído?**	oo serrveessoo ishtah eengklweedoo
Is everything included?	**Está tudo incluído?**	ishtah toodoo eengklweedoo
Do you accept traveller's cheques?	**Aceitam cheques de viagem?**	erssaytahng^{w} shehkersh der vyahzhahng^{y}
Can I pay with this credit card?	**Posso pagar com este cartão de crédito?**	possoo pergahr kawng ayshter kerrtahng^{w} der krehdittoo
Thank you, this is for you.	**Obrigado(a), isto é para si.**	oabriggahdoo(er) eeshtoo eh perrer see
Keep the change.	**Guarde o troco.**	gwahrder oo troakoo
That was a delicious meal.	**A refeição estava deliciosa.**	er rerfayssahng^{w} ishtahver derlissyozzer
We enjoyed it, thank you.	**Gostámos muito, obrigado(a).**	gooshtahmoosh moong^{y}too oabriggahdoo(er)

SERVIÇO INCLUÍDO
SERVICE INCLUDED

TIPPING, see inside back-cover

Snacks—Picnic *Refeições leves—Piquenique*

You may not feel like having a big meal in a restaurant and may just want a quick bite at a snack-bar. You'll find a selection of small pies and fritters, sandwiches and pastries, and also small dishes *(petiscos)* or salads (see pages 41–42). Since most of the snacks are on display, ordering is easy.

I'll have one of these, please.	**Queria um destes, se faz favor.**	kerreeer oong **daysh**tish ser fash fer**voar**
Give me two of these and one of those.	**Dê-me dois destes e um daqueles.**	day mer doysh **daysh**tish ee oong der**kay**lersh
to the left/right	**à esquerda/direita**	ah ish**kayr**der/dir**ray**ter
above/below	**por cima/por baixo**	poor **see**mer/poor **bigh**shoo
It's to take away.	**É para levar.**	eh **per**rer ler**vahr**
I'd like a/some …	**Queria …**	kerreeer
chicken	**um frango**	oong **frahng**goo
half a roast chicken	**meio-frango assado**	mayoo **frahng**goo ers**sah**doo
chicken pie	**uma empada de galinha**	oomer ayng**pah**der der ger**lee**nyer
chips (french fries)	**batatas fritas**	ber**tah**tersh **free**tersh
croquette	**um croquete**	oong krok**keh**ter
cod	**pastel de bacalhau**	persh**tehl** der berker**lyow**
meat	**croquete de carne**	krok**keh**ter der **kah**rner
hamburger	**um hamburger**	oong ahng**boor**gehr
hot dog	**um cachorro (quente)**	oong ker**shoa**rroo (**kayng**ter)
omelete	**uma omelete**	oomer ommer**leh**ter
pancake	**um crepe [uma panqueca]**	oong **kreh**per [oomah pahng**keh**kah]
with sugar	**com açúcar**	kawng ers**soo**kerr
with jam	**com doce [geléia]**	kawng **doa**sser [zhay**lay**ah]
(small) pie	**um pastel**	oong persh**tehl**
meat	**de carne**	der **kah**rner
shrimp	**de camarão**	der kermer**rahng**ʷ
salad	**uma salada**	oomer ser**lah**der
sandwich	**uma [um] sanduíche**	oomer [oong] sahng**dwee**sher
cheese	**de queijo**	der **kay**zhoo
ham	**de fiambre**	der **fyahng**brer
toast	**uma torrada**	oomer too**rrah**der
toasted sandwich	**uma tosta**	oomer **tosh**ter
ham-and-cheese	**tosta mista [um misto quente]**	**tosh**ter **meesh**ter [oong **mees**toa **kayng**ti]

Here's a basic list of food and drink that might come in useful when shopping for a picnic.

Please give me a/an/ some ...	**Por favor, dê-me ...**	poor f**er**voar day mer
apples	**maçãs**	mer**ssahngsh**
bananas	**bananas**	ber**ner**nersh
biscuits (Br.)	**bolachas**	boo**lah**shersh
beer	**cerveja**	serr**vay**zher
bread	**pão**	pahng^{w}
brown	**escuro**	ish**koo**roo
wholemeal (-wheat)	**integral**	eengter**grahl**
butter	**manteiga**	mahng**tay**ger
cake	**um bolo**	oong **boa**loo
cheese	**queijo**	**kay**zhoo
chips (Am.)	**batatas fritas**	ber**tah**tersh **free**tersh
chocolate bar	**uma tablete de chocolate**	oomer tah**bleh**ter der shookoo**lah**ter
coffee	**café**	ker**feh**
instant	**instantâneo**	eengshtahng**ter**nyoo
cold cuts	**carnes frias**	**kahr**nersh **free**ersh
cookies	**bolachas**	boo**lah**shersh
crisps	**batatas fritas**	ber**tah**tersh **free**tersh
eggs	**ovos**	**ov**voosh
frankfurters	**salsichas**	sahl**see**shersh
gherkins (pickles)	**pepinos de conserva**	per**pee**noosh der kawng**sehr**ver
grapes	**uvas**	**oo**versh
ham	**fiambre**	**fyahng**brer
ice-cream	**gelado [sorvete]**	zher**lah**doo [sor**veh**ti]
lemon	**um limão**	oong lim**mahng^{w}**
milk	**leite**	**lay**ter
mustard	**mostarda**	moosh**tahr**der
oranges	**laranjas**	ler**rahng**zhersh
pastries	**bolos**	**boa**loosh
pepper	**pimenta**	pim**mayng**ter
roll	**um papo-seco [pãozinho]**	oong **pah**poo **say**koo [pahng^{w}**zee**nyoa]
salami	**salame**	ser**ler**mer
salt	**sal**	**sahl**
sausage	**um chouriço**	oong shoa**ree**ssoo
soft drink	**um refrigerante**	oong rerfrizzher**rahng**ter
sugar	**açúcar**	er**soo**kerr
tea	**chá**	**shah**
tomatoes	**tomates**	too**mah**tish
yoghurt	**iogurte**	yog**goor**ter

Travelling around

n Brazil, where air transport is almost as common as bus ravel in Portugal, the following expressions might be useful.

lane *Avião*

s there a flight to Rio de Janeiro?	**Há um voo para o Rio de Janeiro?**	ah oong **voaoo perr**er oo **ree**oo der zher**nay**roo
s it a direct flight?	**É um voo directo?**	eh oong **voaoo** di**rreh**too
When's the next flight to São Paulo?	**A que horas é o próximo avião para São Paulo?**	er ker **or**rersh eh oo **pro**ssimmoo er**vyahng**^{w} perrer sahng^{w} powloo
Can I make a connection to Brasília?	**Tenho correspondência [conexão] para Brasília?**	**tay**nyoo koorrershpawng**dayng**syer [konnehk**sahng**^{w}] perrer brer**zee**lyer
I'd like a ticket to Recife.	**Quero um bilhete para Recife.**	**keh**roo oong bi**llyay**ter perrer rer**see**fer
single (one-way)	**ida**	**ee**der
return (roundtrip)	**ida e volta**	**ee**der ee **voll**ter
What time do we take off?	**A que horas sai o avião?**	er ker **or**rersh sigh oo er**vyahng**^{w}
What time do I have to check in?	**A que horas devo apresentar-me?**	er ker **or**rersh **day**voo erprerzayng**tahr** mer
Is there a bus to the airport?	**Há um autocarro [ônibus] para o aeroporto?**	ah oong owto**kkahr**roo [**oa**nibbooss] **perr**er oo erehro**ppoar**too
What's the flight number?	**Qual é o número do voo?**	kwahl eh oo **noo**merroo doo **voaoo**
At what time do we arrive?	**A que horas chegamos?**	er ker **or**rersh sher**ger**moosh
I'd like to ... my reservation.	**Queria ... a marcação do meu lugar.**	ker**ree**er ... er merrker**ssahng**^{w} doo **meh**oo loo**gahr**
cancel	**anular**	ernoo**lahr**
change	**mudar**	moo**dahr**
confirm	**confirmar**	kawngfirr**mahr**

CHEGADA
ARRIVAL

PARTIDA
DEPARTURE

Train *Comboio [trem]*

The Portuguese railway, *Caminhos de Ferro Portugueses (C.P.),* handles practically all rail services. The trains are fast and generally run on time on the main lines. They offer first and second class seats. The Brazilian railways, *Estrada de Ferro Central do Brasil (E.F.C.B.),* are, with the exception of a few lines, not recommended for passengers.

Lisboa-Expresso, TER (lizh**boaer** ish**prehs**soo, tehr)	Express train linking Lisbon with Madrid; reservation compulsory, surcharge payable
Lusitânia-Expresso (loozitternyer ish**prehs**soo)	Express train, links Lisbon to Madrid, early booking advisable
Sud-Express (sood ish**prehss**)	Express train, links Lisbon to Paris, early booking advisable
Internacional (eengterrnerssyoo**nahl**)	A direct train; for a trip abroad you'll have to book a seat in advance, as only one carriage crosses the border.
Rápido (**rah**piddoo)	Direct train, stops only at main stations, early booking advisable
Automotora (owtoamoo**toa**rer)	Small diesel train used on short runs
Correio (koo**rray**oo)	Long-distance postal train, stops at all stations, also takes passengers

To the railway station *Para a estação*

Lisbon has four principal railway stations. International services and trains for northern Portugal leave from Santa Apolónia station. Commuter trains for the western suburbs and Estoril and Cascais leave from Cais do Sodré. Trains for Sintra and the west depart from Rossio station. And the fourth station, Sul e Sueste, has ferryboats which cross the Tagus for trains that go on as far as the Algarve.

Taxi!	**Táxi!**	**tah**ksi
Take me to ... station.	**Leve-me à estação de ...**	**leh**ver mer ah ishter**ssahng**^{w} der

Is this the railway station for trains to ...?	**É esta a estação dos comboios [trens] para ...?**	eh **ehsh**ter er ishter**ssahng**ʷ doosh kawng**boy**oosh [trahngʸss] **per**rer
How much is that?	**Quanto é?**	**kwahng**too eh

ENTRADA	ENTRANCE
SAÍDA	EXIT
ACESSO AOS CAIS [ÀS PLATAFORMAS]	TO THE PLATFORMS
INFORMAÇÕES	INFORMATION

Where's the ...? *Onde é ...?*

Where is/are the ...?	**Onde é/são ...?**	**awng**der eh/sahngʷ
booking office	**a marcação de lugares**	er merrker**ssahng**ʷ der loo**gah**rersh
currency exchange office	**o câmbio**	oo **kahng**byoo
left-luggage office (baggage check)	**o depósito da bagagem**	oo der**pozz**ittoo der ber**gah**zhahngʸ
lost property (lost and found) office	**a secção dos perdidos e achados**	er sehk**sahng**ʷ doosh perr**dee**doosh ee er**shah**doosh
luggage lockers	**o depósito da bagagem automático**	oo der**pozz**ittoo der ber**gah**zhahngʸ owtoo**mah**tikkoo
newsstand	**o quiosque [a banca] de jornais**	oo **kyosh**ker [ah **bahng**kah] der zhoor**nighsh**
reservations office	**a marcação de lugares**	er merrker**ssahng**ʷ der loo**gah**rersh
restaurant	**o restaurante**	oo rishtow**rahng**ter
snack bar	**o snack-bar [a lanchonete]**	oo "snack bar" [ah lahngshoa**neh**ti]
ticket office	**a bilheteira [a bilheteria]**	er billyer**tay**rer [ah billyaytay**ree**ah]
waiting room	**a sala de espera**	er **sah**ler der ish**peh**rer
Where are the toilets?	**Onde são as casas de banho [os banheiros]?**	**awng**der sahngʷ ersh **kah**zersh der **ber**nyoo [oass bah**nyay**roass]

TAXI, see page 21

Inquiries *Informações*

When is the ... train to Faro?	**Quando é o ... comboio* para Faro?**	**kwahng**doo eh oo ... kawng**boy**oo **per**rer **fah**roo
first/last/next	**primeiro/último/ próximo**	prim**may**roo/**ool**timmoo/ **pro**ssimmoo
What time does the train to Braga leave?	**A que horas parte o comboio* para Braga?**	er ker **or**rersh **pahr**ter oo kawng**boy**oo **per**rer **brah**ger
What's the fare to Oporto?	**Qual é o preço do bilhete para o Porto?**	kwahl eh oo **pray**ssoo doo bil**yay**ter **per**rer oo **poar**too
Is it a through train?	**É um comboio* directo?**	eh oong kawng**boy**oo dir**reh**too
Must I pay a surcharge?	**Tenho de pagar um suplemento?**	**tay**nyoo der per**gahr** oong soopler**mayng**too
Is there a connection to ...?	**Há correspondência [conexão] para ...?**	ah koorrershpawng**dayng**syer [konnehk**sahng**ʷ] **per**rer
Do I have to change trains?	**Tenho de mudar de comboio*?**	**tay**nyoo der moo**dahr** der kawng**boy**oo
Is there sufficient time to change?	**Dá tempo para mudar?**	dah **tayng**poo **per**rer moo**dahr**
Is the train running on time?	**O comboio* sai à tabela?**	oo kawng**boy**oo sigh ah ter**beh**ler
What time does the train arrive in Lisbon?	**A que horas chega o comboio* a Lisboa?**	er ker **or**rersh **shay**ger oo kawng**boy**oo er lizh**boa**er
Is there a dining-car on the train?	**O comboio* tem restaurante?**	oo kawng**boy**oo tahngʸ rishtow**rahng**ter
Does the train stop in Obidos?	**O comboio* pára em Óbidos?**	oo kawng**boy**oo **pah**rer ahngʸ **ob**biddoosh
What track does the train to Sintra leave from?	**Qual é a linha do comboio* para Sintra?**	kwahl eh er **lee**nyer doo kawng**boy**oo **per**rer **seeng**trer
What platform does the train from Sintra arrive at?	**Qual é o cais [a plataforma] do comboio* de Sintra?**	kwahl eh oo kighsh [ah plahtah**forr**mah] doo kawng**boy**oo der **seeng**trer
I'd like to buy a timetable.	**Queria comprar um horário.**	ker**ree**er kawng**prahr** oong or**rah**ryoo

* In Brazil: **trem** [trahngʸ]

É um comboio [trem] directo.	It's a through train.
Tem de mudar em ...	You have to change at ...
Mude em ... e apanhe [pegue] um comboio [trem] regional.	Change at ... and get a local train.
O cais [a plataforma] 3 fica ...	Platform 3 is ...
ali/lá em cima **à esquerda/à direita**	over there/upstairs on the left/on the right
Há um comboio [trem] para ... às ...	There's a train to ... at ...
O seu comboio [trem] sai da linha 5.	Your train will leave from track 5.
Há um atraso de ... minutos.	There'll be a delay of ... minutes.
Primeira classe à frente/ao meio/atrás.	First class at the front/in the middle/at the end.

Tickets *Bilhetes*

I'd like a ticket to Oporto.	**Quero um bilhete para o Porto.**	**keh**roo oong bil**lyay**ter perrer oo poartoo
single (one-way)	**ida**	**ee**der
return (roundtrip)	**ida e volta**	**ee**der ee **voll**ter
first class	**primeira classe**	prim**may**rer **klah**sser
second class	**segunda classe**	ser**goong**der **klah**sser
half price	**meio-bilhete**	**may**oo bil**lyay**ter
with surcharge	**com suplemento**	kawng soopler**mayng**too

Reservation *Marcação de lugares*

I want to reserve a ...	**Queria marcar ...**	ker**ree**er merr**kahr**
seat (by the window)	**um lugar (junto à janela)**	oong loo**gahr** (**zhoong**too ah zher**neh**ler)
berth	**um beliche**	oong ber**lee**sher
upper	**superior**	sooper**ryoar**
lower	**inferior**	eengfer**ryoar**
berth in the sleeping car	**um lugar na carruagem-camas [no vagão-leitos]**	oong loo**gahr** ner kerr**wah**zhahng^y **ker**mersh [noa vah**gahng**^{w} **lay**toass]

NUMBERS, see page 147

All aboard *Partida*

Is this the right platform for the train to Faro?	**É este o cais [a plataforma] do comboio* para Faro?**	eh **aysh**ter oo kighsh [ah plahtah**forr**mah] doo kawng**boy**oo **per**rer **fah**roo
Is this the train to Madrid?	**É este o comboio* para Madrid?**	eh **aysh**ter oo kawng**boy**oo **per**rer mer**dreed**
Excuse me. May I get by?	**Com licença. Posso passar?**	kawng li**ssayng**ser. **po**ssoo per**ssahr**
Is this seat taken?	**Este lugar está ocupado?**	**aysh**ter loo**gahr** ish**tah** okkoo**pah**doo

FUMADORES	NÃO FUMADORES
SMOKER	NONSMOKER

I think that's my seat.	**Acho que esse é o meu lugar.**	**ah**shoo ker **ay**sser eh oo **meh**oo loo**gahr**
Would you let me know before we get to Coimbra?	**Pode avisar-me quando chegarmos a Coimbra?**	**po**dder ervi**zzahr** mer **kwahng**doo sher**gahr**moosh er **kweeng**brer
What station is this?	**Que estação é esta?**	ker ishter**ssahng**ʷ eh **ehsh**ter
How long does the train stop here?	**Quanto tempo vai demorar o comboio* aqui?**	**kwahng**too **tayng**poo vigh dermoo**rahr** oo kawng**boy**oo er**kee**
When do we get to Lisbon?	**Quando chegamos a Lisboa?**	**kwahng**doo sher**ger**moosh er lizh**boa**er

Sleeping *Para dormir*

Are there any free compartments in the sleeping car?	**Há compartimentos livres na carruagem-camas [no vagão-leitos].**	ah kawngperrti**mmayng**toosh **lee**vrersh ner ker**rwah**zhahngʸ **ker**mersh [noa vah**gahng**ʷ **lay**toass]
Where's the sleeping car?	**Onde fica a carruagem-camas [o vagão-leitos]?**	**awng**der **fee**ker er ker**rwah**zhahngʸ **ker**mersh [oa vah**gahng**ʷ **lay**toass]
Where's my berth?	**Onde fica o meu beliche?**	**awng**der **fee**ker oo **meh**oo ber**lee**sher

* In Brazil: **trem** [trahngʸ]

I'd like a lower/ upper berth.	**Queria um beliche inferior/superior.**	kerr**ee**er oong berl**ee**sher eengferr**yoar**/sooperr**yoar**
Would you make up our berths?	**Pode preparar-nos os beliches?**	**po**dder prerperr**ahr** noosh oosh berl**ee**shersh
Would you wake me at 7 o'clock?	**Pode acordar-me às 7 horas?**	**po**dder erkoor**dahr** mer ahsh 7 **o**rrersh

Eating *Para comer*

You can get snacks and drinks in the buffet car and a full meal in the dining car. If the train is crowded there may be two sittings.

Where's the dining car/buffet car?	**Onde é a carruagem--restaurante/cantina?**	**awng**der eh er kerr**wah**zhahng^{y} rishtow**rahng**ter/kahng**tee**ner

Baggage and porters *Bagagens e carregadores*

Porter!	**Carregador!**	kerrerger**doar**
Can you help me with my luggage?	**Pode ajudar-me a levar a bagagem?**	**po**dder erzhoo**dahr** mer er ler**vahr** er ber**gah**zhahng^{y}
Where are the luggage trolleys (carts)?	**Onde estão os carrinhos da bagagem?**	**awng**der ish**tahng**^{w} oosh kerr**ee**nyoosh der ber**gah**zhahng^{y}
Where are the luggage lockers?	**Onde é o depósito da bagagem automático?**	**awng**der eh oo der**pozz**ittoo der ber**gah**zhahng^{y} owtoo**mah**tikkoo
Where's the left-luggage office (baggage check)?	**Onde é o depósito da bagagem?**	**awng**der eh oo der**pozz**ittoo der ber**gah**zhahng^{y}
I'd like to leave my luggage, please.	**Queria depositar a minha bagagem, se faz favor.**	kerr**ee**er derpoozi**ttahr** er **mee**nyer ber**gah**zhahng^{y} ser fahsh fer**voar**
I'd like to register (check) my luggage.	**Queria despachar a minha bagagem.**	kerr**ee**er dishper**shahr** er **mee**nyer ber**gah**zhahng^{y}

> **DESPACHO DE BAGAGENS**
> REGISTERING (CHECKING) BAGGAGE

PORTERS, see also page 18

Coach (long-distance bus) *Camioneta [ônibus]*

Inter-city bus and coach services are frequent and cover most of Portugal. Some coaches are run by the Portuguese Transport Company, *Rodoviária Nacional (R.N.)*, others are private. In Brazil coach travel is cheap, but time-consuming.

Where's the coach terminal (bus station)?	Onde é o terminal das camionetas [dos ônibus]?	awngder eh oo terrminnahl dersh kahmyooneetersh [doass oanibbooss]
When's the next inter-city bus to …?	A que horas é o próximo expresso para …?	er ker orrersh eh oo prossimmoo ishprehssoo perrer
Does this coach stop in …?	Esta camioneta [este ônibus] pára em …?	ehshter kahmyoonehter [aysti oanibbooss] pahrer ahngy
How long does the journey (trip) take?	Quanto tempo demora a viagem?	kwahngtoo tayngpoo dermorrer er vyahzhahngy

Note: Most of the phrases on the previous pages can be used or adapted for travelling on local transport.

Bus—Tram (streetcar) *Autocarro [ônibus]—Eléctrico [bonde]*

I'd like a booklet of tickets/tourist pass.	Queria uma caderneta de bilhetes/um passe para turistas.	kerreeer oomer kerderrnayter der billyaytersh/oong pahsser perrer tooreeshtersh
Which tram (streetcar) goes to the town centre?	Qual é o eléctrico [bonde] que vai para o centro da cidade?	kwahl eh oo illehtrikkoo [bawngdi] ker vigh perrer oo sayngtroo der siddahder
Where can I get a bus to …?	Onde posso apanhar [pegar] um autocarro [ônibus] para …?	awngder possoo erpernyahr [paygahr] oong owtokkahrroo [oanibbooss] perrer
Which bus do I take for …?	Que autocarro [ônibus] devo apanhar [pegar] para …?	ker owtokkahrroo [oanibbooss] dayvoo erpernyahr [paygahr] perrer
Where's the bus stop?	Onde é a paragem do autocarro [parada de ônibus]?	awngder eh er perrahzhahngy doo owtokkahrroo [pahrahdah di oanibbooss]

When is the ... bus to ...?	**A que horas é o ... autocarro [ônibus] para ...?**	er ker **or**rersh eh oo ... owto**kkah**rroo [**oa**nibbooss] **per**rer
first/last/next	**primeiro/último/ próximo**	prim**may**roo/**ool**timmoo/ **pro**ssimmoo
How much is the fare to ...?	**Qual é o preço do bilhete para ...?**	kwahl eh oo **pray**ssoo doo bil**lyay**ter **per**rer
Do I have to change buses?	**É preciso mudar de autocarro [ônibus]?**	eh prer**ssee**zoo moo**dahr** der owto**kkah**rroo [**oa**nibbooss]
How many bus stops are there to ...?	**Quantas paragens [paradas] há até ...?**	**kwahng**tersh per**rah**-zhahng^{y}sh [pah**rah**dahss] ah er**teh**
Will you tell me when to get off?	**Pode avisar-me quando devo descer?**	**po**dder ervi**zzahr** mer **kwahng**doo **day**voo dish**sayr**
I want to get off at ...	**Quero descer no(a) ...**	**keh**roo dish**sayr** noo(er)

PARAGEM DE AUTOCARROS [PARADA DE ÔNIBUS]	BUS STOP

Underground (subway) *Metropolitano/Metro*

The underground in Lisbon has two main lines which join at Pombal Square. The fare is the same irrespective of the distance you travel. São Paulo and Rio de Janeiro also have underground systems.

Where's the nearest underground (subway) station?	**Onde é a estação de metro mais próxima?**	**awng**der eh er ishter-**ssahng**^{w} der **meh**troo mighsh **pro**ssimmer?
Does this train go to ...?	**Este metro vai para ...?**	**aysh**ter **meh**troo vigh **per**rer
Where do I change for ...?	**Onde devo mudar para ...?**	**awng**der **day**voo moo**dahr** **per**rer
Is the next station ...?	**A próxima estação é ...?**	er **pro**ssimmer ishter-**ssahng**^{w} eh
Which line should I take for ...?	**Que linha devo tomar para ...?**	ker **lee**nyer **day**voo too**mahr** **per**rer

Boat service *Barcos*

When does the next boat to ... leave?	**Quando sai o próximo barco para ...?**	**kwahng**doo sigh oo **pro**ssimmoo **bahr**koo **per**rer
Where's the embarkation point?	**Onde é o cais de embarque?**	**awng**der eh oo kighsh der ayng**bahr**ker
How long does the crossing take?	**Quanto tempo leva a travessia?**	**kwahng**too **tayng**poo **leh**ver trerver**ssee**er
At which port(s) do we stop?	**Em que porto(s) paramos?**	ahng^{y} ker **poar**too(sh) perr**rer**moosh
I'd like to take a cruise.	**Gostava de fazer um cruzeiro.**	goosh**tah**ver der fer**zayr** oong kroo**zay**roo
bay	**a baía**	er ber**ee**er
cabin	**a cabine**	er kah**bee**ner
single/double	**individual/dupla**	eengdivvi**ddwahl**/**doo**pler
deck	**o convés**	oo kawng**vehsh**
ferry	**o ferry-boat**	oo "ferry-boat"
harbour	**o porto**	oo **poar**too
hovercraft	**o hovercraft**	oo "hovercraft"
hydrofoil	**o hidroplano [aerobarco]**	oo iddro**pler**noo [ahehro**bbahr**koa]
life belt	**o cinto de salvação**	oo **seeng**too der sahlver**ssahng**^{w}
life boat	**o bote salva-vidas**	oo **bot**ter **sahl**ver **vee**dersh
ship	**o navio**	oo ner**vee**oo
steamer	**o vapor**	oo ver**poar**

Other means of transport *Outros meios de transporte*

bicycle	**a bicicleta**	er bissi**kkleh**ter
cable car	**o teleférico**	oo terler**feh**rikkoo
funicular	**o elevador**	oo illerver**doar**
helicopter	**o helicóptero**	oo illi**kko**pterroo
lift (elevator)	**o elevador**	oo illerver**doar**
moped	**a bicicleta motorizada**	er bissi**kkleh**ter mootoori**zzah**der
motorbike	**a motocicleta**	er mottossi**kkleh**ter
scooter	**a scooter**	er "scooter"

Or perhaps you prefer:

to hitchhike	**pedir boleia [carona]**	per**deer** boo**lay**er [kah**roa**nah]
to walk	**andar a pé**	ahng**dahr** er peh

Car *Automóvel*

Roads in Portugal are classified by numbers, the lower the better. Some motorways (expressway) and bridges are subject to tolls *(a portagem)*. On winding mountain roads it's compulsory to sound your horn. Seat belts *(o cinto de segurança)* are obligatory unless you're in a built-up area. In southern Brazil roads are good, the traffic, however, is very intense, and driving requires good nerves.

Where's the nearest filling station?	**Qual é a estação de serviço mais próxima?**	kwahl eh er ishter**ssahng**^{w} der serr**vee**ssoo mighsh **pro**ssimmer
Full tank, please.	**Encha o depósito, se faz favor.**	**ayng**sher oo der**po**zzittoo ser fash fer**voar**
Give me ... litres of petrol (gasoline).	**Dê-me ... litros de gasolina.**	day mer ... **lee**troosh der gerzoo**lee**ner
super (premium)/ regular/unleaded/ diesel	**super/normal sem chumbo/ gasóleo**	**soo**pehr/norr**mahl**/sahng^{y} **shoong**boo/gah**zo**llyoo
Please check the ...	**Verifique ...**	verri**ffee**ker
battery	**a bateria**	er berter**ree**er
brake fluid	**o líquido dos travões [freios]**	oo **lee**kiddoo doosh trer**vawng**^{y}**sh** [**fray**oass]
oil/water	**o óleo/a água**	oo **o**llyoo/er **ah**gwer
Would you check the tyre pressure?	**Pode verificar a pressão dos pneus?**	**po**dder verriffi**kkahr** er prer**ssahng**^{w} doosh **pneh**oosh
1.6 front, 1.8 rear.	**23 à frente, 26 atrás.**	23 ah **frayng**ter 26 er**trahsh**
Please check the spare tyre, too.	**Verifique também o pneu sobresselente, se faz favor.**	verri**ffee**ker tahng**bahng**^{y} oo **pneh**oo soobrersser**layng**ter ser fash fer**voar**
Can you mend this puncture (fix this flat)?	**Pode consertar este furo?**	**po**dder kawngserr**tahr** **aysh**ter **foo**roo
Would you change the ..., please?	**Pode mudar ...?**	**po**dder moo**dahr**
bulb	**a lâmpada**	er **lahng**perder
fan belt	**a correia da ventoinha**	er koo**rray**er der vayng**twee**nyer

CAR HIRE, see page 20

spark(ing) plugs	**as velas**	ersh **veh**lersh
tyre	**o pneu**	oo **pneh**oo
wipers	**os limpa-vidros**	oosh **leeng**per **vee**droosh
Would you clean the windscreen (windshield)?	**Pode limpar o pára-brisas?**	**pod**der leeng**pahr** oo **pah**rer **bree**zersh

Asking the way—Street directions *Para perguntar o caminho*

Can you tell me the way to ...?	**Pode indicar-me o caminho para ...?**	**pod**der eengdik**kahr** mer oo ker**mee**nyoo **per**rer
How do I get to ...?	**Como se vai para ...?**	**koa**moo ser vigh **per**rer
Are we on the right road for ...?	**É esta a estrada para ...?**	eh **ehsh**ter er ish**trah**der **per**rer
How far is the next village?	**A que distância fica a próxima povoação?**	er ker dish**tahng**syer **fee**ker er **pro**ssimmer poovwer**ssahng**[w]
Is there a road with little traffic?	**Há alguma estrada com pouco trânsito?**	ah ahl**goo**mer ish**trah**der kawng **poa**koo **trahng**zittoo
How far is it to ... from here?	**A que distância estamos de ...?**	er ker dish**tahng**syer ish**ter**moosh der
Is there a motorway (expressway)?	**Há uma auto--estrada?**	ah **oo**mer **ow**to ish**trah**der
How long does it take by car/on foot?	**Quanto tempo se leva de carro/a pé?**	**kwahng**too **tayng**poo ser **leh**ver der **kah**rroo/er peh
Can I drive to the centre of town?	**Posso ir de carro até ao centro da cidade?**	**po**ssoo eer der **kah**rroo er**teh** ow **sayng**troo der sid**dah**der
Can you tell me where ... is?	**Pode dizer-me onde fica ...?**	**pod**der diz**zayr** mer **awng**der **fee**ker
How can I find this place/address?	**Como posso encontrar este lugar/endereço?**	**koa**moo **po**sso ayngkawng**trahr ay**shter loo**gahr**/ ayngder**ray**ssoo
Where's this?	**Onde fica isto?**	**awng**der **fee**ker **eesh**too
Can you show me on the map where I am?	**Pode mostrar-me no mapa onde estou?**	**pod**der moosh**trahr** mer noo **mah**per **awng**der ish**toa**
Can you show me on the map where ... is?	**Pode mostrar-me no mapa onde fica ...?**	**pod**der moos**trahr** mer noo **mah**per **awng**der **fee**ker

Enganou-se na estrada.	You're on the wrong road.
Vá sempre em frente.	Go straight ahead.
É ali à esquerda/à direita.	It's down there on the left/right.
em frente de/atrás de ... **ao lado de/depois de ...**	opposite/behind ... next to/after ...
norte/sul/(l)este/oeste	north/south/east/west
Vá até ao primeiro/ segundo cruzamento.	Go to the first/second crossroads (intersection).
Vire à esquerda nos semáforos.	Turn left at the traffic lights.
Vire à direita na próxima esquina.	Turn right at the next corner.
Apanhe a estrada para ...	Take the ... road to.
É uma rua de sentido único.	It's a one-way street.
Tem de voltar atrás até ...	You have to go back to ...
Siga a direcção Sul Ponte.	Follow signs for Sul Ponte.

Parking *Estacionamento*

Where can I park?	**Onde posso estacionar?**	**awng**der **po**ssoo ishterssyoo**nahr**
Is there a car park nearby?	**Há um parque de automóveis aqui perto?**	ah oong **pahr**ker der owtoo**mo**vvaysh er**kee** **pehr**too
May I park here?	**Posso estacionar aqui?**	**po**ssoo ishterssyoo**nahr** er**kee**
How long can I park here?	**Quanto tempo posso ficar aqui estacionado?**	**kwahng**too **tayng**poo **po**ssoo fi**kkahr** er**kee** ishterssyoo**nah**doo
What's the charge per hour?	**Qual é o preço à hora?**	kwahl eh oo **pray**ssoo ah **o**rrer
Do you have some change for the parking meter?	**Tem dinheiro trocado para o parcómetro?**	tahng^y di**nnyay**roo troo**kah**doo **pe**rrer oo perr**ko**mmertroo

Breakdown—Road assistance *Avarias—Asistência na estrada*

Where's the nearest garage?	**Onde é a garagem mais próxima?**	**awng**der eh er ger**rah**-zhahng^{y} mighsh **pro**ssimmer
Excuse me. My car has broken down.	**Desculpe. O meu carro avariou-se.**	dish**kool**per. oo **meh**oo **kah**rroo erver**ryoa** ser
I've had a breakdown at ...	**Tive uma avaria em ...**	**tee**ver **oo**mer erverr**ee**er ahng^{y}
Can you send a mechanic?	**Pode mandar-me um mecânico?**	**po**dder mahng**dahr** mer oong mer**ker**nikkoo
My car won't start.	**O motor não pega.**	oo moo**toar** nahng^{w} **peh**ger
The battery is dead.	**A bateria está descarregada.**	er berterr**ee**er ish**tah** dishkerrer**gah**der
I've run out of petrol (gasoline).	**Acabou-se-me a gasolina.**	erker**boa** ser mer er gerzoo**lee**ner
I have a flat tyre.	**Tenho um pneu vazio.**	**tay**nyoo oong **pneh**oo ver**zee**oo
The engine is overheating.	**O motor aquece demais.**	oo moo**toar** er**keh**sser der**mighsh**
There is something wrong with the ...	**Há um defeito qualquer ...**	ah oong der**fay**too kwahl**kehr**
brakes	**nos travões [freios]**	noosh trer**vawng^{y}sh** [**fray**oass]
carburettor	**no carburador**	noo kerrboorer**doar**
exhaust pipe	**no tubo de escape**	noo **too**boo der ish**kah**per
radiator	**no radiador**	noo rerdyer**doar**
steering wheel	**no volante**	**noo voolahng**ter
wheel	**numa roda**	**noo**mer **ro**dder
Can you send a breakdown van (tow truck)?	**Pode mandar-me um pronto-socorro?**	**po**dder mahng**dahr** mer oong **prawng**too soo**koa**rroo
How long will you be?	**Quanto tempo vai demorar?**	**kwahng**too **tayng**poo vigh dermoo**rahr**

Accident—Police *Accidentes—Polícia*

Please call the police.	**Por favor, chame a polícia.**	poor fer**voar sher**mer er poo**lee**ssyer
There's been an accident. It's about 2 km. from ...	**Houve um acidente. A cerca de 2 km de ...**	**oa**ver oong erssi**ddayng**ter. er **sayr**ker der 2 ki**llo**mmertroosh der

Where is there a telephone?	**Onde há um telefone?**	**awng**der ah oong terler**fo**nner
Call a doctor/an ambulance quickly.	**Chame um médico/ uma ambulância, depressa.**	**sher**mer oong **meh**dikkoo/ **oo**mer ahngboo**lahng**syer der**preh**sser
There are people injured.	**Há feridos.**	ah fer**ree**doosh
Here's my driving licence.	**Aqui está a minha carta de condução [carteira de motorista].**	er**kee** ish**tah** er **mee**nyer **kahr**ter der kawngdoo**ssahng**[w] [kahr**tay**rah di moatoa**rees**tah]
What's your name and address?	**Qual é o seu nome e endereço?**	kwahl eh oo **seh**oo **noa**mer ee ayngder**ray**ssoo
What's your insurance company?	**Qual é a sua companhia de seguros?**	kwahl eh er **soo**er kawngper**nyee**er der ser**goo**roosh

Road signs *Sinais de trânsito*

AFROUXE	Slow down
BERMAS ALTAS	Soft shoulder
CUIDADO	Caution
CURVAS	Bends (curves)
DESCIDA PERIGOSA	Steep hill
DESVIO	Diversion (detour)
DEVAGAR	Slow
ESTACIONAMENTO PERMITIDO/PROIBIDO	Parking allowed/ No parking
OBRAS	Road works (men working)
PASSAGEM DE NÍVEL	Level (railroad) crossing
PEDÁGIO (Braz.)	Toll
PEDESTRES (Braz.)	Pedestrians
PEÕES	Pedestrians
PORTAGEM	Toll
... PROIBIDO	No ...
QUEDA DE PEDRAS	Falling rocks
SAÍDA DE CAMI[NH]ÕES	Lorry (truck) exit
SIGA PELA DIREITA	Keep right
SEM SAÍDA	No through road
SEMÁFOROS	Traffic lights ahead
SILÊNCIO	Silence zone
TRABALHOS	Road works (men working)
TRÂNSITO PROIBIDO	Road closed
VEÍCULOS PESADOS	Heavy vehicles

Sightseeing

Where's the tourist office?	**Onde é o turismo?**	**awng**der eh oo too**reezh**moo
What are the main points of interest?	**O que há de mais interessante para se ver?**	oo ker ah der mighsh eeng-terrer**ssahng**ter perrer ser vayr
We're here for ...	**Ficamos aqui ...**	fikker**moosh** er**kee**
only a few hours	**só algumas horas**	saw ahl**goo**mersh **or**rersh
a day	**um dia**	oong **dee**er
a week	**uma semana**	**oo**mer ser**mer**ner
Can you recommend a sightseeing tour/ an excursion?	**Pode recomendar-me um circuito turístico/uma excursão?**	**po**dder rerkoomayng**dahr** mer oong sirr**kooy**too too**reesh**tikkoo/**oo**mer ishkoor**sahng**^{w}
Where's the point of departure?	**De onde é a partida?**	der **awng**der eh er perr**tee**der
Will the bus pick us up at the hotel?	**A camioneta [o ônibus] vem buscar-nos ao hotel?**	er kahmyoo**neh**ter [oa **oa**nibbooss] vahng^{y} boosh-**kahr** noosh ow o**ttehl**
How much does the tour cost?	**Quanto custa a excursão?**	**kwahng**too **koosh**ter er ishkoor**sahng**^{w}
What time does the tour start?	**A que horas começa a excursão?**	er ker **or**rersh koo**meh**sser er ishkoor**sahng**^{w}
Is lunch included?	**O almoço está incluído?**	oo ahl**moa**ssoo ish**tah** eeng**klwee**doo
What time do we get back?	**A que horas regressamos?**	er ker **or**rersh rergrer**sser**moosh
Do we have free time in ...?	**Temos algum tempo livre em ...?**	**tay**moosh ahl**goong** **tayng**-poo **lee**vrer ahng^{y}
Is there an English-speaking guide?	**Há algum guia que fale inglês?**	ah ahl**goong** **ghee**er ker **fah**ler eeng**glaysh**
I'd like to hire a private guide for ...	**Queria um guia particular por ...**	ker**ree**er oong **ghee**er perrtikkoo**lahr** poor
half a day	**meio-dia**	**may**oo **dee**er
a full day	**um dia inteiro**	oong **dee**er eeng**tay**roo

Where is/are the ...?	Onde fica/ficam ...?	awngder feeker/feekahng[w]
aquarium	o aquário	oo erkwahryoo
art gallery	a galeria de arte	er gerlerreeer der ahrter
artists' quarter	o bairro dos artistas	oo bighrroo doosh errteeshtersh
basilica	a basílica	er berzeelikker
botanical gardens	o jardim botânico	oo zherrdeeng booternikkoo
building	o edifício	oo iddiffeessyoo
bullring	a praça de touros	er prahsser der toaroosh
business district	o centro de negócios	oo sayngtroo der nergossyoosh
castle	o castelo	oo kershtehloo
cathedral	a sé/catedral	er seh/kerterdrahl
cemetery	o cemitério	oo sermittehryoo
city centre	o centro da cidade	oo sayngtroo der siddahder
chapel	a capela	er kerpehler
church	a igreja	er iggrayzher
concert hall	a sala de concertos	er sahler der kawngsayrtoosh
convent	o convento	oo kawngvayngtoo
court house	o palácio de justiça	oo perlahssyoo der zhooshteesser
downtown area	o centro da cidade	oo sayngtroo der siddahder
exhibition	a exposição	er ishpoozissahng[w]
factory	a fábrica	er fahbrikker
fair	a feira	er fayrer
flea market	a feira da ladra	er fayrer der lahdrer
fortress	a fortaleza	er foorterlayzer
fountain	a fonte	er fawngter
gardens	o jardim	oo zherrdeeng
harbour	o porto	oo poartoo
library	a biblioteca	er bibblyootehker
market	o mercado	oo merrkahdoo
memorial	o monumento comemorativo	oo moonoomayngtoo koomermoorerteevoo
monastery	o mosteiro	oo mooshtayroo
monument	o monumento	oo moonoomayngtoo
museum	o museu	oo moozehoo
old town	a cidade velha	er siddahder vehlyer
opera house	o teatro da ópera	oo tyahtroo der opperrer
palace	o palácio	oo perlahssyoo
park	o parque	oo pahrker
parliament building	a assembleia nacional	er erssayngblayer nerssyoonahl
planetarium	o planetário	oo plernertahryoo
ruins	as ruínas	ersh rweenersh

shopping area	**a zona comercial**	er **zoa**ner koomerr**syahl**
square	**a praça**	er **prah**sser
stadium	**o estádio**	oo ish**tah**dyoo
statue	**a estátua**	er ish**tah**twer
stock exchange	**a bolsa**	er **boal**ser
theatre	**o teatro**	oo **tyah**troo
tomb	**o túmulo**	oo **too**mooloo
tower	**a torre**	er **toa**rrer
town hall	**a câmara municipal**	er **ker**merrer moonissi**ppahl**
university	**a universidade**	er oonivverrsi**ddah**der
zoo	**o jardim zoológico**	oo zherr**deeng** zoo**lo**zhikkoo

Admission *À entrada*

Is ... open on Sundays?	**... está aberto aos domingos?**	ish**tah** er**behr**too owsh doo**meeng**goosh
What are the opening hours?	**Quais são as horas de abertura?**	kwighsh sahng^{w} ersh orrersh der erberr**too**rer
When does it close?	**A que horas fecha?**	er ker orrersh **fay**sher
How much is the entrance fee?	**Quanto custa a entrada [o ingresso]?**	**kwahng**too **koosh**ter er ayng**trah**der [oo eeng**greh**ssoa]
Is there any reduction for ...?	**Há desconto para ...?**	ah dish**kawng**too **per**rer
children	**crianças**	kr**yahng**ssersh
the disabled	**deficientes físicos**	derfiss**yayng**tish **fee**zikkoosh
groups	**grupos**	**groo**poosh
pensioners	**reformados [aposentados]**	rerfoor**mah**doosh [ahpoozayng**tah**doass]
students	**estudantes**	ishtoo**dahng**tish
Have you a guidebook (in English)?	**Tem um guia (em inglês)?**	tahng^{y} oong **ghee**er (ahng^{y} eeng**glaysh**)
Can I buy a catalogue?	**Posso comprar um catálogo?**	**po**ssoo kawng**prahr** oong ker**tah**loogoo
Is it all right to take pictures?	**É permitido tirar fotografias?**	eh perrmi**ttee**doo ti**rrahr** footoogrer**fee**ersh

ENTRADA LIVRE	ADMISSION FREE
É PROIBIDO TIRAR FOTOGRAFIAS	NO CAMERAS ALLOWED

Who—What—When? *Quem—Que—Quando?*

What's that building?	**Que edifício é aquele?**	ker iddi**ffee**ssyoo eh er**kay**ler
Who was the ...?	**Quem foi ...?**	kahng^{y} foy
architect	**o arquitecto**	oo errki**tteh**too
artist	**o artista**	oo err**teesh**ter
painter	**o pintor**	oo peeng**toar**
sculptor	**o esculptor**	oo ishkool**toar**
Who built it?	**Quem o construiu?**	kahng^{y} oo kawngsh**trwee**oo
Who painted that picture?	**Quem pintou aquele quadro?**	kahng^{y} peeng**toa** er**kay**ler **kwah**droo
When did he live?	**Em que época viveu?**	ahng^{y} ker **eh**pooker vi**vveh**oo
When was it built?	**Quando foi construído?**	**kwahng**doo foy kawngsh**trwee**doo
Where's the house where ... lived?	**Onde fica a casa onde viveu ...?**	**awng**der **fee**ker er **kah**zer **awng**der vi**vveh**oo
We're interested in ...	**Estamos interessados em ...**	ish**ter**moosh eengterrer**ssah**doosh ahng^{y}
antiques	**antiguidades**	ahngtiggwi**ddah**dersh
archaeology	**arqueologia**	errkyooloo**zhee**er
art	**arte**	**ahr**ter
botany	**botânica**	boo**ter**nikker
ceramics	**cerâmica**	se**rrer**mikker
coins	**numismática**	noomizh**mah**tikker
fine arts	**belas-artes**	**beh**lersh **ahr**tish
furniture	**mobiliário**	moobi**llyah**ryoo
geology	**geologia**	zhyooloo**zhee**er
handicrafts	**artesanato**	errterzer**nah**too
history	**história**	ish**to**rryer
maritime history	**história marítima**	ish**to**rryer me**rree**timmer
medicine	**medicina**	merdi**ssee**ner
music	**música**	**moo**zikker
natural history	**ciências naturais**	**syayng**syersh nertoo**righsh**
ornithology	**ornitologia**	orrnittooloo**zhee**er
painting	**pintura**	peeng**too**rer
pottery	**olaria**	olle**rree**er
religion	**religião**	rerli**zhyahng**^{w}
sculpture	**esculptura**	ishkool**too**rer
zoology	**zoologia**	zoo-ooloo**zhee**er
Where's the ... department?	**Onde é a secção de ...?**	**awng**der eh er sehk**sahng**^{w} der

It's ...	**É ...**	eh
amazing	**espantoso**	ishpahng**toa**zoo
awful	**horroroso**	orroo**roa**zoo
beautiful	**lindo**	**leeng**doo
gloomy	**lúgubre**	**loo**goobrer
impressive	**impressionante**	eengprerssyoo**nahng**ter
interesting	**interessante**	eengterrer**ssahng**ter
magnificent	**magnífico**	mer**gnee**fikkoo
pretty	**bonito**	boo**nee**too
strange	**estranho**	ish**trer**nyoo
superb	**estupendo**	ishtoo**payng**doo
terrifying	**pavoroso**	pervoo**roa**zoo
tremendous	**tremendo**	trer**mayng**doo
ugly	**feio**	**fay**oo

Religious services *Serviços religiosos*

Portugal, predominantly Roman Catholic, is rich in cathedrals and churches worth visiting. Fátima—probably the most famous pilgrimage centre in the Iberian peninsula—is about 130 km. north-east of Lisbon. Brazil is also largely Roman Catholic. Most places are open for the public to view except, of course, during mass. If you're interested in taking photographs, you should get permission first.

Is there a ... near here?	**Há ... aqui perto?**	ah ... er**kee pehr**too
Catholic church	**uma igreja católica**	oomer ig**gray**zher ker**to**llikker
Protestant church	**uma igreja protestante**	oomer ig**gray**zher prootish**tahng**ter
mosque	**uma mesquita**	oomer mish**kee**ter
synagogue	**uma sinagoga**	oomer sinner**go**gger
At what time is ...?	**A que horas é ...?**	er ker **o**rrersh eh
mass/the service	**a missa/ o culto**	er **mee**sser/oo **kool**too
Where can I find a ... who speaks English?	**Onde posso encontrar um ... que fale inglês?**	**awng**der **po**ssoo ayngkawng**trahr** oong ... ker **fah**ler eeng**glaysh**
priest/minister	**padre/pastor**	**pah**drer/persh**toar**
rabbi	**rabino**	rer**bee**noo
I'd like to visit the church.	**Queria visitar a igreja.**	ker**ree**er vizzi**ttahr** er ig**gray**zher

In the countryside *No campo*

Is there a scenic route to ...?	**Há algum itinerário turístico para ...?**	ah ahl**goong** ittinner**rah**ryoo too**reesh**tikkoo **per**rer
How far is it to ...?	**A que distância fica ...?**	er ker dish**tahng**syer **fee**ker
Can we walk?	**Podemos ir a pé?**	poo**day**moosh eer er peh
How high is that mountain?	**Qual é a altitude daquela montanha?**	kwahl eh er ahlti**ttoo**der der**keh**ler mawng**ter**nyer
What's the name of that ...?	**Qual é o nome ...?**	kwahl eh oo **noa**mer
animal/bird	**daquele animal/ pássaro**	der**kay**ler erni**mmahl/ pah**sserroo
flower/tree	**daquela flor/árvore**	der**keh**ler floar/**ahr**voorer

Landmarks *Pontos de referência*

bridge	**a ponte**	er **pawng**ter
cliff	**a falésia**	er fer**leh**zyer
coast	**a costa**	er **kosh**ter
farm	**a quinta [fazenda]**	er **keeng**ter [fah**zayng**dah]
field	**o campo**	oo **kahng**poo
footpath	**o caminho pedestre**	oo ker**mee**nyoo per**dehsh**trer
forest	**a floresta**	er floo**rehsh**ter
garden	**o jardim**	oo zherr**deeng**
hill	**a colina**	er koo**lee**ner
house	**a casa**	er **kah**zer
lake	**o lago**	oo **lah**goo
meadow	**o prado**	oo **prah**doo
mountain range	**a serra**	er **seh**rrer
path	**o caminho**	oo ker**mee**nyoo
peak	**o pico/cume**	oo **pee**koo/**koo**mer
rain forest	**a selva**	er **sehl**ver
river	**o rio**	oo **ree**oo
road	**a estrada**	er ish**trah**der
sea	**o mar**	oo mahr
spring	**a nascente**	er nersh**sayng**ter
valley	**o vale**	oo **vah**ler
village	**a aldeia**	er ahl**day**er
vineyard	**a vinha**	er **vee**nyer
wall	**o muro**	oo **moo**roo
waterfall	**a cascada**	er kersh**kah**der
windmill	**o moinho**	oo **mwee**nyoo
wood	**a mata**	er **mah**ter

ASKING THE WAY, see page 76

Relaxing

Cinema (movies)—Theatre *Cinema—Teatro*

In Portugal, films are usually shown in the original language, with Portuguese subtitles. Separate performances are the rule, beginning about 3 p.m., with the last show at around 9.30 p.m. In Brazil showings are normally continuous, starting at 2 p.m.

In Portuguese theatres, there are matinées and two evening performances on Sundays. Revues are very popular.

You can find out what's playing from newspapers and billboards.

What's on at the cinema tonight?	**O que dão no cinema hoje à noite?**	oo ker dahng^{w} noo sin**nay**mer **oa**zher ah **noy**ter
What's playing at the ... theatre?	**O que está em cena no teatro ...?**	oo ker ish**tah** ahng^{y} **say**ner noo **tyah**troo
What sort of play is it?	**Que género de peça é?**	ker **zheh**nerroo der **peh**sser eh
Who's it by?	**Quem é o autor?**	kahng^{y} eh oo ow**toar**
Can you recommend (a) ...?	**Pode recomendar-me ...?**	**po**dder rerkoomayng**dahr** mer
good film	**um bom filme**	oong bawng **feel**mer
comedy	**uma comédia**	**oo**mer koo**meh**dyer
musical	**uma comédia musical**	**oo**mer koo**meh**dyer moozi**kkahl**
revue	**uma revista**	**oo**mer rer**veesh**ter
Where's that film directed by ... being shown?	**Em que cinema está sendo exibido o filme de ...?**	ahng^{y} ker sin**nay**mer ish**tah** **sayng**doo izzi**bbee**doo oo **feel**mer der
Who's in it?	**Quem são os actores?**	kahng^{y} sahng^{w} oosh ah**toa**rersh
Who's playing the lead?	**Quem desempenha o papel principal?**	kahng^{y} derzayng**pay**nyer oo per**pehl** preengsi**ppahl**
Who's the director?	**Quem é o realizador?**	kahng^{y} eh oo ryerlizzer**doar**
At which theatre is that play by ... being performed?	**Em que teatro está sendo representada a peça de ...?**	ahng^{y} ker **tyah**troo ish**tah** **sayng**doo rerprerzayng**tah**der er **peh**sser der

Is there a sound-and-light show on somewhere?	**Há algum espectáculo de luzes e som em qualquer lado?**	ah ahl**goong** ishpeh**tah**kooloo der **loo**zersh ee sawng ahng^{y} kwahl**kehr lah**doo
What time does it begin/finish?	**A que horas começa/acaba?**	er ker **or**rersh koo**meh**sser/er**kah**ber
Are there any seats for tonight?	**Há ainda bilhetes para hoje à noite?**	ah er**eeng**der bil**lyay**tish **per**rer **oa**zher ah **noy**ter
How much are the seats?	**Qual é o preço dos lugares?**	kwahl eh oo **pray**ssoo doosh loo**gah**rersh
I'd like to reserve 2 seats for the show on Friday evening.	**Quero reservar 2 lugares para o espectáculo de sexta-feira à noite.**	**keh**roo rerzerr**vahr** 2 loo**gah**rersh **per**rer oo ishpeh**tah**kooloo der **saysh**ter **fay**rer ah **noy**ter
Can I have a ticket for the matinée on Tuesday?	**Pode dar-me um bilhete para a matinée de terça-feira?**	**pod**der dahr mer oong bil**lyay**ter **per**rer er mahti**nneh** der **tayr**ser **fay**rer
I'd like a seat in the stalls (orchestra).	**Quero um lugar na plateia.**	**keh**roo oong loo**gahr** ner pler**tay**er
Not too far back.	**Não muito atrás.**	nahng^{w} **moong**^{y}too er**trahsh**
Somewhere in the middle.	**Mais ou menos ao meio.**	mighsh oa **may**noosh ow **may**oo
How much are the seats in the circle (mezzanine)?	**Qual é o preço dos lugares no balcão?**	kwahl eh oo **pray**ssoo doosh loo**gah**rersh noo bahl**kahng^{w}**
May I have a programme, please?	**Pode dar-me um programa?**	**pod**der dahr mer oong proo**grer**mer
Where's the cloakroom?	**Onde é o vestiário?**	**awng**der eh oo vish**tyah**ryoo

Lamento, mas a lotação está esgotada.	I'm sorry, we're sold out.
Restam apenas alguns lugares no balcão.	There are only a few seats left in the circle (mezzanine).
Pode mostrar-me o bilhete?	May I see your ticket?
Este é o seu lugar.	This is your seat.

DAYS OF THE WEEK, see page 151

Opera—Ballet—Concert *Ópera—Ballet—Concerto*

Can you recommend a/an ...?	**Pode recomendar--me ...?**	po**dder** rerkoomayng**dahr** mer
ballet	**um ballet**	oong bah**leh**
concert	**um concerto**	oong kawng**sayr**too
opera	**uma ópera**	**oo**mer **op**perrer
operetta	**uma opereta**	**oo**mer opper**ray**ter
Where's the opera house/the concert hall?	**Onde fica o teatro da ópera/a sala de concertos?**	**awng**der **fee**ker oo **tyah**troo der **op**perrer/er **sah**ler der kawng**sayr**toosh
What's on at the opera tonight?	**O que está em cena na ópera hoje à noite?**	oo ker ish**tah** ahng^{y} **say**ner ner **op**perrer **oa**zher ah **noy**ter
Who's singing/dancing?	**Quem canta/dança?**	kahng^{y} **kahng**ter/**dahng**ser
Which orchestra is playing?	**Qual é a orquestra?**	kwahl eh er orr**kehsh**trer
What are they playing?	**O que vão tocar?**	oo ker vahng^{w} too**kahr**
Who's the conductor/soloist?	**Quem é o chefe [regente] de orquestra/o solista?**	kahng^{y} eh oo **sheh**fer [ray**zhayng**ti] der orr**kehsh**trer/oo soo**leesh**ter

Fado—Nightclubs—Discos *Fado—Boîtes—Discotecas*

In Portugal, you will find the usual range of nightclubs and discotheques along the coast and in large towns. You can have a night out in a casino, or visit a *casa de fados,* an intimate, late-night restaurant where your meal is accompanied by the haunting melodies of the *fado,* the national folk song. Gambling is illegal in Brazil, but having fun isn't. There are many nightclubs, particularly in Rio de Janeiro.

Can you recommend a good nightclub?	**Pode recomendar-me uma boa boîte/casa de fados?**	po**dder** rerkoomayng**dahr** mer **oo**mer **boa**er **bwah**ter/ **kah**zer der **fah**doosh
Is there a floor show?	**Há variedades?**	ah verryer**dah**dish
Is evening dress required?	**É preciso traje de noite?**	eh prer**ssee**zoo **trah**zher der **noy**ter

Where can we go dancing?	**Onde podemos ir dançar?**	awngder poodaymoosh eer dahngsahr
Is there a discotheque in town?	**Há alguma discoteca na cidade?**	ah ahlgoomer dishkoo-tehker ner siddahder
Would you like to dance?	**Quer dançar?**	kehr dahngsahr
I'd like to see some folk dancing.	**Gostava de ver danças folclóricas.**	gooshtahver der vayr dahngsersh follklorrikkersh
Where's the casino?	**Onde é o casino?**	awngder eh oo kerzeenoo

Bullfight *A tourada*

The Portuguese version of the bullfight *(corrida à Portuguesa* or *tourada)* is quite different from the Spanish *corrida.* In Spain, the fashion has always been to fight the bull on foot whereas in Portugal the characteristic style is on horseback, and killing the bull is actually forbidden.

The best (and most expensive) seats are located in the shade *(sombra)* and in the front rows *(barreira).* Next come the *sol e sombra* (sun and shade) seats.

Bullfighting takes place—from Easter to October—almost every Sunday afternoon in many places.

I'd like to see a bullfight.	**Queria ver uma tourada.**	kerreeer vayr oomer toarahder
I want a seat in the shade/in the sun.	**Queria um lugar à sombra/ao sol.**	kerreeer oong loogahr ah sawngbrer/ow sol

Sports *Desportos [esportes]*

The Portuguese and Brazilians are great football (soccer) fans. Portugal is well known for its splendid golf courses.

Is there a football (soccer) match anywhere this Saturday?	**Há algum jogo de futebol no sábado?**	ah ahlgoong zhoagoo der footerboll no sahberdoo
Which teams are playing?	**Quais são as equipas que jogam?**	kwighsh sahng^w ersh ikkeepersh ker zhoggahng^w

Can you get me a ticket?	**Pode arranjar-me [arrumar-me] um bilhete?**	**po**dder errahng**zhahr** mer [ahrroo**mahr** mi] oong bil**lyay**ter

basketball	**o basquetebol**	oo bahshkeht**boll**
boxing	**o boxe**	oo boks
car racing	**as corridas de automóveis**	ersh koo**rree**dersh der owtoo**mo**vvaysh
cycling	**o ciclismo**	oo sik**kleezh**moo
football (soccer)	**o futebol**	oo footer**boll**
(horseback) riding	**a equitação**	er ikkitter**ssahng**ʷ
horse racing	**as corridas de cavalos**	ersh koo**rree**dersh der ker**vah**loosh
swimming	**a natação**	er nerter**ssahng**ʷ
tennis	**o ténis**	oo **teh**nish
volleyball	**o voleibol**	oo vollay**boll**

I'd like to see a boxing match.	**Gostava de ver um combate de boxe.**	goosh**tah**ver der vayr oong kawng**bah**ter der boks
What's the admission charge?	**Quanto custa a entrada [o ingresso]?**	**kwahng**too **koosh**ter er ayng**trah**der [oa eeng**greh**ssoa]
Where's the nearest golf course?	**Onde é o campo de golfe mais próximo?**	**awng**der eh oo **kahng**poo der **goal**fer mighsh **pro**ssimmoo
Where are the tennis courts?	**Onde são os campos de ténis?**	**awng**der sahngʷ oosh **kahng**poosh der **teh**nish
What's the charge per ...?	**Qual é o preço por ...?**	kwahl eh oo **pray**ssoo poor
day/round/hour	**dia/jogo/hora**	**dee**er/**zhoa**goo/**o**rrer
Can I hire (rent) golf clubs/rackets?	**Posso alugar clubes de golfe/raquetes?**	**po**ssoo erloo**gahr** **kloo**bersh der **goal**fer/rah**keh**tish
Where's the race course (track)?	**Onde é o hipódromo?**	**awng**der eh oo ip**po**ddroomoo
Is there any good fishing/hunting around here?	**Há algum bom lugar para pescar/caçar aqui perto?**	ah ahl**goong** bawng loo**gahr** **per**rer pish**kahr**/ker**ssahr** er**kee** **pehr**too
Do I need a permit?	**É preciso licença?**	eh prer**ssee**zoo li**ssayng**ser
Where can I get one?	**Onde posso arranjar [arrumar] uma?**	**awng**der **po**ssoo errahng**zhahr** [ahrroo**mahr**] **oo**mer
Is there a swimming pool here?	**Há aqui uma piscina?**	ah er**kee** **oo**mer pish**see**ner

Is it open-air or indoor?	**É ao ar livre ou coberta?**	eh ow ahr **lee**vrer oa koo**behr**ter
Is it heated?	**É aquecida?**	eh erkeh**ssee**der
What's the temperature of the water?	**Qual é a temperatura da água?**	kwahl eh er tayngperrer**too**rer der **ah**gwer

On the beach *Na praia*

Is it safe for swimming?	**Pode-se nadar sem perigo?**	**po**dder ser ner**dahr** sahng^{y} per**ree**goo
Is there a lifeguard?	**Há um banheiro [salva-vidas]?**	ah oong ber**nyay**roo [**sahl**vah **vee**dahss]
Is it safe for children?	**Não há perigo para as crianças?**	nahng^{w} ah per**ree**goo **per**rer ersh **kryahng**sersh
The sea is calm.	**O mar é calmo.**	oo mahr eh **kahl**moo
There are some big waves.	**Há ondas grandes.**	ah **awng**dersh **grahng**dish
Are there any dangerous currents?	**Há correntes perigosas?**	ah koo**rrayng**tish perri**ggo**zzersh
What time is high tide/low tide?	**A que horas é a maré alta/maré baixa?**	er ker **o**rrersh eh er mer**reh ahl**ter/mer**reh bigh**sher
I want to hire a/an/some ...	**Quero alugar ...**	**keh**roo erloo**gahr**
bathing hut (cabana)	**uma barraca**	**oo**mer be**rrah**ker
deck chair	**uma cadeira de encosto**	**oo**mer ker**day**rer der ayng**koash**too
motorboat	**um barco a motor**	oong **bahr**koo er moo**toar**
rowing boat	**um barco a remos**	oong **bahr**koo er **reh**moosh
sailing boat	**um barco à vela**	oong **bahr**koo ah **veh**ler
skin-diving equipment	**um equipamento para pesca submarina**	oong ikkipper**mayng**too **per**rer **pehsh**ker soobmer**ree**ner
sunshade (umbrella)	**um chapéu de sol**	oong sher**peh**oo der soll
surfboard	**uma prancha de surf**	**oo**mer **prahng**sher der serrf
waterskis	**uns esquis aquáticos**	oongsh ish**keesh** er**kwah**tikkoosh
windsurfer	**uma prancha à vela**	**oo**mer **prahng**sher ah **veh**ler

PRAIA PRIVADA	PRIVATE BEACH
É PROIBIDO TOMAR BANHO	NO SWIMMING

Making friends

Introductions *Apresentações*

May I introduce ...?	**Posso apresentar--lhe ...?**	**po**ssoo erprerzayng**tahr** lyer
John, this is ...	**João, apresento--lhe ...**	zhwahng^w erprer**zayng**too lyer
My name is ...	**Chamo-me ...**	**sher**moo mer
Pleased to meet you.	**Muito prazer em conhecê-lo(la).**	**moong^y**too prer**zayr** ahng^y koonyer**ssay** loo(ler)
What's your name?	**Como se chama?**	**koa**moo ser **sher**mer
How are you?	**Como está?**	**koa**moo ish**tah**
Fine, thanks. And you?	**Bem, obrigado(a). E o Senhor (a Senhora)?**	bahng^y oabri**ggah**doo(er). ee oo si**nnyoar** (er si**nnyoar**er)

Follow up *Para quebrar o silêncio*

How long have you been here?	**Há quanto tempo está aqui?**	ah **kwahng**too **tayng**poo ish**tah** er**kee**
We've been here a week.	**Estamos aqui há uma semana.**	ish**ter**moosh er**kee** ah **oo**mer ser**mer**ner
Are you enjoying your stay?	**Gosta de estar cá?**	**gosh**ter der ish**tahr** kah
Yes, I like it very much.	**Sim, gosto muito.**	seeng **gosh**too **moong^y**too
I like the land-scape/region a lot.	**Gosto muito da paisagem/região.**	**gosh**too **moong^y**too der pigh**zah**zhahng^y/rer**zhyahng^w**
What do you think of the country/people?	**O que é que acha do país/das pessoas?**	oo ker eh ker **ah**sher doo per**eesh**/dersh per**ssoa**ersh
Where do you come from?	**Donde é?**	**dawng**der eh
I'm from ...	**Sou de ...**	soa der
What nationality are you?	**De que nacionalidade é?**	der ker nerssyoonerli**ddah**der eh

COUNTRIES, see page 146

I'm ...	**Sou ...**	soa
American	**americano**	ermerri**kker**noo
British	**britânico**	britt**er**nikkoo
Canadian	**canadiano**	kerner**dyer**noo
English	**inglês**	eeng**glaysh**
Irish	**irlandês**	irrlahng**daysh**
Are you on your own?	**Está sozinho(a)?**	ish**tah** saw**zee**nyoo(er)
I'm with my ...	**Estou com ...**	ish**toa** kawng
wife	**a minha mulher**	er **mee**nyer mool**yehr**
husband	**o meu marido**	oo **meh**oo mer**ree**doo
family	**a minha família**	er **mee**nyer fer**mee**lyer
children	**os meus filhos**	oosh **meh**oosh **fee**lyoosh
parents	**os meus pais**	oosh **meh**oosh pighsh
boyfriend/girlfriend	**o meu namorado/a minha namorada**	oo **meh**oo nermoo**rah**doo/er **mee**nyer nermoo**rah**der

grandfather/grandmother	**o avô/a avó**	oo er**voa**/er er**vaw**
father/mother	**o pai/a mãe**	oo pigh/er mahng^{y}
son/daughter	**o filho/a filha**	oo **fee**lyoo/er **fee**lyer
brother/sister	**o irmão/a irmã**	oo irr**mahng**^{w}/er irr**mahng**
uncle/aunt	**o tio/ a tia**	oo **tee**oo/er **tee**er
nephew/niece	**o sobrinho/a sobrinha**	oo soo**bree**nyoo/er soo**bree**nyer
cousin	**o primo/ a prima**	oo **pree**moo/er **pree**mer

Are you married/single?	**É casado(a)/solteiro(a)?**	eh ker**zah**doo(er)/soll**tay**roo(er)
Do you have children?	**Tem filhos?**	tahng^{y} **fee**lyoosh
What do you do?	**Qual é a sua profissão?**	kwahl eh er **soo**er proofi**ssahng**^{w}
I'm a student.	**Sou estudante.**	soa ishtoo**dahng**ter
What are you studying?	**O que é que está a estudar?**	oo ker eh ker ish**tah** er ishtoo**dahr**
I'm here on a business trip.	**Estou aqui em viagem de negócios.**	ish**toa** er**kee** ahng^{y} **vyah**zhahng^{y} der ner**go**ssyoosh
Do you travel a lot?	**Viaja muito?**	**vyah**zher **moong**^{y}too
Do you play chess/cards?	**Joga xadrez/às cartas?**	**zho**gger sher**draysh**/ahsh **kahr**tersh

The weather *O tempo*

What a lovely day!	**Que lindo dia!**	ker **leeng**doo **dee**er
What awful weather!	**Que tempo horrível!**	ker **tayng**poo or**ree**vehl
Isn't it cold/ hot today?	**Que frio/calor está hoje!**	ker **free**oo/ker**loar** ish**tah oa**zher
Is it usually as warm as this?	**Está sempre assim tanto calor?**	ish**tah sayng**prer er**sseeng tahng**too ker**loar**
Do you think it's going to ...?	**Acha que vai ...?**	**ah**sher ker vigh
be a nice day	**estar bom tempo**	ish**tahr** bawng **tayng**poo
rain	**chover**	shoo**vayr**
What is the weather forecast?	**Quais são as previsões do tempo?**	kwighsh sahng^{w} ersh prer-vizz**awng^{y}sh** doo **tayng**poo

cloud	**a nuvem**	er **noo**vahng^{y}
fog	**o nevoeiro**	oo ner**vway**roo
ice	**o gelo**	oo **zhay**loo
lightning	**o relâmpago**	oo rer**lahng**pergoo
moon	**a lua**	er **loo**er
rain	**a chuva**	er **shoo**ver
sky	**o céu**	oo **se**hoo
star	**a estrela**	er ish**tray**ler
sun	**o sol**	oo soll
thunder	**o trovão**	oo troo**vahng^{w}**
thunderstorm	**a trovoada**	er troo**vwah**der
wind	**o vento**	oo **vayng**too

Invitations *Convites*

Would you like to have dinner with us on ...?	**Quer jantar connosco ...?**	kehr zhahng**tahr** koa**noash**koo
May I invite you for lunch?	**Posso convidá-lo(la) para almoçar?**	**po**ssoo kawngvi**ddah** loo (ler) **per**rer ahlmoo**ssahr**
Can you come round for a drink this evening?	**Pode cá vir hoje à noite tomar uma bebida?**	**po**dder kah veer **oa**zher ah **noy**ter too**mahr oo**mer ber**bee**der
There's a party. Are you coming?	**Há uma festa. Quer vir?**	ah **oo**mer **fehsh**ter. kehr veer

DAYS OF THE WEEK, see page 151

That's very kind of you.	**É muito amável da sua parte.**	eh **moong^{y}**too er**mah**vehl der **soo**er **pahr**ter
Great. I'd love to come.	**Óptimo. Virei com muito prazer.**	**o**ttimmoo. vi**rray** kawng **moong^{y}**too prer**zayr**
What time shall we come?	**A que horas vimos?**	er ker **o**rrersh **vee**moosh
May I bring a friend/ a girlfriend?	**Posso trazer um amigo/uma amiga?**	**po**ssoo trer**zayr** oong er**mee**goo/**oo**mer er**mee**ger
I'm afraid we've got to leave now.	**Lamento, mas temos de nos ir já embora.**	ler**mayng**too mersh **tay**-moosh der noosh eer zhah ayng**bo**rrer
Next time you must come to visit us.	**Para a próxima vez, são vocês que vêm ver-nos.**	**per**rer er **pro**ssimmer vaysh sahng^{w} vo**ssaysh** ker **vahng^{y}**ahng^{y} vayr noosh
Thanks for the evening. It was great.	**Obrigado(a) pela festa. Foi óptima.**	oabri**ggah**doo(er) **pay**ler **fehsh**ter. foy **o**ttimmer

Dating *Encontros*

Do you mind if I smoke?	**Importa-se que eu fume?**	eeng**porr**ter ser ker **e**hoo **foo**mer
Would you like a cigarette?	**Quer um cigarro?**	kehr oong si**ggah**rroo
Do you have a light, please?	**Tem lume, por favor?**	tahng^{y} **loo**mer poor fer**voar**
Why are you laughing?	**Porque está a rir?**	**poor**ker ish**tah** er reer
Is my pronunciation that bad?	**A minha pronúncia é assim tão má?**	er **mee**nyer proo**noong**syer eh er**sseeng** tahng^{w} mah
Do you mind if I sit here?	**Importa-se que eu me sente aqui?**	eeng**porr**ter ser ker **e**hoo mer **sayng**ter er**kee**
Can I get you a drink?	**Posso oferecer-lhe uma bebida?**	**po**ssoo offerrer**ssayr** lyer **oo**mer ber**bee**der
Are you waiting for someone?	**Está à espera de alguém?**	ish**tah** ah ish**peh**rer der ahl**gahng^{y}**
Are you free this evening?	**Está livre hoje à noite?**	ish**tah** **lee**vrer **oa**zher ah **noy**ter
Would you like to go out with me tonight?	**Quer sair comigo hoje à noite?**	kehr ser**eer** koo**mee**goo **oa**zher ah **noy**ter

Would you like to go dancing?	**Quer ir dançar?**	kehr eer dahng**sahr**
I know a good discotheque.	**Conheço uma boa discoteca.**	koo**nyay**ssoo **oo**mer **boa**er dishkoo**teh**ker
Shall we go to the cinema (movies)?	**Vamos ao cinema?**	**ver**moosh ow sin**nay**mer
Would you like to go for a drive?	**Quer ir dar um passeio de carro?**	kehr eer dahr oong per**ssay**oo der **kah**rroo
Where shall we meet?	**Onde nos encontramos?**	**awng**der noosh ayngkawng**trer**moosh
I'll pick you up at your hotel.	**Vou buscá-la ao seu hotel.**	voa boosh**kah** ler ow **seh**oo ot**tehl**
Where are you staying?	**Onde está hospedado?**	**awng**der ish**tah** oshper**dah**doo
I'll call for you at 8.	**Vou buscá-la às 8.**	voa boosh**kah** ler ash 8
May I take you home?	**Posso acompanhá-la a casa?**	**po**ssoo erkawngper**nyah** ler er **kah**zer
Can I see you again tomorrow?	**Posso voltar a vê-la amanhã?**	**po**ssoo voll**tahr** er vay ler ahmer**nyahng**
I hope we'll meet again.	**Espero que nos voltemos a ver.**	ish**peh**roo ker noosh voll**tay**moosh er vayr

... and you might answer:

I'd love to, thank you.	**Com muito prazer, obrigado(a).**	kawng **moong**^{y}too prer**zayr** oabrig**gah**doo(er)
Thank you, but I'm busy.	**Obrigado(a), mas tenho que fazer.**	oabrig**gah**doo(er) mersh **tay**nyoo ker fer**zayr**
No, I'm not interested, thank you.	**Obrigado(a), mas não estou interessada.**	oabrig**gah**doo(er) mersh nahng^{w} ish**toa** eengterrer**ssah**der
Leave me alone, please!	**Deixe-me em paz, se faz favor!**	**day**sher mer ahng^{y} pash ser fash fer**voar**
Thank you, it's been a wonderful evening.	**Obrigado(a), passei uma noite maravilhosa.**	oabrig**gah**doo(er) per**ssay** **oo**mer **noy**ter merrervi**llyo**zzer
I've enjoyed myself.	**Diverti-me muito.**	divverr**tee** mer **moong**^{y}too

Shopping Guide

This shopping guide is designed to help you find what you want with ease, accuracy and speed. It features:

1. A list of all major shops, stores and services (p. 98).
2. Some general expressions required when shopping to allow you to be specific and selective (p. 100).
3. Full details of the shops and services most likely to concern you. Here you'll find advice, alphabetical lists of items, and conversion charts listed under the headings below.

LAUNDRY, see page 29/HAIRDRESSER'S, see page 30

Shops, stores and services *Lojas e serviços*

Most shops are open from about 9 a.m. to 7 p.m., with a lunch break from 1 to 3 p.m. Very few remain open on Saturday afternoon. Brazilian stores are open from 8 a.m. to 9 p.m. and close at noon on Saturdays.

Where's the nearest ...?	**Onde é ... mais próximo(a)?**	**awng**der eh ... mighsh prossimmoo(er)
antique shop	**o antiquário**	oo ahngti**kkwah**ryoo
art gallery	**a galeria de arte**	er gerler**reeer** der **ahr**ter
baker's	**a padaria**	er pahder**reeer**
bank	**o banco**	oo **bahng**koo
barber's	**o barbeiro**	oo berr**bay**roo
beauty salon	**o instituto de beleza**	oo eengshti**ttoo**too der ber**lay**zer
bookshop	**a livraria**	er livvrer**ree**er
butcher's	**o talho [açougue]**	oo **tah**lyoo [ah**ssoa**ghi]
cake shop	**a pastelaria**	er pershterler**reeer**
camera shop	**a loja de artigos fotográficos**	er **lo**zher der err**tee**goosh footoo**grah**fikkoosh
chemist's	**a farmácia**	er ferr**mah**ssyer
dairy	**a leitaria**	er layter**reeer**
delicatessen	**a salsicharia**	er sahlsisher**reeer**
dentist	**o dentista**	oo dayng**teesh**ter
department store	**o grande armazém**	oo **grahng**der ahrmer**zahng**ʸ
drugstore	**a farmácia**	er ferr**mah**ssyer
dry cleaner's	**a lavandaria a seco**	er lervahngder**reeer** er **say**koo
electrician	**o electricista**	oo illehtri**ssee**shter
fishmonger's	**a peixaria**	er paysher**reeer**
florist's	**a florista**	er floo**reesh**ter
furrier's	**a casa de peles**	er **kah**zer der **peh**lersh
greengrocer's	**o lugar de frutas e legumes [a quitanda]**	oo loo**gahr** der **froo**tersh ee ler**goo**mersh [ah ki**ttahng**dah]
grocery	**a mercearia**	er merrsyer**reeer**
hairdresser's (ladies/men)	**o cabeleireiro (para senhoras/homens)**	oo kerberlay**ray**roo (**per**rer si**nnyoa**rersh/**om**mahngʸs
hardware store	**a loja de ferrajens**	er **lo**zher der fer**rah**zhahngʸsh
health food shop	**a loja de produtos dietéticos**	er **lo**zher der proo**doo**toosh dyay**teh**tikkoosh
hospital	**o hospital**	oo oshpi**ttahl**
ironmonger's	**a loja de ferragens**	er **lo**zher der fer**rah**zhahngʸsh

eweller's	a ourivesaria	er oarivverzer**reeer**
aunderette	a lavandaria automática	er lervahngder**reeer** owtoo**mah**tikker
aundry	a lavandaria	er lervahngder**reeer**
ibrary	a biblioteca	er bibblyoo**teh**ker
narket	o mercado	oo merr**kah**doo
iewsstand	o quiosque [a banca] de jornais	oo **kyosh**ker [ah **bahng**kah] der zhoor**nighsh**
ptician	o oculista	oo okkoo**leesh**ter
astry shop	a pastelaria	er pershterler**reeer**
hotographer	o fotógrafo	oo foo**tog**grerfoo
olice station	o posto da polícia	oo **poash**too der poo**lee**ssyer
ost office	a estação de correios	er ishter**ssahng**^{w} der koo**rray**oosh
econd-hand shop	a loja de velharias	er **lo**zher der vehlyer**ree**ersh
hoemaker's (repairs)	o sapateiro	oo serper**tay**roo
hoe shop	a sapataria	er serperter**reeer**
hopping centre	o centro comercial	oo **sayng**troo koomerr**syahl**
ouvenir shop	a loja de lembranças	er **lo**zher der layng**brahng**sersh
porting goods shop	a loja de artigos desportivos [esportivos]	er **lo**zher der err**tee**goosh dishpoor**tee**voosh [aysporr**tee**voass]
tationer's	a papelaria	er perperler**reeer**
upermarket	o supermercado	oo soopehrmerr**kah**doo
elegraph office	estação telegráfica	ishter**ssahng**^{w} terler**grah**fikker
obacconist's	a tabacaria	er terberker**reeer**
oy shop	a loja de brinquedos	er **lo**zher der breeng**kay**doosh
ravel agency	a agência de viagens	er er**zhayng**syer der **vyah**zhahng^{y}sh
egetable store	o lugar de frutas e e legumes [a quitanda]	oo loo**gahr** der **froo**tersh ee ler**goo**mersh [ah kit**tahng**dah]
eterinarian	o veterinário	oo verterrin**nah**ryoo
vatchmaker's	a relojoaria	er rerloozhwer**reeer**
vine merchant's	o comerciante de vinhos	oo koomerr**syahng**ter der **vee**nyoosh

ENTRADA	ENTRANCE
SAÍDA	EXIT
SAÍDA DE EMERGÊNCIA	EMERGENCY EXIT

General expressions *Expressões gerais*

Where? *Onde?*

Where's there a good ...?	**Onde há um bom/ uma boa ...?**	awngder ah oong bawng/ oomer boaer
Where can I find a ...?	**Onde posso encontrar um/uma ...?**	awngder possoo ayngkawngtrahr oong/oomer
Where's the main shopping area?	**Onde é a zona comercial?**	awngder eh er zoaner koomerrsyahl
Is it far from here?	**É longe daqui?**	eh lawngzher derkee
How do I get there?	**Como posso ir até lá?**	koamoo possoo eer erteh lah

SALDOS SALE

Service *Serviços*

Can you help me?	**Pode ajudar-me?**	podder erzhoodahr mer
I'm just looking.	**Estou só a ver.**	ishtoa saw er vayr
Do you sell ...?	**Vende ...?**	vayngder
I want to buy ...	**Quero comprar ...**	kehroo kawngprahr
Can you show me some ...?	**Pode mostrar-me ...?**	podder mooshtrahr mer
Do you have any ...?	**Tem ...?**	tahng[y]
Where's the ... department?	**Onde é a secção ...?**	awngder eh er sehksahng[w]
Where is the lift (elevator)/escalator?	**Onde é o elevador/ a escada rolante?**	awngder eh oo illerverdoar/ er ishkahder roolahngter

That one *Aquele*

Can you show me ...?	**Pode mostrar-me ...?**	podder mooshtrahr mer
this/that	**isto/aquilo**	eeshtoo/erkeeloo
the one in the window/in the display case	**o que está na vitrina/na banca**	oo ker ishtah ner vittreener/ ner bahngker

Defining the article *Descrição do artigo*

I'd like a ... one.	**Quero um ...**	**keh**roo oong
big	**grande**	**grahng**der
cheap	**barato**	ber**rah**too
dark	**escuro**	ish**koo**roo
good	**bom**	bawng
heavy	**pesado**	per**zah**doo
large	**grande**	**grahng**der
light (weight)	**leve**	**leh**ver
light (colour)	**claro**	**klah**roo
oval	**oval**	ov**vahl**
rectangular	**rectangular**	rehtahnggoo**lahr**
round	**redondo**	rer**dawng**doo
small	**pequeno**	per**kay**noo
square	**quadrado**	kwer**drah**doo
sturdy	**resistente**	rerzish**tayng**ter

Preference *Preferências*

Can you show me some more?	**Pode mostrar-me mais alguns?**	podder moosh**trahr** mer mighsh ahl**goongsh**
Haven't you anything ...?	**Não tem nada ...?**	nahng^w tahng^y **nah**der
cheaper/better	**mais barato/melhor**	mighsh ber**rah**too/mi**llyor**
larger/smaller	**maior/mais pequeno [menor]**	may**or**/mighsh per**kay**noo [meh**nor**]

How much? *Quanto custa?*

How much is this?	**Quanto custa isto?**	**kwahng**too **koosh**ter **eesh**too
How much are they?	**Quanto custam?**	**kwahng**too **koosh**tahng^w
I don't understand.	**Não compreendo.**	nahng^w kawng**pryayng**doo
Please write it down.	**Pode escrever num papel?**	podder ishkrer**vayr** noong per**pehl**
I don't want anything too expensive.	**Não quero nada muito caro.**	nahng^w **keh**roo **nah**der **moong**^{y} too **kah**roo
I don't want to spend more than ... escudos/cruzados.	**Não quero gastar mais que ... escudos/ cruzados.**	nahng^w **keh**roo gersh**tahr** mighsh ker ... ish**koo**doosh/ kroo**zah**doass

COLOURS, see page 113

Decision *Decisão*

It's not quite what I want.	Não é bem o que quero.	nahng^w eh bahng^w oo ker kehroo
No, I don't like it.	Não, não gosto.	nahng^w nahng^w goshtoo
I'll take it.	Fico com ele.	feekoo kawng ayler

Ordering *Encomenda*

Can you order it for me?	Pode encomendar--mo?	podder ayngkoomayngdahr moo
How long will it take?	Quanto tempo demora?	kwahngtoo tayngpoo dermorrer

Delivery *Entrega*

I'll take it with me.	Levo-o já.	lehvoo oo zhah
Deliver it to the ... Hotel.	Mande entregá-lo no Hotel ...	mahngder ayngtrergah loo noo ottehl
Please send it to this address.	Mande-o para este endereço, por favor.	mahngder oo perrer ayshter ayngderrayssoo poor fervoar
Will I have any difficulty with the customs?	Terei dificuldades na alfândega?	terray diffikkooldahdersh ner ahlfahngderger

Paying *Pagamento*

How much is it?	Quanto é?	kwahngtoo eh
Can I pay by traveller's cheque?	Posso pagar com cheques de viagem?	possoo pergahr kawng shehkersh der vyahzhahng^y
Do you accept dollars/pounds?	Aceitam dólares/libras?	erssaytahng^w dollerrsh/leebrersh
Do you accept credit cards?	Aceitam cartões de crédito?	erssaytahng^w kerrtawng^ysh der krehdittoo
Do I have to pay the VAT (sales tax)?	Tenho de pagar o IVA?	taynyoo der pergahr oo eever
Isn't there a mistake in the bill?	Não se enganou na conta?	nahng^w ser aynggernoa ner kawngter

Anything else? *Mais alguma coisa?*

No, thanks, that's all.	**Não, obrigado(a)*, é tudo.**	nahng^{w} oabri**ggah**doo/er eh **too**doo
Yes, I'd like ...	**Sim, quero ...**	seeng **keh**roo
Show me ...	**Mostre-me ...**	**mosh**trer mer
May I have a bag, please?	**Pode dar-me um saco, por favor?**	**po**dder dahr mer oong **sah**koo poor fer**voar**
Could you wrap it up for me, please?	**Pode embrulhar, se faz favor?**	**po**dder ayngbroo**lyahr** ser fahsh fer**voar**

Dissatisfied? *Insatisfeito?*

Can you exchange this, please?	**Pode trocar isto?**	**po**dder troo**kahr eesh**too
I want to return this.	**Quero devolver isto.**	**keh**roo dervoll**vayr eesh**too
I'd like a refund. Here's the receipt.	**Quero que me reembolsem. Aqui está o recibo.**	**keh**roo ker mer ryayng**boal**sahng^{y}. er**kee** ish**tah** oo rers**see**boo

Em que posso servi-lo(la)?	Can I help you?
O que deseja?	What would you like?
Que ... deseja?	What ... would you like?
cor/forma qualidade/quantidade	colour/shape quality/quantity
Lamento, mas não temos.	I'm sorry, we haven't any.
Esse artigo está esgotado.	We're out of stock.
Deseja que o encomendemos?	Shall we order it for you?
Quer levá-lo já ou deseja que lho enviemos?	Will you take it with you or shall we send it?
Mais alguma coisa?	Anything else?
São ... escudos/cruzados.	That's ... escudos/cruzados.
A caixa é ali.	The cash desk is over there.

* A woman would say **obrigada.**

Bookshop—Stationer's *Livraria—Papelaria*

In Portugal and Brazil, bookshops and stationer's are usually separate, though the latter will often sell paperbacks. Newspapers and magazines are sold at newsstands.

Where's the nearest ...?	Onde é ... mais próximo(a)?	awngder eh ... mighsh prossimmoo(er)
bookshop	a livraria	er livvrerreeer
stationer's	a papelaria	er perperlerreeer
newsstand	o quiosque [a banca] de jornais	oo kyoshker [ah bahngkah] der zhoornighsh
Where can I buy an English-language newspaper?	Onde posso comprar um jornal em inglês?	awngder possoo kawng-prahr oong zhoornahl ahng^y eengglaysh
Where do you keep the English books?	Onde estão os livros em inglês?	awngder ishtahng^w oosh leevroosh ahng^y eengglaysh
Do you have second-hand books?	Tem livros em segunda mão?	tahng^y leevroosh ahng^y sergoongder mahng^w
I want to buy a/an/ some ...	Quero comprar ...	kehroo kawngprahr
address book	um livrinho de endereços	oong livvreenyoo der ayngderrayssoosh
ball-point pen	uma esferográfica	oomer ishfehroggrahfikker
book	um livro	oong leevroo
calendar	um calendário	oong kerlayngdahryoo
cellophane tape	fita adesiva	feeter erderzeever
crayons	lápis de cor	lahpish der koar
dictionary	um dicionário	oong dissyoonahryoo
Portuguese-English	português-inglês	poortoogaysh eengglaysh
pocket	de bolso	der boalsoo
drawing paper	papel de desenho	perpehl der derzaynyoo
drawing pins	pioneses [tachas]	pyoonehzersh [tahshahss]
envelopes	uns envelopes	oongsh ayngverloppish
eraser	uma borracha	oomer boorrahsher
exercise book	um caderno	oong kerdehrnoo
felt-tip pen	uma caneta feltro	oomer kernayter fayltroo
fountain pen	uma caneta de tinta permanente*	oomer kernayter der teeng-ter perrmernayngter
glue	cola	koller
grammar book	uma gramática	oomer grermahtikker

* In Brazil: **uma caneta-tinteiro** (oomah kahnaytah teengtayroa)

guidebook	um guia turístico	oong **gheeer** too**reesh**tikkoo
ink	tinta	**teeng**ter
red/blue	vermelha/azul	verr**maylyer**/er**zool**
(adhesive) labels	etiquetas (autocolantes)	itti**kkay**tersh (owtokkoo**lahng**tish)
magazine	uma revista	oomer rer**veesh**ter
map	um mapa	oong **mah**per
map of the town	uma planta da cidade	oomer **plahng**ter der sid**dah**der
road map of ...	um mapa das estradas de ...	oong **mah**per dersh ish**trah**dersh der
mechanical pencil	uma lapiseira	oomer lerpi**zzay**rer
newspaper	um jornal	oong zhoor**nahl** ermerri-kkernoo/eeng**glaysh**
American/English	americano/inglês	
notebook	um bloco de apontamentos	oong **blo**kkoo der erpawngter**mayng**toosh
note paper	papel de carta	per**pehl** der **kahr**ter
paintbox	uma caixa de tintas	oomer **kigh**sher der **teeng**tersh
paper	papel	per**pehl**
paperback	um livro de bolso	oong **lee**vroo der **boal**soo
paperclips	clipes	**klee**pish
paper napkins	guardanapos de papel	gwerrder**nah**poosh der per**pehl**
paste	cola	koller
pen	uma caneta	oomer ker**nay**ter
pencil	um lápis	oong **lah**pish
pencil sharpener	um apara-lápis [apontador]	oong er**pah**rer **lah**pish [ahpawngtah**doar**]
playing cards	cartas de jogar	**kahr**tersh der zhoo**gahr**
pocket calculator	uma calculadora de bolso	oomer kahlkooler**doa**rer der **boal**soo
postcard	um bilhete postal	oong bi**llyay**ter poosh**tahl**
propelling pencil	uma lapiseira	oomer lerpi**zzay**rer
refill (for a pen)	uma carga (para caneta)	oomer **kahr**ger (perrer ker**nay**ter
rubber	uma borracha	oomer boo**rrah**sher
ruler	uma régua	oomer **reh**gwer
staples	agrafos [grampos]	er**grah**foosh [**grahng**poass]
string	cordel [barbante]	koor**dehl** [bahr**bahng**ti]
thumbtacks	pioneses [tachas]	pyoo**neh**zersh [**tah**shahss]
travel guide	um guia turístico	oong **gheeer** too**reesh**tikkoo
typewriter ribbon	uma fita para máquina de escrever	oomer **fee**ter perrer **mah**kinner der ishkrer**vayr**
typing paper	papel para máquina de escrever	per**pehl** perrer **mah**kinner der ishkrer**vayr**
writing pad	um bloco de papel	oong **blo**kkoo der per**pehl**

Camping equipment *Equipamento de campismo*

I'd like a/an/some ...	**Queria ...**	ker**ree**er
backpack	**uma mochila**	**oo**mer moo**shee**ler
bottle-opener	**um abre-garrafas [abridor de garrafas]**	oong **ah**brer ger**rah**fersh [ahbri**ddoar** di gah**rrah**fahss]
butane gas	**gás butano**	gahsh boo**ter**noo
campbed	**uma cama de campismo**	**oo**mer **ker**mer der kahng**peezh**moo
can opener	**um abre-latas [abridor de latas]**	oong **ah**brer **lah**tersh [ahbri**ddoar** di **lah**tersh]
candles	**velas**	**veh**lersh
(folding) chair	**uma cadeira (de fechar)**	**oo**mer ker**day**rer (der fi**shahr**)
charcoal	**carvão de lenha**	kerr**vahng**^{w} der **lay**nyer
clothes pegs	**molas da roupa**	**mo**llersh der **roa**per
compass	**uma bússola**	**oo**mer **boo**ssooler
cool box	**uma mala frigorífica**	**oo**mer **mah**ler friggoo**ree**fikker
corkscrew	**um saca-rolhas**	oong **sah**ker **roa**lyersh
deck chair	**uma cadeira de encosto**	**oo**mer ker**day**rer der ayng**koash**too
dishwashing detergent	**detergente para a louça**	derterr**zhayng**ter **per**rer er **loa**sser
first-aid kit	**um estojo de primeiros-socorros**	oong ish**toa**zhoo der prim**may**roosh soo**ko**rroosh
fishing tackle	**apetrechos de pesca**	erper**tray**shoosh der **pehsh**ker
flashlight	**uma lanterna de bolso**	**oo**mer lahng**teh**rner der **boal**soo
food box	**uma caixa para alimentos**	**oo**mer **kigh**sher **per**rer erlim**mayng**toosh
frying pan	**uma frigideira**	**oo**mer frizhi**ddayrer**
groundsheet	**um tapete**	oong ter**pay**ter
hammer	**um martelo**	oong merr**teh**loo
hammock	**uma cama de rede [uma rede]**	**oo**mer **ker**mer der **ray**der [**oo**mer **ray**di]
ice pack	**uma placa frigorífica**	**oo**mer **plah**ker friggoo**ree**fikker
kerosene	**petróleo**	per**tro**llyoo
lantern	**uma lanterna**	**oo**mer lahng**teh**rner
matches	**fósforos**	**fosh**fooroosh
mattress	**um colchão**	oong koal**shahng**^{w}
methylated spirits	**álcool desnaturado**	**ahl**koll dizhnertoo**rah**doo
mosquito net	**um mosquiteiro**	oong mooshki**ttay**roo

CAMPING, see page 32

araffin	**petróleo**	pertrollyoo
enknife	**um canivete**	oong kernivvehter
icnic basket	**um cesto de piquenique**	oong sayshtoo der pikkerneeker
lastic bag	**um saco de plástico**	oong sahkoo der plahshtikkoo
ɔpe	**uma corda**	oomer korrder
ucksack	**uma mochila**	oomer moosheeler
aucepan	**um tacho**	oong tahshoo
leeping bag	**um saco-cama**	oong sahkoo kermer
folding) table	**uma mesa (de fechar)**	oomer mayzer der fishahr
ent	**uma tenda**	oomer tayngder
ent pegs	**umas estacas de tenda**	oomersh ishtahkersh der tayngder
ent pole	**um mastro de tenda**	oong mahshtroo der tayngder
nfoil	**papel de alumínio**	perpehl der erloomeenyoo
n opener	**um abre-latas [abridor de latas]**	oong ahbrer lahtersh [ahbriddoar di lahtahss]
ɔrch	**uma lanterna de bolso**	oomer lahngtehrner der boalsoo
acuum flask	**um termo [uma garrafa térmica]**	oong tayrmoo [oomah gahrrahfah tehrmikkah]
vashing powder	**detergente para a roupa**	derterrzhayngter perrer er roaper
vater flask	**um cantil**	oong kahngteel
vood alcohol	**álcool desnaturado**	ahlkoll dizhnertoorahdoo

Crockery *Louça*

cups	**chávenas [xícaras]**	shahvernersh [sheekahrahss]
mugs	**canecas**	kernehkersh
plates	**pratos**	prahtoosh
saucers	**pires**	peerersh
tumblers	**copos**	koppoosh

Cutlery *Talheres*

forks	**garfos**	gahrfoosh
knives	**facas**	fahkersh
spoons	**colheres**	koolyehrersh
teaspoons	**colheres de chá**	koolyehrersh der shah
(made of) plastic/ stainless steel	**(de) plástico/ aço inoxidável**	(der) plahshtikkoo/ ahssoo innoksiddahvehl

Chemist's (drugstore) *Farmácia*

Portuguese chemists' don't normally stock the great range of goods you would find in Britain or the U.S., for example photographic equipment or books. For perfume, makeup etc., you must go to a *perfumaria* (perrfoomer**reeer**). Otherwise, toilet and household articles can be bought from a *drogaria* (drooger**reeer**).

This section is divided into two parts:

1. Pharmaceutical—medicine, first-aid, etc.
2. Toiletry—toilet articles, cosmetics

General *Generalidades*

Where's the nearest (all-night) chemist's?	**Onde fica a farmácia (de serviço) mais próxima?**	**awng**der **fee**ker er ferr**mah**ssyer (der serr**vee**ssoo) mighsh **pro**ssimmer
What time does the chemist's open/close?	**A que horas abre/fecha a farmácia?**	er ker **o**rrersh **ah**brer/**fay**sher er ferr**mah**ssyer

1—Pharmaceutical *Produtos farmacêuticos*

I want something for ...	**Quero qualquer coisa para ...**	**keh**roo kwahl**kehr koay**zer **per**rer
a cold	**a constipação [o resfriado]**	er kawngshtipper**ssahng**^{w} [oo rays**fryah**doa]
a cough	**a tosse**	er **to**sser
hay fever	**a febre dos fenos**	er **feh**brer doosh **fay**noosh
insect bites	**as picadas de insectos**	ersh pi**kkah**dersh der eeng**seh**toosh
sunburn	**as queimaduras do sol**	ersh kaymer**doo**rersh doo soll
travel sickness	**o enjoo (da viagem)**	oo ayng**zhoa**oo (der **vyah**zhahng^{y})
an upset stomach	**a indigestão**	er eengdizhersh**tahng**^{w}
Can you make up this prescription for me?	**Pode aviar-me esta receita?**	**po**dder er**vyahr** mer **eh**ster rer**ssay**ter
Can I get it without a prescription?	**É preciso receita médica?**	eh prer**ssee**zoo rer**ssay**ter **meh**dikker
Shall I wait?	**Tenho que esperar?**	**tay**nyoo ker ishper**rahr**

DOCTOR, see page 137

Can I have a/an/some ...?	Pode dar-me ...?	podder dahr mer
analgesic	um analgésico	oong ernahlzhehzikkoo
antiseptic cream	uma pomada anti-séptica	oomer poomahder ahngti sehtikker
aspirin	aspirinas	ershpirreenersh
(elastic) bandage	uma ligadura [atadura] (elástica)	oomer liggerdoorer [ahtahdoorah] (illahshtikker)
Band-Aids	pensos rápidos [bandaids]	payngsoosh rahpiddoosh [bahngdaydss]
contraceptives	contraceptivos	kawngtrerssehteevoosh
corn plasters	pensos para os calos	payngsoosh perrer oosh kahloosh
cotton wool (absorbent cotton)	algodão hidrófilo	ahlgoodahngʷ iddroffilloo
cough drops	pastilhas para a tosse	pershteelyersh perrer er tosser
disinfectant	um desinfectante	oong derzeengfehtahngter
Elastoplast	pensos rápidos [bandaids]	payngsoosh rahpiddoosh [bahngdaydss]
eye drops	gotas para os olhos	goatersh perrer oosh ollyoosh
gauze	gaze	gahzer
insect repellent/spray	um produto insectífugo/spray insecticida	oong proodootoo eengsehteefoogoo/"spray" eengsehtisseeder
iodine	tintura de iodo	teengtoorer der yoadoo
laxative	um laxativo	oong lersherteevoo
mouthwash	um gargarejo	oong gerrgerrayzhoo
nose drops	gotas para o nariz	goatersh perrer oo nerreesh
sanitary towels (napkins)	pensos higiénicos [toalhas higiénicas]	payngsoosh izhyehnikkoosh [twahlyahss izhyehnikkahss]
suppositories	supositórios	soopoozittorryoosh
... tablets	comprimidos ...	kawngprimmeedoosh
tampons	tampões higiénicos	tahngpawngʸsh izhyehnikkoosh
thermometer	um termómetro	oong terrmommertroo
throat lozenges	pastilhas para a garganta	pershteelyersh perrer er gerrgahngter
vitamin pills	vitaminas	vittermeenersh

VENENO	POISON
PARA USO EXTERNO	FOR EXTERNAL USE ONLY

2—Toiletry *Produtos de higiene e cosméticos*

I'd like a/an/some ...	**Queria ...**	kerreeer
after-shave lotion	**uma loção para depois da barba**	oomer loo**ssahng**^{w} **per**rer der**poysh** der **bahr**ber
blusher	**um blusher**	oong "blusher"
bubble bath	**um banho de espuma**	oong **ber**nyoo der ish**poo**mer
cosmetic	**um cosmético**	oong koozh**meh**teekoo
cream	**um creme**	oong **kreh**mer
cleansing cream	**creme de limpeza**	**kreh**mer der leeng**pay**zer
foundation cream	**creme de base**	**kreh**mer der **bah**zer
moisturizing cream	**creme hidratante**	**kreh**mer iddrer**tahng**ter
night cream	**creme de noite**	**kreh**mer der **noy**ter
cuticle remover	**um produto para tirar as cutículas**	oong proo**doo**too **per**rer tir**rahr** ersh koo**tee**koolersh
deodorant	**um desodorizante [desodorante]**	oong derzoddoori**zzahng**ter [dayzoadoa**rahng**ti]
emery board	**uma lima [lixa] de unhas**	oomer **lee**mer [**lee**shah] der **oo**nyersh
eyebrow pencil	**um lápis para os olhos**	oong **lah**pish **per**rer oosh **o**llyoosh
eye shadow	**uma sombra para os olhos**	oomer **sawng**brer **per**rer oosh **o**llyoosh
face powder	**pó de arroz**	paw der er**roash**
foot/hand cream	**um creme para os pés/as mãos**	oong **kreh**mer **per**rer oosh **pehsh**/ersh **mahng**^{w}sh
lipsalve	**um bâton para o cieiro**	oong bah**tawng** **per**rer oo **syay**roo
lipstick	**um bâton**	oong bah**tawng**
make-up remover pads	**discos de algodão**	**deesh**koosh der ahlgoo**dahng**^{w}
nail brush	**uma escova de unhas**	oomer ish**koa**ver der **oo**nyersh
nail clippers	**um corta-unhas**	oong **korr**ter **oo**nyersh
nail file	**uma lima [lixa] de unhas**	oomer **lee**mer [**lee**shah] der **oo**nyersh
nail polish	**um verniz [esmalte] de unhas**	oong verr**neesh** [ismahlti] der **oo**nyersh
nail polish remover	**um dissolvente de verniz [esmalte]**	oong dissoll**vayng**ter der verr**neesh** [is**mahl**ti]
nail scissors	**uma tesoura de unhas**	oomer ter**zoa**rer der **oo**nyersh
perfume	**um perfume**	oong perr**foo**mer
powder	**pó**	paw
razor	**uma gilete [um barbeador]**	oomer zhi**lleh**ter [oong bahrbyah**doar**]

azor blades	**lâminas de barbear**	**ler**minnersh der berr**byahr**
afety pins	**alfinetes-de-ama**	ahlfi**nnay**tersh der **er**mer
having cream	**um creme da barba**	oong **kreh**mer der **bahr**ber
oap	**um sabonete**	oong serboo**nay**ter
ponge	**uma esponja**	**oo**mer ish**pawng**zher
un-tan cream/oil	**um creme/óleo para bronzear**	oong **kreh**mer/ollyoo perrer brawng**zyahr**
alcum powder	**pó de talco**	paw der **tahl**koo
issues	**lenços de papel**	**layng**soosh der per**pehl**
oilet paper	**papel higiénico**	per**pehl** **izhyeh**nikkoo
oilet water	**uma água-de-colónia**	**oo**mer **ah**gwer der koo**lo**nnyer
oothbrush	**uma escova de dentes**	**oo**mer ish**koa**ver der **dayng**tish
oothpaste	**uma pasta de dentes**	**oo**mer **pahsh**ter der **dayng**tish
owel	**uma toalha**	**oo**mer **twah**lyer
weezers	**uma pinça para depilar**	**oo**mer **peeng**ser **per**rer derpi**llahr**

For your hair *Para o cabelo*

obby pins	**ganchos [grampos]**	**gahng**shoosh [**grahng**poass]
comb	**um pente**	oong **payng**ter
dry shampoo	**um shampoo [xampu] seco**	oong shahng**poa** [shahng**poo**] **say**koo
airbrush	**uma escova de cabelo**	**oo**mer ish**koa**ver der ker**bay**loo
airgrips	**ganchos [grampos]**	**gahng**shoosh [**grahng**poass]
air lotion	**uma loção capilar**	**oo**mer loo**ssahng**^{w} kerpi**llahr**
air slide	**um travessão [clipe]**	oong trerver**ssahng**^{w} [**klee**pi]
air spray	**laca [laquê]**	**lah**ker [lah**kay**]
etting lotion	**um fixador**	oong fikser**doar**
hampoo	**um shampoo [xampu]**	oong shahng**poa** [shahng-**poo**]
for dry/greasy (oily) hair	**para cabelo seco/ oleoso**	**per**rer ker**bay**loo **say**koo/olly**oa**zoo
int	**um produto colorante**	oong proo**doo**too kooloo**rahng**ter
wig	**uma peruca**	**oo**mer per**roo**ker

For the baby *Para o bebé [nenê]*

baby food	**comida para bebé [nenê]**	koo**mee**der **per**rer beh**beh** [nay**nay**]
dummy (pacifier)	**uma chupeta**	**oo**mer shoo**pay**ter
feeding bottle	**um biberon**	oong bibber**rawng**
nappies (diapers)	**fraldas**	**frahl**dersh

Clothing *Vestuário*

If you want to buy something specific, prepare yourself i advance. Look at the list of clothing on page 116. Get som idea of the colour, material and size you want. They're al listed on the next few pages.

General *Generalidades*

I'd like ...	**Queria ...**	ker**reeer**
I want ... for a 10-year-old boy/girl.	**Quero ... para um menino/uma menina de 10 anos.**	**keh**roo ... **per**rer oong mer**nee**noo/**oo**mer mer**nee**-ner der 10 **er**noosh
I want something like this.	**Quero qualquer coisa neste género.**	**keh**roo kwahl**kehr koy**zer **naysh**ter **zheh**nerroo
I like the one in the window.	**Gosto do que está na vitrina.**	**gosh**too doo ker ish**tah** ner vit**tree**ner
How much is that per metre?	**A como [Quanto] é o metro?**	er **koa**moo [**kwahng**too] eh oo **meh**troo

1 centimetre (cm.)	= 0.39 in.	1 inch =	2.54 cm.
1 metre (m.)	= 39.37 in.	1 foot =	30.5 cm.
10 metres	= 32.81 ft.	1 yard =	0.91 m.

Colour *Cores*

I want a darker/ lighter shade.	**Quero um tom mais escuro/mais claro.**	**keh**roo oong tawng mighsh ish**koo**roo/mighsh **klah**roo
I want something to match this.	**Quero qualquer coisa que condiga com isto.**	**keh**roo kwahl**kehr koy**zer ker kawng**dee**ger kawng **eesh**too
I don't like the colour/pattern.	**Não gosto da cor/ do padrão.**	nahng^{w} **gosh**too der koar/ doo per**drahng**^{w}

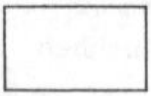

liso
(**lee**zoo)

às riscas
(ahsh **reesh**-kersh)

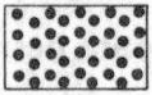

às bolas
(ahsh bo**llersh**)

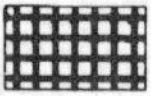

xadrez
(sher**draysh**)

estampado
(ishtahng-**pah**doo)

beige	**bege**	**beh**zher
black	**preto**	**pray**too
blue	**azul**	er**zool**
brown	**castanho [marrom]**	kersh**ter**nyoo [mah**rrawng**]
fawn	**castanho dourado**	kersh**ter**nyoo doa**rah**doo
golden	**dourado**	doa**rah**doo
green	**verde**	**vayr**der
grey	**cinzento**	seeng**zayng**too
mauve	**lilás**	lil**lahsh**
orange	**cor-de-laranja**	koar der ler**rahng**zher
pink	**cor-de-rosa**	koar der **ro**zzer
purple	**roxo**	**roa**shoo
red	**vermelho**	verr**may**lyoo
scarlet	**escarlate**	ishkerr**lah**ter
silver	**prateado**	prer**tyah**doo
turquoise	**azul-turquesa**	er**zool** toor**kay**zer
white	**branco**	**brahng**koo
yellow	**amarelo**	ermer**reh**loo
light ...	**... claro**	... **klah**roo
dark ...	**... escuro**	... ish**koo**roo

Fabrics *Tecidos*

Do you have anything in ...?	**Tem alguma coisa de ...?**	tahng[y] ahl**goo**mer **koy**zer der
Is that ...?	**É ...?**	eh
handmade	**feito à mão**	**fay**too ah mahng[w]
imported	**importado**	eengpoor**tah**doo
made here	**feito aqui**	**fay**too er**kee**
pure cotton/wool	**algodão puro/ pura lã**	ahlgoo**dahng**[w] **poo**roo/ **poo**rer lahng
synthetic	**sintético**	seeng**teh**tikkoo
colourfast	**de cor fixa**	der koar **fee**kser
Is it hand washable/ machine washable?	**Pode lavar-se à mão/ à máquina?**	**po**dder ler**vahr** ser ah mahng[w]/ah **mah**kinner
Will it shrink?	**Não encolhe?**	nahng[w] ayng**ko**llyer
Is it wrinkle-resistant?	**Não amarrota?**	nahng[w] ermer**ro**tter
I want something thinner.	**Quero qualquer coisa mais fina.**	**keh**roo kwahl**kehr koy**zer mighsh **fee**ner
Do you have anything of better quality?	**Tem uma qualidade melhor?**	tahng[y] **oo**mer kwerlid**dah**-der mi**llyor**

cambric	**cambraia**	kahng**brigh**der
camel-hair	**pêlo de camelo**	payloo der ker**may**loo
chiffon	**chiffon**	shif**fawng**
corduroy	**bombazina**	bawngber**zee**ner
cotton	**algodão**	ahlgoo**dahng**ʷ
crepe	**crepe**	**kreh**per
denim	**sarja**	**sahr**zher
felt	**feltro**	**fayl**troo
flannel	**flanela**	fler**neh**ler
gabardine	**gabardine**	gerbahr**dee**ner
lace	**renda**	**rayng**der
leather	**cabedal [couro]**	kerber**dahl** [**koa**roo]
linen	**linho**	**lee**nyoo
poplin	**popelina**	popper**lee**ner
satin	**cetim**	ser**teeng**
silk	**seda**	**say**der
suede	**camurça**	ker**moor**ser
terrycloth	**pano turco [tecido felpudo]**	**per**noo **toor**koo [tay**ssee**doa fehl**poo**doa]
velvet	**veludo**	ver**loo**doo
velveteen	**veludo de algodão**	ver**loo**doo der ahlgoo**dahng**ʷ
wool	**lã**	lahng
worsted	**lã cardada**	lahng kerr**dah**der

Size *Medidas*

Sizes can vary from one manufacturer to another, so be sure to try on shoes and clothing before you buy.

I take size 38.	**O meu número é o 38.**	oo **meh**oo **noo**merroo eh oo 38
Could you measure me?	**Pode tirar-me as medidas?**	**pod**der ti**rrahr** mer ersh mer**dee**dersh
I don't know the Portuguese/ Brazilian sizes.	**Não conheço as medidas portuguesas/ brasileiras.**	nahngʷ koo**nyay**ssoo ersh mer**dee**dersh poortoo**gay**zersh/brahzi**llay**rahss
Can I try it on?	**Posso provar?**	**pos**soo proo**vahr**
Where's the fitting room?	**Onde é a cabine de provas?**	**awng**der eh er kah**bee**ner der **prov**versh
Is there a mirror?	**Há um espelho?**	ah oong ish**pay**lyoo

t fits very well.	**Fica muito bem.**	feeker moong^{y}too bahng^{y}
t doesn't fit.	**Não fica bem.**	nahng^{w} feeker bahng^{y}
t's too ...	**Está muito ...**	ishtah moong^{y}too
hort/long	**curto/comprido**	koortoo/kawngpreedoo
ight/loose	**apertado/largo**	erperrtahdoo/lahrgoo
low long will it take o alter?	**Quanto tempo leva para modificar?**	kwahngtoo tayngpoo lehver perrer moodiffikkahr

Vomen *Senhoras*

	Dresses/Suits					
American	8	10	12	14	16	18
British	10	12	14	16	18	20
Portuguese	36	38	40	42	44	46
Brazilian	38	40	42	44	46	48

	Stockings			Shoes			
American / British	8–8½	9–9½	10–10½	4½ / 3	5½ / 4	6½ / 5	7½ / 6
Portuguese / Brazilian	36–38	38–40	40–42	36	37	38	39

Men *Homens*

	Suits/Overcoats						Shirts			
American / British	36	38	40	42	44	46	15	16	17	18
Portuguese / Brazilian	46	48	50	52	54	56	38	41	43	45

	Shoes				
American / British	5	6	7	8	8½
Portuguese / Brazilian	38	39	41	42	43

NUMBERS, see page 147

Clothes and accessories *Roupas e acessórios*

I'd like a/an/some ...	**Queria ...**	ker**ree**er
bathing cap	**uma touca de banho**	**oo**mer **toa**ker der **ber**nyoo
bathing suit	**um fato [maiô] de banho**	oong **fah**too [migh**oa**] der **ber**nyoo
blouse	**uma blusa**	**oo**mer **bloo**zer
bra	**um soutien**	oong soo**tyahng**
braces	**uns suspensórios**	oongsh sooshpayng**so**rryoosh
briefs	**umas calças [calcinhas]**	**oo**mersh **kahl**sersh [kahl**see**nyahss]
cap	**um boné**	oong bon**neh**
cardigan	**um casaco de malha**	oong ker**zah**koo der **mahl**yer
coat	**um casaco comprido**	oong ker**zah**koo kawng**pree**doo
dress	**um vestido**	oong versh**tee**doo
evening dress (woman's)	**um vestido de noite**	oong versh**tee**doo der **noy**ter
girdle	**uma cinta**	**oo**mer **seeng**ter
gloves	**umas luvas**	**oo**mersh **loo**versh
handbag	**uma mala de mão [bolsa]**	**oo**mer **mah**ler der mahng^{w} [**boal**sah]
hat	**um chapéu**	oong sher**peh**oo
jacket	**um casaco**	oong ker**zah**koo
jeans	**uns jeans**	oongsh "jeans"
nightdress	**uma camisa de dormir [camisola]**	**oo**mer ker**mee**zer der door**meer** [kahmi**zzo**llah]
pair of ...	**um par de ...**	oong pahr der
panties	**umas calças [calcinhas]**	**oo**mersh **kahl**sersh [kahl**see**nyahss]
pants (Am.)	**umas calças compridas**	**oo**mersh **kahl**sersh kawng**pree**dersh
panty girdle	**uma cinta-calça**	**oo**mer **seeng**ter **kahl**ser
panty hose	**um collant**	oong col**lahng**
pullover	**uma camisola de malha [um pulôver]**	**oo**mer kermi**zzo**ller der **mahl**yer [oong poo**loa**veh]
roll-neck (turtle-neck)	**de gola alta**	der **go**ller **ahl**ter
round-neck/V-neck	**de decote redondo/ em bico**	der der**ko**tter rer**dawng**doo/ahng^{y} **bee**koo
with long/short sleeves	**de mangas compridas/curtas**	der **mahng**gersh kawng**pree**dersh/**koor**tersh
sleeveless	**sem mangas**	sahng^{y} **mahng**gersh
pyjamas	**um pijama**	oong pi**zher**mer

raincoat	**uma capa da chuva**	oomer **kah**per der **shoo**ver
scarf	**um lenço de pescoço**	ooṅg **layng**soo der pish**koa**ssoo
shirt	**uma camisa**	oomer ker**mee**zer
shorts	**uns calções**	oongsh kahl**sawng^{y}sh**
skirt	**uma saia**	oomer **sigh**er
slip	**uma saia de baixo**	oomer **sigh**er der **bigh**shoo
socks	**umas peúgas [meias curtas]**	oomersh **pyoo**gersh [**may**ahss **koor**tahss]
stockings	**umas meias**	oomersh **may**ersh
suit (man's)	**um fato [terno]**	oong **fah**too [**tehr**noa]
suit (woman's)	**um fato [terno] de saia e casaco**	oong **fah**too [**tehr**noa] der **sigh**er ee ker**zah**koo
suspenders (Am.)	**uns suspensórios**	oongsh sooshpayng**so**rryoosh
sweatshirt	**uma camisola [um suéter] de algodão**	oomer kermi**zzo**ller [oong **sweh**tehr] der ahlgoo**dahng^{w}**
swimming trunks/ swimsuit	**um fato [maiô] de banho**	oong **fah**too [mighoa] der **ber**nyoo
T-shirt	**uma camiseta**	oomer kermi**zzay**ter
tie	**uma gravata**	oomer grer**vah**ter
tights	**um collant**	oong ko**llahng**
tracksuit	**um fato de treino [um training]**	oong **fah**too der **tray**noo [oong **tray**neengg]
trousers	**umas calças compridas**	oomersh **kahl**sersh kawng**pree**dersh
umbrella	**um guarda-chuva**	oong **gwahr**der **shoo**ver
underpants	**umas cuecas**	oomersh **kweh**kersh
undershirt	**uma camisola interior [camiseta]**	oomer kermi**zzo**ller eengter**ryoar** [kahmi**zzay**tah]
vest (Am.)	**um colete**	oong koo**lay**ter
vest (Br.)	**uma camisola interior [camiseta]**	oomer kermi**zzo**ller eengter**ryoar** [kahmi**zzay**tah]
waistcoat	**um colete**	oong koo**lay**ter

belt	**um cinto**	oong **seeng**too
buckle	**uma fivela**	oomer fi**vveh**ler
button	**um botão**	oong boo**tahng^{w}**
collar	**um colarinho**	oong kooler**ree**nyoo
pocket	**um bolso**	oong **boal**soo
press stud (snap fastener)	**um botão de mola [de pressão]**	oong boo**tahng^{w}** der **mo**ller [der pray**ssahng^{w}**]
zip (zipper)	**um fecho éclair**	oong **fay**shoo ay**klehr**

Shoes *Sapatos*

I'd like a pair of ...	**Queria um par de ...**	ker**ree**er oong pahr der
boots	**botas**	**bo**ttersh
moccasins	**mocassins**	mokkah**ssahngsh**
plimsolls (sneakers)	**ténis**	**teh**nish
sandals	**sandálias**	sahng**dah**lyersh
shoes	**sapatos**	ser**pah**toosh
flat	**de salto raso**	der **sahl**too **rah**zoo
with a heel	**de salto alto**	der **sahl**too **ahl**too
with leather/ rubber soles	**de sola de cabedal [couro]/de borracha**	der **so**ller der kerber**dahl** [**koa**roo]/der boo**rrah**sher
slippers	**chinelos**	shi**nneh**loosh
These are too ...	**Estes são ... demais.**	**aysh**tish sahng^{w} ... der**mighsh**
narrow/wide	**apertados/largos**	erperr**tah**doosh/**lahr**goosh
large/small	**grandes/pequenos**	**grahng**dish/per**kay**noosh
Do you have a larger/smaller size?	**Tem um número maior/mais pequeno [menor]?**	tahng^{y} oong **noo**merroo may**or**/mighsh per**kay**noo [meh**nor**]
Do you have the same in black?	**Tem os mesmos em preto?**	tahng^{y} oosh **mayzh**moosh ahng^{y} **pray**too
cloth	**em tela**	ahng^{y} **teh**ler
leather	**em cabedal [couro]**	ahng^{y} kerber**dahl** [**koa**roo]
rubber	**em borracha**	ahng^{y} boo**rrah**sher
suede	**em camurça**	ahng^{y} ker**moor**ser
Is it genuine leather?	**É cabedal [couro] autêntico?**	eh kerber**dahl** [**koa**roo] ow**tayng**tikkoo
I need some shoe polish/shoelaces.	**Preciso de graxa/ atacadores [cordões] de sapatos.**	prer**ssee**zoo der **grah**sher/ erterker**doa**rersh [kor**dawng^{y}sh**] der ser**pah**toosh

Shoes worn out? Here's the key to getting them fixed again:

Can you repair these shoes?	**Pode consertar estes sapatos?**	**po**dder kawngserr**tahr** **aysh**tish ser**pah**toosh
Can you stitch this?	**Pode coser isto?**	**po**dder koo**zayr** **eesh**too
I want new soles and heels.	**Quero que ponha solas e saltos novos.**	**keh**roo ker **poa**nyer **sol**lersh ee **sahl**toos **nov**voosh
When will they be ready?	**Quando estarão prontos?**	**kwahng**doo ishte**rrahng^{w}** **prawng**toosh

COLOURS, see page 113

Electrical appliances *Aparelhos eléctricos*

The standard current in Portugal is 220-volt, 50-cycle A.C. In most places in Brazil the current is 110-volt, 60-cycles.

What's the voltage?	**Qual é a voltagem?**	kwahl eh er vol**tah**zhahng^{Y}
Do you have a battery for this?	**Tem uma pilha para isto?**	tahng^{Y} **oo**mer **pee**lyer perrer **eesh**too
Can you repair this?	**Pode consertar isto?**	**po**dder kawngserr**tahr** **eesh**too
Can you show me how it works?	**Pode mostrar-me como funciona?**	**po**dder moosh**trahr** mer **koa**moo foong**syo**nner
I'd like a/an/some ...	**Queria ...**	ker**ree**er
adaptor	**um adaptador**	oong erderpter**doar**
amplifier	**um amplificador**	oong ahngpliffikker**doar**
bulb	**uma lâmpada**	**oo**mer **lahng**perder
clock-radio	**um rádio-despertador**	oong **rah**dyoo dishperr-ter**doar**
electric toothbrush	**uma escova de dentes eléctrica**	**oo**mer ish**koa**ver der **dayng**tish **illeh**trikker
extension lead (cord)	**uma extensão**	**oo**mer ishtayng**sahng**^{W}
hair dryer	**um secador de cabelo**	oong ser**ker**doar der ker**bay**loo
headphones	**uns auscultadores [fones]**	oongsh owshkoolter**doa**rersh [**fo**nniss]
(travelling) iron	**um ferro de engomar (de viagem)**	oong **feh**rroo der aynggoo**mahr** (der **vyah**zhahng^{Y})
lamp	**um candeeiro [abajur]**	oong kahng**dyay**roo [ahbah**zhoor**]
plug	**uma ficha**	**oo**mer **fee**sher
portable ...	**... portátil**	... poor**tah**till
radio	**um rádio**	oong **rah**dyoo
record player	**um gira-discos [toca-discos]**	oong **zhee**rer **deesh**koosh [**to**kkah **dees**koass]
shaver	**uma máquina de barbear**	**oo**mer **mah**kinner der berr**byahr**
speakers	**uns alto-falantes**	oongsh **ahl**too fer**lahng**tish
(cassette) tape recorder	**um gravador (de cassetes)**	oong grerver**doar** (der kah**sseh**tish)
(colour) television	**uma televisão (a cores)**	**oo**mer terlervi**zzahng**^{W} (er **koa**rersh)
transformer	**um transformador**	oong trahngshfoormer**doar**
video cassette	**uma videocassete**	**oo**mer viddyokkah**sseh**ter
video recorder	**um gravador vídeo**	oong grerver**doar** **vee**dyoo

Grocery *Mercearia*

I'd like some bread, please.	**Queria pão, se faz favor.**	kerr**ee**er pahng^{w} ser fahsh fervoar
What sort of cheese do you have?	**Que género de queijo tem?**	ker **zheh**nerroo der **kay**zhoo tahng^{y}
A piece of ...	**Um pedaço ...**	oong per**dah**ssoo
that one	**daquele**	der**kay**ler
the one on the shelf	**do que está na prateleira**	doo ker is**tah** ner prerter**lay**rer
I'll have one of those, please.	**Dê-me um desses, por favor.**	day mer oong **day**ssersh poor fer**voar**
May I help myself?	**Posso servir-me?**	possoo serr**veer** mer
I'd like ...	**Queria ...**	kerr**ee**er
a kilo of apples	**um quilo de maçãs**	oong **kee**loo der mer**ssahngs**
half a kilo of tomatoes	**meio-quilo de tomates**	**may**oo **kee**loo der too**mah**tish
100 grams of butter	**100 gramas de manteiga**	100 **grer**mersh der mahng**tay**ger
a litre of milk	**um litro de leite**	oong **lee**troo der **lay**ter
4 slices of ham	**4 fatias de fiambre**	4 fer**tee**ersh der **fyahng**brer
a packet of tea	**um pacote de chá**	oong per**kot**ter der shah
a jar of honey	**um frasco de mel**	oong **frahsh**koo der mehl
a tin (can) of peaches	**uma lata de pêssegos**	**oo**mer **lah**ter der **pay**ssergoosh
a tube of mustard	**um tubo de mostarda**	oong **too**boo der moosh**tahr**der
a box of chocolates	**uma caixa de chocolates**	**oo**mer **kigh**sher der shookoo**lah**tish

1 kilogram or kilo (kg.) = 1000 grams (g.)

100 g. = 3.5 oz.	½ kg. = 1.1 lb.
200 g. = 7.0 oz.	1 kg. = 2.2 lb.

1 oz. = 28.35 g.
1 lb. = 453.60 g.

1 litre (l.) = 0.88 imp. quarts = 1.06 U.S. quarts

1 imp. quart = 1.14 l.	1 U.S. quart = 0.95 l.
1 imp. gallon = 4.55 l.	1 U.S. gallon = 3.8 l.

FOOD, see also page 63

Jeweller's—Watchmaker's *Ourivesaria—Relojoaria*

Could I see that, please?	**Posso ver aquilo ali?**	**po**ssoo vayr er**kee**loo er**lee**
Do you have anything in gold?	**Tem alguma coisa em ouro?**	tahng^{y} ahl**goo**mer **koy**zer ahng^{y} **o**aroo
How many carats is this?	**Quantos quilates tem isto?**	**kwahng**toosh ki**llah**tish tahng^{y} **eesh**too
Is this real silver?	**É prata de lei?**	eh **prah**ter der lay
Can you repair this watch?	**Pode consertar este relógio?**	**po**dder kawngserr**tahr ay**shter rer**lo**zhyoo
I'd like a/an/some ...	**Queria ...**	ker**ree**er
alarm clock	**um despertador**	oong dishperrter**doar**
bangle	**um bracelete**	oong brahsser**leh**ter
battery	**uma pilha**	**oo**mer **pee**lyer
bracelet	**uma pulseira**	**oo**mer pool**say**rer
chain bracelet	**uma corrente de pulso**	**oo**mer koo**rrayng**ter der **pool**soo
charm bracelet	**uma pulseira de berloques**	**oo**mer pool**say**rer der berr**lo**kkersh
brooch	**um broche**	oong **bro**sher
chain	**uma corrente**	**oo**mer koo**rrayng**ter
charm	**um berloque**	oong berr**lo**kker
cigarette case	**uma cigarreira**	**oo**mer sigger**ray**rer
cigarette lighter	**um isqueiro**	oong ish**kay**roo
clip	**um broche de mola**	oong **bro**sher der **mo**ller
clock	**um relógio**	oong rer**lo**zhyoo
cross	**uma cruz**	**oo**mer kroosh
cuff links	**uns botões de punho [abotoaduras]**	oongsh boo**tawng^{y}sh** der **poo**nyoo [ahboatwah**doo**rahss]
cutlery	**uns talheres**	oongsh ter**lyeh**rersh
earrings	**uns brincos**	oongsh **breeng**koosh
filigree jewellery	**as filigranas**	ersh filli**ggrer**nersh
gem	**uma pedra preciosa**	**oo**mer **peh**drer prers**syo**zzer
jewel box	**um cofre de jóias**	oong **ko**ffrer der **zhoy**ersh
necklace	**um colar**	oong koo**lahr**
pendant	**um pingente**	oong peeng**zhayng**ter
pin	**um alfinete**	oong ahlfi**nnay**ter
pocket watch	**um relógio de bolso**	oong rer**lo**zhyoo der **boal**soo
powder compact	**uma caixinha de pó de arroz**	**oo**mer kigh**shee**nyer der paw der er**roash**

ring	um anel	oong ernehl
engagement ring	um anel de noivado	oong ernehl der noyvahdoo
signet ring	um anel de sinete	oong ernehl der sinnayter
wedding ring	uma aliança	oomer erlyahngser
rosary	um rosário	oong roozahryoo
silverware	umas pratas	oomersh prahtersh
tie clip/pin	uma mola/um alfinete de gravata	oomer moller/oong ahlfinnayter der grervahter
watch	um relógio	oong rerlozhyoo
automatic	automático	owtoomahtikkoo
digital	digital	dizhittahl
quartz	quartzo	kwahrtzoo
with a second hand	com ponteiro de segundos	kawng pawngtayroo der sergoongdoosh
waterproof	à prova de água	ah provver der ahgwer
watchstrap (watchband)	uma correia de relógio	oomer koorrayer der rerlozhyoo
wristwatch	um relógio de pulso	oong rerlozhyoo der poolsoo

amber	âmbar	ahngberr
amethyst	ametista	ermerteeshter
chromium	cromo	krommoo
copper	cobre	kobbrer
coral	coral	koorahl
crystal	cristal	krishtahl
diamond	diamante	dyermahngter
emerald	esmeralda	izhmerrahlder
enamel	esmalte	izhmahlter
glass	vidro	veedroo
gold	ouro	oaroo
gold-plated	banhado a ouro	bernyahdoo er oaroo
ivory	marfim	merrfeeng
jade	jade	zhahder
onyx	ónix	onniks
pearl	pérola	pehrooler
pewter	estanho	ishternyoo
platinum	platina	plerteener
ruby	rubi	roobee
sapphire	safira	serfeerer
silver	prata	prahter
silver-plated	banhado a prata	bernyahdoo er prahter
stainless steel	aço inoxidável	ahssoo innoksiddahvehl
topaz	topázio	toopahzyoo
turquoise	turqueza	toorkayzer

)ptician *Oculista*

've broken my lasses.	**Parti [Quebrei] os óculos.**	perr**tee** [kay**bray**] oosh okkooloosh
Can you repair them or me?	**Pode consertá-los?**	podder kawngserr**tah** loosh
When will they be eady?	**Quando estarão prontos?**	**kwahng**doo ishter**rahng**^{w} **prawng**toosh
Can you change the enses?	**Pode mudar as lentes?**	podder moo**dahr** ersh **layng**tish
want tinted lenses.	**Quero lentes de cor.**	**keh**roo **layng**tish der koar
The frame is proken.	**A armação está partida [quebrada].**	er errmer**ssahng**^{w} ish**tah** perr**tee**der [kay**brah**dah]
'd like a spectacle case.	**Queria uma caixa de óculos.**	ker**ree**er **oo**mer **kigh**sher der okkooloosh
'd like to have ny eyesight checked.	**Queria fazer um exame à vista.**	ker**ree**er fer**zayr** oong izzermer ah **veesh**ter
'm short-sighted/ ong-sighted.	**Sou míope/presbita.**	soa **mee**ooper/prersh**bee**ter
want some contact enses.	**Quero lentes de contacto.**	**keh**roo **layng**tish der kawng**tah**ktoo
've lost one of my contact lenses.	**Perdi uma lente de contacto.**	perr**dee** **oo**mer **layng**ter der kawng**tah**ktoo
Could you give me another one?	**Pode dar-me outra?**	podder dahr mer **oa**trer
have hard/soft enses.	**Tenho lentes de contacto rígidas/ flexíveis.**	**tay**nyoo **layng**tish der kawng**tah**ktoo **ree**zhid-dersh/ flehk**see**vaysh
Have you any con- act-lens fluid?	**Tem um líquido para lentes de contacto?**	tahng^{y} oong **lee**kiddoo **per**rer **layng**tish der kawng**tah**ktoo
'd like to buy a pair of sunglasses.	**Queria comprar um par de óculos de sol.**	ker**ree**er kawng**prahr** oong pahr der okkooloosh der soll
May I look in a nirror?	**Posso ver-me ao espelho?**	possoo vayr mer ow ish**pay**lyoo
'd like to buy a pair of binoculars.	**Queria comprar uns binóculos.**	ker**ree**er kawng**prahr** oongsh binnokkooloosh

Photography *Fotografia*

I want a/an ... camera.	**Quero uma máquina fotográfica ...**	kehroo oomer mahkinner footoograhfikker
automatic	**automática**	owtoomahtikker
inexpensive	**barata**	berrahter
simple	**simples**	seengplersh
Show me some cine (movie) cameras.	**Mostre-me algumas máquinas de filmar.**	moshtrer mer ahlgoomersh mahkinnersh der filmahr
I'd like to have some passport photos taken.	**Queria tirar fotografias de passaporte.**	kerreeer tirrahr footoogrerfeeersh der persserporrter

Film *Rolos [Filmes]*

I'd like a film for this camera.	**Queria um rolo para esta máquina.**	kerreeer oong roaloo perrer ehshter mahkinner
black and white	**a preto e branco**	er praytoo ee brahngkoo
colour	**a cores**	er koarersh
colour negative	**para negativos a cores**	perrer nergerteevoosh er koarersh
colour slide	**para slides**	perrer slighdersh
cartridge	**um rolo-cassete**	oong roaloo kahssehter
disc film	**um disco-película**	oong deeshkoo perleekooler
roll film	**um rolo**	oong roaloo
video cassette	**uma videocassete**	oomer viddyokkahssehter
24/36 exposures	**24/36 fotografias**	veengter ee kwahtroo/ treengter ee saysh footoogrerfeeersh
this size	**deste tamanho**	dayshter termernyoo
this ASA/DIN number	**este número de ASA/DIN**	ayshter noomerroo der ahzer/deen
artificial light type	**para luz artificial**	perrer loosh errtiffissyahl
daylight type	**para luz do dia**	perrer loosh doo deeer
fast (high-speed)	**ultra-rápido**	ooltrer rahpiddoo
fine grain	**de grão fino**	der grahng^{w} feenoo

Developing *Revelação*

What's the charge for processing?	**Quanto custa a revelação?**	kwahngtoo kooshter er rerverlerssahng^{w}

'd like ... prints of each negative.	**Quero ... cópias de cada negativo.**	**keh**roo ... **kop**pyersh der **ker**der nerger**tee**voo
with a mat finish	**mates**	**mah**tish
with a glossy finish	**brilhantes**	bri**llyahng**tish
Will you enlarge this, please?	**Pode ampliar isto, por favor?**	**po**dder ahng**plyahr eesh**too poor fer**voar**
When will the photos be ready?	**Quando estarão prontas?**	**kwahng**doo ishter**rahng^{w}** **prawng**tersh

Accessories and repairs *Acessórios e consertos*

'd like a/an/some ...	**Quero ...**	**keh**roo
battery	**uma pilha**	**oo**mer **pee**lyer
cable release	**um disparador**	**oong** dishperrer**doar**
camera case	**uma capa (de máquina fotográfica)**	**oo**mer **kah**per (der **mah**kinner footoo**grah**fikker)
(electronic) flash	**um flash (electrónico)**	**oong** flahsh (illeh**tro**nnikkoo)
filter	**um filtro**	**oong feel**troo
for black and white	**para preto e branco**	**per**rer **pray**too ee **brahng**koo
for colour	**para cores**	**per**rer **koa**rersh
lens	**uma objectiva**	**oo**mer obzheh**tee**ver
telephoto lens	**uma teleobjectiva**	**oo**mer tehlehobzheh**tee**ver
wide-angle lens	**uma objectiva grande angular**	**oo**mer obzheh**tee**ver **grahng**der ahnggoo**lahr**
lens cap	**uma tampa para a objectiva**	**oo**mer **tahng**per **per**rer er obzheh**tee**ver
Can you repair this camera?	**Pode consertar esta máquina?**	**po**dder kawngserr**tahr ehsh**ter **mah**kinner
The film is jammed.	**O rolo está encravado.**	oo **roa**loo ish**tah** ayngkrer**vah**doo
There's something wrong with the ...	**Há qualquer avaria ...**	ah kwahl**kehr** erverr**ee**er
exposure counter	**no contador**	noo kawngter**doar**
film winder	**no botão de bobinagem**	noo boo**tahng^{w}** der bobbi**nnah**zhahng^{y}
flash attachment	**no encaixe do flash**	noo ayng**kigh**sher doo flahsh
lens	**na objectiva**	ner obzheh**tee**ver
light meter	**no fotómetro**	noo foo**to**mmertroo
rangefinder	**no telémetro**	noo ter**leh**mertroo
shutter	**no obturador**	noo obtoorer**doar**

NUMBERS, see page 147

Tobacconist's *Tabacaria*

Other than at tobacconist's you can buy cigarettes at newsstands, hotels and bars. Foreign brands are heavily taxed.

A packet of cigarettes, please.	**Um maço de cigarros, se faz favor.**	oong **mah**ssoo der sig**gahr**roosh ser fahsh fer**voar**
Do you have any American/English cigarettes?	**Tem cigarros americanos/ingleses?**	tahng^{y} sig**gahr**roosh ermerri**kker**noosh/eeng**glay**zersh
I'd like a carton.	**Queria um pacote.**	ker**ree**er oong per**ko**tter
I'd like a/some ...	**Queria ...**	ker**ree**er
candy	**rebuçados [balas]**	rerboo**ssah**doosh [**bah**lahss]
chewing gum	**pastilhas elásticas [chicletes]**	persh**tee**lyersh i**llahsh**tikkersh [shi**kkleh**tiss]
chewing tobacco	**tabaco [fumo] de mascar**	ter**bah**koo [**foo**moa] der mersh**kahr**
chocolate	**chocolate**	shookoo**lah**ter
cigarette case	**uma cigarreira**	**oo**mer sigger**ray**rer
cigarette holder	**uma boquilha [piteira]**	**oo**mer boo**kee**lyer [pit**tay**rah]
cigarettes	**cigarros**	sig**gah**rroosh
filter-tipped	**com filtro**	kawng **feel**troo
without filter	**sem filtro**	sahng^{y} **feel**troo
mild/strong	**suaves/fortes**	**swah**versh/**forr**tish
menthol	**mentolados**	mayngtoo**lah**doosh
king-size	**gigantes**	zhig**gahng**tish
cigars	**charutos**	sher**roo**toosh
lighter	**um isqueiro**	oong ish**kay**roo
lighter fluid/gas	**gasolina/gás para isqueiro**	gerzoo**lee**ner/gash **per**rer ish**kay**roo
matches	**fósforos**	**fosh**fooroosh
pipe	**um cachimbo**	oong ker**sheeng**boo
pipe cleaners	**limpa-cachimbos**	oong **leeng**per ker**sheeng**boosh
pipe tobacco	**tabaco [fumo] para cachimbo**	ter**bah**koo [**foo**moa] **per**rer ker**sheeng**boo
pipe tool	**um esgaravatador de cachimbos**	oong izhgerrerverter**doar** der ker**sheeng**boosh
postcard	**um bilhete postal**	oong bi**llyay**ter poosh**tahl**
snuff	**rapé**	rer**peh**
stamps	**selos**	**say**loosh
sweets	**rebuçados [balas]**	rerboo**ssah**doosh [**bah**lahss]
wick	**uma torcida**	**oo**mer toor**see**der

liscellaneous *Miscelânea*

ouvenirs *Lembranças*

Iere are some suggestions for articles which you might like o bring back as a souvenir or a gift.

d like to buy a ift for ...	**Queria comprar um presente para ...**	kerr**ee**er kawng**prahr** oong prerzayngter perrer
omething typically ortuguese/Brazilian.	**Algo tipicamente português/brasileiro.**	**ahl**goo tippikker**mayng**ter poortoo**gaysh**/brahzil**lay**roo
hina	**a porcelana**	er poorser**ler**ner
orkware	**os artigos de cortiça**	oosh err**tee**goosh der koor**tee**sser
ostumes	**os trajos típicos**	oosh **trah**zhoosh **tee**pikkoosh
mbroidery	**os bordados**	oosh boor**dah**doosh
iligree jewellery	**as filigranas**	ersh filli**ggrer**nersh
andkerchieves	**os lenços**	oosh **layng**soosh
eadscarves	**os lenços de pescoço**	oosh **layng**soosh der pish**koa**ssoo
ace	**as rendas**	ersh **rayng**dersh
eatherwork	**os artigos de couro**	oosh err**tee**goosh der ish**ter**nyoo
ottery	**a loiça de barro**	er **loy**sser der **bahr**roo
ugs	**os tapetes**	oosh ter**pay**tish
iles	**os azulejos**	oosh erzoo**lay**zhoosh
vickerware	**os artigos de verga**	oosh err**tee**goosh der **vayr**ger
voodwork	**os artigos de madeira**	oosh err**tee**gosh der mer**day**rer
voven materials	**os artigos de tear manual [tecelagem]**	oosh err**tee**goosh der tyahr mer**nwahl** [tayssay**lah**zhayng^{y}]

Records—Cassettes *Discos – Cassetes*

)o you have any ecords by ...?	**Tem discos de ...?**	tahng^{y} **deesh**koosh der
'd like a ...	**Queria ...**	kerr**ee**er
cassette	**uma cassete**	**oo**mer kahs**seh**ter
video cassette	**uma videocassete**	**oo**mer viddyokkah**sseh**ter
compact disc	**um disco compacto**	oong **deesh**koo kawng**pahk**too

L.P. (33 rpm)	**um L.P. (33 rotações)**	oong **eh**ler pay (33 rooter**ssawng^{y}sh**)
E.P. (45 rpm)	**um maxi-single (45 rotações)**	oong "maxi-single" (45 rooter**ssawng^{y}sh**)
single	**um single (45 rotações)**	oong "single" (45 rooter**ssawng^{y}sh**)

Do you have any songs by ...?	**Tem canções de ...?**	tahng^y kahng**sawng^{y}sh** der
Can I listen to this record?	**Posso ouvir este disco?**	**po**ssoo oa**veer aysh**ter **deesh**koo
chamber music	**música de câmara**	**moo**zikker der **ker**merrer
classical music	**música clássica**	**moo**zikker **klah**ssikker
folk music	**música folclórica**	**moo**zikker fol**klo**rrikker
instrumental music	**música instrumental**	**moo**zikker eengshtroo-mayng**tahl**
light music	**música ligeira**	**moo**zikker li**zhay**rer
orchestral music	**música sinfónica**	**moo**zikker seeng**fo**nnikker
pop music	**música pop**	**moo**zikker pop

Toys *Brinquedos*

I'd like a toy/ game ...	**Queria um brinquedo/jogo ...**	ker**ree**er oong breeng**kay**doo/**zhoa**goo
for a boy	**para um menino**	**per**rer oong mer**nee**noo
for a 5-year-old girl	**para uma menina de 5 anos**	**per**rer **oo**mer mer**nee**ner der 5 **er**noosh
ball	**uma bola**	**oo**mer **bo**ller
beach ball	**um balão**	oong ber**lahng^w**
bucket and spade (pail and shovel)	**um balde e uma pá**	oong **bahl**der ee **oo**mer pah
building blocks (bricks)	**um jogo de construções**	oong **zhoa**goo der kawngshtroo**ssawng^{w}sh**
card game	**um baralho de cartas**	oong ber**rah**lyoo der **kahr**tersh
chess set	**um jogo de xadrez**	oong **zhoa**goo der sher**draysh**
doll	**uma boneca**	**oo**mer boo**neh**ker
electronic game	**um jogo electrónico**	oong **zhoa**goo illeh**tro**nnikkc
flippers	**umas barbatanas**	**oo**mersh berrber**ter**nersh
roller skates	**uns patins de rodas**	oongsh per**teengsh** der **ro**ddersh

Your money: banks—currency

In Portugal the usual banking hours are from 8.30 to 11.45 a.m. and from 1 to 2.45 p.m., Monday to Friday. In Brazil banking hours are normally from 10 a.m. to 4.30 p.m. Monday to Friday.

You'll find currency exchange offices *(câmbio)* in most Portuguese and Brazilian tourist centres, and they often stay open longer, especially during the summer season, for the benefit of tourists.

The basic unit of currency in Portugal is the *escudo* (ishkoodoo) divided into 100 *centavos* (sayng**tah**voosh). *Escudo* is abbreviated to *esc*.

Coins: 50 centavos, 1, 2½, 5 and 25 escudos.
Banknotes: 20, 50, 100, 500, 1,000 and 5,000 escudos.

Brazil's monetary unit is the *cruzado* (kroo**zah**doa), abbreviated *CZ$*, and introduced into the country in February 1986. While the old currency continues to circulate, visitors should note that its value is one thousandth that of the new currency (1 *cruzado* = 1000 *cruzeiros*).

Coins: 10, 20, 100, 200 and 500 cruzeiros.
Banknotes: 100, 200, 500, 1,000, 5,000, 10,000, 50,000 and 100,000 cruzeiros.

Credit cards may be used in an increasing number of hotels, restaurants, shops, etc. Signs are posted indicating which cards are accepted.

Traveller's cheques are accepted by hotels, travel agents and many shops, although the exchange rate is invariably better at a bank. Be sure to take your passport with you for identification. You may also cash Eurocheques in Portugal.

Where's the nearest bank?	**Onde é o banco mais próximo?**	**awng**der eh oo **bahng**koo mighsh **pro**ssimmoo
Where's the nearest currency exchange office?	**Onde é a agência de câmbio mais próxima?**	**awng**der eh er er**zhayng**-syer der **kahng**byoo mighsh **pro**ssimmer

At the bank *No banco*

I want to change some dollars/pounds.	**Quero trocar dólares/libras.**	keh**roo** troo**kahr** dollersh/**lee**brersh
I want to cash a traveller's cheque.	**Quero levantar um cheque de viagem.**	kehroo lervahng**tahr** oong **sheh**ker der **vyah**zhahng^y
What's the exchange rate?	**A como [quanto] está o câmbio?**	er **koa**moo [**kwahng**toa] ish**tah** oo **kahng**byoo
How much commission do you charge?	**Que comissão cobram?**	ker koomi**ssahng**^{w} **kob**brahng^w
Can you telex my bank in London?	**Pode mandar um telex para o meu banco em Londres?**	**pod**der mahng**dahr** oong teh**lehks per**rer oo **meh**oo **bahng**koo ahng^y **lawng**-drersh
I have a/an/some ...	**Tenho ...**	**tay**nyoo
bank card	**um cartão bancário**	oong kerr**tahng**^{w} bahng**kah**ryoo
credit card	**um cartão de crédito**	oong kerr**tahng**^{w} der **kreh**dittoo
Eurocheques	**Eurocheques**	ehooro**sheh**kersh
introduction from ...	**uma carta de apresentação de ...**	oomer **kahr**ter der erprer-zayngter**ssahng**^{w} der
letter of credit	**uma carta de crédito**	oomer **kahr**ter der **kreh**dittoo
I'm expecting some money from New York. Has it arrived?	**Estou à espera de dinheiro de Nova Iorque. Já chegou?**	ish**toa** ah ish**peh**rer der din**nyay**roo der **nov**ver york. zhah sher**goa**
Please give me some ...	**Se faz favor, dê-me ...**	ser fahsh fer**voar** day mer
coins	**moedas**	**mweh**dersh
notes (bills)	**notas**	**not**tersh
small change	**dinheiro trocado**	din**nyay**roo troo**kah**doo

Deposits—Withdrawals *Depósitos—Levantamentos*

I want to ...	**Quero ...**	**keh**roo
open an account	**abrir uma conta**	er**breer oo**mer **kawng**ter
withdraw ... escudos/cruzados	**levantar ... escudos/cruzados**	lervahng**tahr** ish**koo**doosh/kroo**zah**doash
Where should I sign?	**Onde devo assinar?**	**awng**der **day**voo erssi**nnahr**

NUMBERS, see page 147

I want to deposit this in my account.	**Quero depositar isto na minha conta.**	**keh**roo derpoozit**tahr eesh**-too ner **mee**nyer **kawng**ter

Business terms *Termos comerciais*

My name is ...	**O meu nome é ...**	oo **meh**oo **noa**mer eh
Here's my card.	**Aqui está o meu cartão.**	er**kee** ish**tah** oo **meh**oo kerr**tahng**^{w}
I have an appointment with ...	**Tenho um encontro marcado com ...**	**tay**nyoo oong ayng**kawng**-troo merr**kah**doo kawng
Can you give me an estimate of the cost?	**Pode dar-me uma estimação do custo?**	**po**dder dahr mer **oo**mer ishtimmer**ssahngg**^{w} doo **koosh**too
What's the rate of inflation?	**Qual é o índice de inflação?**	kwahl eh oo **eeng**disser der eengflah**ssahng**^{w}
Can you provide me with an interpreter?	**Pode arranjar-me [arrumar-me] um intérprete?**	**po**dder errahng**zhahr** mer [ahrroo**mahr** mi] oong eeng**tehr**prerter
Where can I make photocopies?	**Onde posso fazer fotocópias?**	**awng**der **po**ssoo fer**zayr** fotto**kko**ppyersh

amount	**a importância**	er eengpoor**tahng**syer
balance	**o balanço**	oo ber**lahng**soo
bond	**a obrigação**	er oabrigger**ssahng**^{w}
capital	**o capital**	oo kerpi**ttahl**
cheque book	**o livro de cheques**	oo **lee**vroo der **sheh**kersh
contract	**o contrato**	oo kawng**trah**too
discount	**o desconto**	oo dish**kawng**too
expenses	**as despesas**	ersh dish**pay**zersh
interest	**o juro**	oo **zhoo**roo
investment	**o investimento**	oo eengvershti**mmayng**too
invoice	**a factura**	er fah**too**rer
loss	**a perda**	er **payr**der
mortgage	**a hipoteca**	er ippoo**teh**ker
payment	**o pagamento**	oo perger**mayng**too
percentage	**a percentagem**	er perrsayng**tah**zhahng^{y}
profit	**o lucro**	oo **loo**kroo
purchase	**a compra**	er **kawng**prer
sale	**a venda**	er **vayng**der
share	**a acção**	er ah**ssahng**^{w}
transfer	**a transferência**	er trahngshfer**rayng**syer
value	**o valor**	oo ver**loar**

At the post office

Post offices in Portugal are indicated by the letters CTT *(Correios e Telecomunicações)* and are generally open from 9 a.m. to 7 p.m., Monday to Friday. Stamps can also be bought at tobacconist's and souvenir stands. Letter boxes (mailboxes) on the street follow the British pillar-box design; they're painted red, too.

In Brazil, post offices bear a sign ECT *(Empresa Brasileira de Correios e Telégrafos)* and are generally open from 8 a.m. to 6 p.m. Monday to Friday, till noon on Saturdays. You can also buy stamps at some newsstands and snack bars displaying the sign *Correios* or *Aqui vendemos selos*. Streetcorner letter boxes are yellow.

Where's the nearest post office?	**Onde fica a estação de correios mais próxima?**	awngder feeker er ishterssahng[w] der koorrayoosh mighsh prossimmer
What time does the post office open/close?	**A que horas abre/fecha o correio?**	er ker orrersh ahbrer/faysher oo koorrayoo
A stamp for this letter/postcard, please.	**Um selo para esta carta/este bilhete postal, por favor.**	oong sayloo perrer ehshter kahrter/ayshter billyayter pooshtahl poor fervoar
A ... escudo stamp, please.	**Um selo de ... escudos, por favor.**	oong sayloo der ... ishkoodoosh poor fervoar
What's the postage for a letter to London?	**Qual é a franquia de uma carta para Londres?**	kwahl eh er frahngkeeer der oomer kahrter perrer lawngdrersh
What's the postage for a postcard to Los Angeles?	**Qual é a franquia de um bilhete postal para Los Angeles?**	kwahl eh er frahngkeeer der oong billyayter pooshtahl perrer "Los Angeles"
Where's the letter box (mailbox)?	**Onde é a caixa do correio?**	awngder eh er kighsher doo koorrayoo

I want to send this parcel.	**Quero enviar esta encomenda [este pacote].**	**keh**roo ayng**vyahr ehsh**ter ayngkoo**mayng**der [**ay**sti] pah**ko**tti]
I want to send this by ...	**Quero mandar isto ...**	**keh**roo mahng**dahr eesh**too
airmail	**por avião**	poor er**vyahng**[w]
express (special delivery)	**por expresso**	poor ish**preh**ssoo
registered mail	**registado**	rerzhish**tah**doo
At which counter can I cash an international money order?	**Em que guiché posso levantar um vale de correio internacional?**	ahng[y] ker ghi**sheh po**ssoo lervahng**tahr** oong **vah**ler der koo**rray**oo eengterrnerssyoo**nahl**
Where's the poste restante (general delivery)?	**Onde é a posta restante?**	**awng**der eh er **posh**ter rish**tahng**ter
Is there any post (mail) for me? My name is ...	**Há correio para mim? O meu nome é ...**	ah koo**rray**oo **per**rer meeng. oo **meh**oo **noa**mer eh

SELOS	STAMPS
ENCOMENDAS [PACOTES]	PARCELS
VALES DE CORREIO	MONEY ORDERS

Telegrams *Telegramas*

In Portugal and Brazil telegrams are sent through the post office.

I want to send a telegram/telex.	**Queria mandar um telegrama/telex.**	ker**ree**er mahng**dahr** oong terler**grer**mer/teh**lehks**
May I have a form, please?	**Pode dar-me um formulário?**	**po**dder dahr mer oong foormoo**lah**ryoo
How much is it per word?	**Qual é a taxa por palavra?**	kwahl eh er **tah**sher poor per**lah**vrer
How long will a cable to Boston take?	**Quanto tempo leva um telegrama para chegar a Boston?**	**kwahng**too **tayng**poo **leh**ver oong terler**grer**mer **per**rer sher**gahr** er "Boston"
How much will this telex cost?	**Quanto custará este telex?**	**kwahng**too kooshte**rrah ay**shter teh**lehks**

Telephoning *Telefones*

In Portugal, coin telephones are found in bars, restaurants and on the street. International calls can be made through the clerk at any post office or at your hotel. In major cities you'll find a few English-speaking operators. But if you must say a number in Portuguese, give it in digits, e.g. 87912 = *oito, sete, nove, um, dois*. Dialling codes are listed in the directory.

To use a public telephone in Brazil you must buy tokens, which are sold at most newsstands. Long-distance and overseas calls can be made from public telephone offices *(estação telefônica)* or your hotel.

Where's the telephone?	**Onde é o telefone?**	**awng**der eh oo terler**fo**nner
I'd like ... telephone tokens.	**Queria ... fichas (de telefone).**	ker**ree**er ... **fee**sherss (der terler**fo**nner)
Where's the nearest telephone booth?	**Onde fica a cabine telefónica mais próxima?**	**awng**der **fee**ker er kah**bee**ner terler**fo**nnikker mighsh **pro**ssimmer
May I use your phone?	**Posso utilizar o seu telefone?**	**po**ssoo ootilli**zzahr** oo **se**hoo terler**fo**nner
Do you have a telephone directory for Faro?	**Tem uma lista telefónica de Faro?**	tahng^y **oo**mer **leesh**ter terler**fo**nnikker der **fah**roo
What's the dialling (area) code for ...?	**Qual é o indicativo de ...?**	kwahl eh oo eengdikker**tee**voo der
How do I get the international operator?	**Como posso obter o serviço internacional?**	**koa**moo **po**ssoo ob**tayr** oo serr**vee**ssoo eengterrnerssyoo**nahl**

Operator *Telefonista*

Good morning, I want São Paulo 23 45 67.	**Bom dia, quero ligar para o 23 45 67 em São Paulo.**	bawng **dee**er **ke**hroo li**ggahr** **pe**rrer oo 23 45 67 ahng^y sahng^w **pow**loo
Can you help me get this number?	**Pode ajudar-me a ligar para este número?**	**po**dder erzhoo**dahr** mer er li**ggahr** **pe**rrer **aysh**ter **noo**merroo

NUMBERS, see page 147

I want to place a personal (person-to-person) call.	**Quero uma comunicação com pré-aviso.**	kehroo oomer koomoo-nikkerssahng^{w} kawng preh erveezoo
I want to reverse the charges (call collect).	**Quero uma comunicação pagável no destino.**	kehroo oomer koomoo-nikkerssahng^{w} pergahvehl noo dishteenoo

Telephone alphabet *Alfabeto telefónico*

A	**Aveiro**	ahvayroo	N	**Nazaré**	nerzerreh
B	**Braga**	brahger	O	**Ovar**	ovvahr
C	**Coimbra**	kweengbrer	P	**Porto**	poartoo
D	**Dafundo**	dahfoongdoo	Q	**Queluz**	kehloosh
E	**Évora**	ehvoorer	R	**Rossio**	roosseeoo
F	**Faro**	fahroo	S	**Setúbal**	sertooberl
G	**Guarda**	gwahrder	T	**Tavira**	terveerer
H	**Horta**	orrter	U	**Unidade**	ooniddahder
I	**Itália**	ittahlyer	V	**Vidago**	viddahgoo
J	**José**	zhoozeh	W	**Waldemar**	vahldermahr
K	**Kodak**	koddahk	X	**Xavier**	shervyehr
L	**Lisboa**	lizhboaer	Y	**York**	"york"
M	**Maria**	merreeer	Z	**Zulmira**	zoolmeerer

Speaking *Ao telefone*

Hello, this is ... speaking.	**Está [Alô]? Aqui fala ...**	ishtah [ahloa]. erkee fahler
I'd like to speak to ...	**Queria falar com ...**	kerreeer ferlahr kawng
I'd like extension ...	**Queria o interno [ramal] ...**	kerreeer oo eengtehrnoo [rahmahl]
Speak louder/more slowly, please.	**Pode falar mais alto/mais devagar?**	podder ferlahr mighsh ahltoo/mighsh dervergahr

Bad luck *Pouca sorte*

Would you try again later, please?	**Pode voltar a chamar um pouco mais tarde?**	podder voltahr er shermahr oong poakoo mighsh tahrder
Operator, you gave me the wrong number.	**A menina [senhorita] deu-me um número errado.**	er merneener [sinnyoareetah] dehoo mer oong noomerroo irrahdoo

Operator, we were cut off.	**Cortaram-nos a ligação.**	koor**tah**rahng[w] noosh er liger**ssahng**[w]

Not there *A pessoa não está*

When will he/she be back?	**Quando é que ele/ ela estará de volta?**	**kwahng**doo eh ker **ay**ler/ **eh**ler ishter**rah** der **voll**ter
Will you tell him/her I called? My name is …	**Pode dizer-lhe que eu telefonei? O meu nome é …**	**po**dder di**zzayr** lyer ker ehoo terlerfoo**nay** oo **meh**oo **noa**mer eh
Would you ask him/her to call me?	**Pode pedir-lhe para me telefonar?**	**po**dder per**deer** lyer **per**rer mer terlerfoo**nahr**
Would you take a message, please?	**Pode dar-lhe um recado?**	**po**dder dahr lyer oong rer**kah**doo

Charges *Taxas*

What was the cost of that call?	**Qual foi o preço da chamada?**	kwahl foy oo **pray**ssoo der sher**mah**der
I want to pay for the call.	**Quero pagar a chamada.**	**keh**roo per**gahr** er sher**mah**der

Há uma chamada para o senhor/a senhora.	There's a telephone call for you.
Que número deseja?	What number are you calling?
A linha está impedida [ocupada].	The line's engaged.
Ninguém atende.	There's no answer.
Enganou-se no número.	You've got the wrong number.
O telefone está avariado [com defeito].	The phone is out of order.
É só um momento.	Just a moment.
Não desligue, por favor.	Hold on, please.
Ele/Ela não está neste momento.	He's/She's out at the moment.

Doctor

Make sure your health insurance policy covers any illness or accident while on holiday. If it doesn't, ask your insurance representative, automobile association or travel agent for details of special health insurance.

General *Generalidades*

Can you get me a doctor?	**Pode chamar-me um médico?**	**po**dder sher**mahr** mer oong **meh**dikkoo
Is there a doctor here?	**Há aqui um médico?**	ah er**kee** oong **meh**dikkoo
I need a doctor, quickly.	**Preciso de um médico, depressa.**	prers**see**zoo der oong **meh**dikkoo der**preh**sser
Where can I find a doctor who speaks English?	**Onde posso encontrar um médico que fale inglês?**	**awng**der **po**ssoo ayngkawng**trahr** oong **meh**dikkoo ker **fah**ler eeng**glaysh**
Where's the surgery (doctor's office)?	**Onde é o consultório médico?**	**awng**der eh oo kawngsool**to**rryoo **meh**dikkoo
What are the surgery (office) hours?	**Qual é o horário das consultas?**	kwahl eh oo o**rrah**ryoo dersh kawng**sool**tersh
Could the doctor come to see me here?	**O médico pode vir consultar-me aqui?**	oo **meh**dikkoo **po**dder veer kawngsool**tahr** mer er**kee**
What time can the doctor come?	**A que horas pode vir o médico?**	er ker **o**rrersh **po**dder veer oo **meh**dikkoo
Can you recommend a/an ...?	**Pode recomendar-me ...?**	**po**dder rerkoomayng**dahr** mer
general practitioner	**um médico de clínica geral**	oong **meh**dikkoo der **klee**nikker zher**rahl**
children's doctor	**um pediatra**	oong per**dyah**trer
eye specialist	**um oftalmologista**	oong ofterlmooloo**zheesh**ter
gynaecologist	**um ginecologista**	oong zhinnerkooloo**zheesh**ter
Can I have an appointment ...?	**Posso ter uma consulta ...?**	**po**ssoo tayr **oo**mer kawng**sool**ter
right now	**agora**	er**go**rrer
tomorrow	**amanhã**	ahmer**nyahng**
as soon as possible	**o mais depressa possível**	oo mighsh der**preh**sser poo**ssee**vehl

CHEMIST'S, see page 108

Parts of the body *Partes do corpo*

appendix	**o apêndice**	oo er**payng**disser
arm	**o braço**	oo **brah**ssoo
back	**as costas**	ersh **kosh**tersh
bladder	**a bexiga**	er ber**shee**ger
bone	**o osso**	oo **oa**ssoo
bowel	**o intestino**	oo eengtersh**tee**noo
breast	**o seio**	oo **say**oo
chest	**o peito**	oo **pay**too
ear	**a orelha**	er oa**ray**lyer
eye	**o olho**	oo **oa**lyoo
face	**o rosto**	oo **roash**too
finger	**o dedo**	oo **day**doo
foot	**o pé**	oo peh
genitals	**os órgãos genitais**	oosh **orr**gahng^{w}sh zherni**ttighsh**
gland	**a glândula**	er **glahng**dooler
hand	**a mão**	er mahng^{w}
head	**a cabeça**	er ker**bay**sser
heart	**o coração**	oo koorer**ssahng^{w}**
jaw	**a maxila**	er mahk**see**ler
joint	**a articulação**	er errtikkooler**ssahng^{w}**
kidney	**o rim**	oo reeng
knee	**o joelho**	oo **zhway**lyoo
leg	**a perna**	er **pehr**ner
lip	**o lábio**	oo **lah**byoo
liver	**o fígado**	oo **fee**gerdoo
lung	**o pulmão**	oo pool**mahng^{w}**
mouth	**a boca**	er **boa**ker
muscle	**o músculo**	oo **moosh**kooloo
neck	**o pescoço**	oo pish**koa**ssoo
nerve	**o nervo**	oo **nayr**voo
nervous system	**o sistema nervoso**	oo sish**tay**mer nerr**voa**zoo
nose	**o nariz**	oo ner**reesh**
rib	**a costela**	er koosh**teh**ler
shoulder	**o ombro**	oo **awng**broo
skin	**a pele**	er **peh**ler
spine	**a coluna vertebral**	er koo**loo**ner verrter**brahl**
stomach	**o estômago**	oo ish**toa**mergoo
tendon	**o tendão**	oo tayng**dahng^{w}**
thigh	**a coxa**	er **koa**sher
throat	**a garganta**	er gerr**gahng**ter
thumb	**o polegar**	oo pooler**gahr**
toe	**o dedo do pé**	oo **day**doo doo peh
tongue	**a língua**	er **leeng**gwer
tonsils	**as amígdalas**	ersh er**mee**derlersh

Accident—Injury *Acidentes—Ferimentos*

There has been an accident.	**Houve um acidente.**	oaver oong erssiddayngter
My son/daughter has had a fall.	**O meu filho/a minha filha deu uma queda.**	oo mehoo feelyoo/er mee-nyer feelyer dehoo oomer kehder
He/She has hurt his/her head.	**Ele/Ela feriu a cabeça.**	ayler/ehler ferreeoo er kerbaysser
He's/She's unconscious.	**Ele/Ela está sem sentidos.**	ayler/ehler ishtah sahng^{y} sayngteedoosh
He's/She's bleeding (heavily).	**Ele/Ela está a sangrar (muito).**	ayler/ehler ishtah er sahnggrahr (moong^{y}too)
He's/She's (seriously) injured.	**Ele/Ela está (gravemente) ferido(a).**	ayler/ehler ishtah (grah-vermayngter) ferreedoo(er)
His/Her arm is broken.	**Ele/Ela tem o braço partido [quebrado].**	ayler/ehler tahng^{y} oo brahssoo perrteedoo [kaybrahdoa]
His/Her ankle is swollen.	**Ele/Ela tem o tornozelo inchado.**	ayler/ehler tahng^{y} oo toornoozayloo eengshahdoo
I've been stung.	**Fui picado.**	fooy pikkahdoo
I've got something in my eye.	**Tenho qualquer coisa no olho.**	taynyoo kwahlkehr koyzer noo oalyoo
I've got a/an ...	**Tenho ...**	taynyoo
blister	**uma bolha**	oomer boalyer
boil	**um furúnculo**	oong fooroongkooloo
bruise	**uma contusão**	oomer kawngtoozahng^{w}
burn	**uma queimadura**	oomer kaymerdoorer
cut	**um corte**	oong korrter
graze	**uma esfoladela**	oomer ishfoolerdehler
lump	**um galo/um alto**	oong gahloo/oong ahltoo
rash	**uma erupção**	oomer irroopsahng^{w}
sting	**uma picada**	oomer pikkahder
swelling	**um inchaço**	oong eengshahssoo
wound	**uma ferida**	oomer ferreeder
Could you have a look at it?	**Pode dar uma olhadela?**	podder dahr oomer ollyer-dehler
I can't move my ...	**Não posso mexer o/a/os/as ...**	nahng^{w} possoo mershayr oo/er/oosh/ersh
It hurts.	**Dói-me.**	doy mer

Onde lhe dói?	Where does it hurt?
Que género de dor sente?	What kind of pain is it?
crónica/aguda	dull/sharp
lancinante/persistente	throbbing/constant
intermitente	on and off
Está ...	It's ...
partido [quebrado]/torcido	broken/sprained
deslocado/rasgado	dislocated/torn
É preciso fazer uma radiografia.	I want you to have an X-ray.
É preciso pôr gesso.	You'll get a plaster.
Está infectado.	It's infected.
Está vacinado contra o tétano?	Have you been vaccinated against tetanus?
Vou dar-lhe um anti-séptico/ um analgésico.	I'll give you an antiseptic/ a painkiller.

Illness *Doenças*

I'm not feeling well.	Não me sinto bem.	nahng^w mer seengtoo bahng^Y
I'm ill.	Estou doente.	ishtoa dwayngter
I feel ...	Tenho ...	taynyoo
dizzy	vertigens	verrteezhahng^Ysh
nauseous	náuseas	nowzyersh
shivery	calafrios	kerlerfreeoosh
I've got a fever.	Tenho febre.	taynyoo fehbrer
My temperature is 38 degrees.	Tenho 38 de febre.	taynyoo 38 der fehbrer
I've been vomiting.	Vomitei.	voomittay
I'm constipated.	Tenho prisão de ventre [Estou constipado(a)].	taynyoo prizzahng^w der vayngtrer [istoa kawngstippahdoa(ah)]
I've got diarrhoea.	Tenho diarreia.	taynyoo dyerrayer
My ... hurts.	Dói-me o/a ...	doy mer oo/er

I've got (a/an) ...	**Tenho ...**	**tay**nyoo
backache	**dor nas costas**	**doar** nersh **kosh**tersh
cold	**uma constipação [um resfriado]**	**oo**mer kawngshtipper**ssahng**^{w} [oong rays**fryah**doa]
cough	**tosse**	**to**sser
cramps	**cãibras**	**kahng**^{y}brersh
earache	**dor de ouvidos**	doar der oa**vee**doosh
hay fever	**a febre dos fenos**	er **feh**brer doosh **fay**noosh
headache	**dor de cabeça**	doar der ker**bay**sser
indigestion	**uma indigestão**	**oo**mer eengdizhersh**tahng**^{w}
nosebleed	**uma hemorragia nasal**	**oo**mer immoorrer**zhee**er ner**zahl**
palpitations	**palpitações**	pahlpitter**ssawng**^{y}**sh**
rheumatism	**reumatismo**	rehoomer**teezh**moo
sore throat	**dor de garganta**	doar der gerr**gahng**ter
stiff neck	**um torcicolo**	oong toorsi**kko**lloo
stomach ache	**dor de estômago**	doar der ish**toa**mergoo
I have difficulties breathing.	**Tenho dificuldade em respirar.**	**tay**nyoo diffikkool**dah**der ahng^{y} rishpi**rrahr**
I have a pain in my chest.	**Sinto uma dor no peito.**	**seeng**too **oo**mer doar noo **pay**too
I had a heart attack ... years ago.	**Tive um ataque cardíaco há ... anos.**	**tee**ver oong er**tah**ker kerr**dee**erkoo ah ... **er**noosh
My blood pressure is too high/too low.	**Tenho uma tensão arterial muito alta/baixa.**	**tay**nyoo **oo**mer tayng**sahng**^{w} errter**ryahl** **moong**^{y}too **ahl**ter/**bigh**sher
I'm allergic to ...	**Sou alérgico(a) a ...**	soa er**lehr**zhikkoo(er) er
I'm diabetic.	**Sou diabético(a).**	soa dyer**beh**tikkoo(er)

Women's section *Sector da mulher*

I have period pains.	**Tenho dores menstruais.**	**tay**nyoo **doa**rersh mayngsh**trwighsh**
I have a vaginal infection.	**Tenho uma infecção vaginal.**	**tay**nyoo **oo**mer eengfeh**ssahng**^{w} verzhi**nnahl**
I'm on the pill.	**Tomo a pílula.**	**to**mmoo er **pee**looler
I haven't had my period for 2 months.	**Há 2 meses que não tenho menstruação.**	ah 2 **may**zersh ker nahng^{w} **tay**nyoo mayngshtrwer**ssahng**^{w}
I'm pregnant.	**Estou grávida.**	ish**toa** **grah**vidder

👉	👈
Há quanto tempo se sente assim?	How long have you been feeling like this?
É a primeira vez que sente isso?	Is this the first time you've had this?
Vou tirar-lhe a temperatura/ a tensão arterial.	I'll take your temperature/ blood pressure.
Arregace a manga, por favor.	Roll up your sleeve, please.
Dispa-se (da cintura para cima), se faz favor.	Please undress (down to the waist).
Deite-se ali, se faz favor.	Please lie down over here.
Abra a boca.	Open your mouth.
Respire fundo.	Breathe deeply.
Tussa, por favor.	Cough, please.
Onde é que lhe dói?	Where does it hurt?
Tem ...	You've got (a/an) ...
uma apendicite	appendicitis
asma	asthma
uma cistite	cystitis
uma doença venérea	venereal disease
uma gastrite	gastritis
uma gripe	flu
uma icterícia	jaundice
uma inflamação de ...	inflammation of ...
uma insolação	sunstroke
uma intoxicação alimentar	food poisoning
uma pneumonia	pneumonia
sarampo	measles
(Não) é contagioso.	It's (not) contagious.
Vou dar-lhe uma injecção.	I'll give you an injection.
Quero uma amostra do seu sangue/das suas fezes/da sua urina.	I want a specimen of your blood/stools/urine.
Deve ficar na cama durante ... dias.	You must stay in bed for ... days.
Quero que consulte um especialista.	I want you to see a specialist.

Prescription—Treatment *Receita—Tratamento*

This is my usual medicine.	**Este é o meu medicamento habitual.**	ayshter eh oo mehoo merdikkermayngtoo erbittwahl
Can you give me a prescription for this?	**Pode dar-me uma receita para isto?**	podder dahr mer oomer rerssayter perrer eeshtoo
Can you prescribe a/an/some ...?	**Pode receitar-me ...**	podder rerssaytahr mer
antidepressant	**um antidepressivo**	oong ahngtidderprer-sseevoo
sleeping pills	**um sonífero**	oong sooneeferroo
tranquillizer	**um calmante**	oong kahlmahngter
I'm allergic to antibiotics/penicillin.	**Sou alérgico(a) a antibióticos/ à penicilina.**	soa erlehrzhikkoo(er) er ahngtibbyottikkoosh/ ah pernissilleener
I don't want anything too strong.	**Não quero nada muito forte.**	nahng^{W} kehroo nahder moong^{Y}too forrter
How many times a day should I take it?	**Quantas vezes devo tomá-lo por dia?**	kwahngtersh vayzersh dayvoo toomah loo poor deeer
Must I swallow them whole?	**Devo engoli-los inteiros?**	dayvoo aynggoolee loosh eengtayroosh

Que tratamento está a fazer?	What treatment are you having?
Que remédio está a tomar?	What medicine are you taking?
Em injecção ou por via oral?	By injection or orally?
Tome ... colheres de chá deste remédio ...	Take ... teaspoons of this medicine ...
Tome um comprimido com um copo de água ...	Take one pill with a glass of water ...
de 2 em 2 horas	every 2 hours
3 vezes por dia	3 times a day
antes/depois das refeições	before/after each meal
de manhã/à noite	in the morning/at night
se tiver dores	if there is any pain
durante 7 dias	for 7 days

CHEMIST'S, see p. 108

Fee *Honorários*

How much do I owe you?	**Quanto lhe devo?**	**kwahng**too lyer **day**voo
May I have a receipt for my health insurance?	**Pode passar-me um recibo para o meu seguro de doença?**	podder per**ssahr** mer oong rer**ssee**boo **per**rer oo meho sergooroo der **dwayng**ser
Can I have a medical certificate?	**Pode passar-me um certificado médico?**	podder per**ssahr** mer oong serrtiffi**kkah**doo **meh**dikkoo
Would you fill in this health insurance form, please?	**Pode preencher esta folha de seguro?**	podder pryayng**shayr ehsh**ter **foa**lyer der ser**goo**roo

Hospital *Hospital*

Please notify my family.	**Por favor, avise a minha família.**	poor fer**voar** er**vee**zer er **mee**nyer fer**mee**lyer
What are the visiting hours?	**Quais são as horas de visita?**	kwighsh sahng^w ersh orrersh der viz**zee**ter
When can I get up?	**Quando posso levantar-me?**	**kwahng**doo **po**ssoo lervahng**tahr** mer
When will the doctor come?	**Quando vem o médico?**	**kwahng**doo vahng^y oo **meh**dikkoo
I'm in pain.	**Estou com dores.**	ish**toa** kawng **doa**rersh
I can't eat/sleep.	**Não posso comer/ dormir.**	nahng^w **po**ssoo koo**mayr**/ door**meer**
Where is the bell?	**Onde está a campainha?**	**awng**der ish**tah** er kahngper**ee**nyer

nurse	**a enfermeira**	er ayngferr**may**rer
patient	**o(a) paciente**	oo(er) per**ssyayng**ter
anaesthesia	**a anestesia**	er ernershter**zee**er
blood transfusion	**a transfusão de sangue**	er trahngshfoo**zahng^w** der **sahng**ger
injection	**a injecção**	er eengzheh**ssahng^w**
operation	**a operação**	er opperrer**ssahng^w**
bed	**a cama**	er **ker**mer
bedpan	**a bacia de cama**	er ber**ssee**er der **ker**mer
thermometer	**o termómetro**	oo terr**mo**mmertroo

Dentist *Dentista*

Can you recommend a good dentist?	**Pode recomendar-me um bom dentista?**	podder rerkoomayngdahr mer oong bawng dayngteeshter
Can I make an (urgent) appointment to see Dr. ...?	**Posso marcar uma consulta (urgente) com o Dr. ...?**	possoo merrkahr oomer kawngsoolter (oorzhayngter) kawng oo doatoar
Couldn't you make it earlier than that?	**Não pode ser antes?**	nahng^{w} podder sayr ahngtish
I have a bad tooth.	**Tenho um dente furado.**	taynyoo oong dayngter foorahdoo
I have a broken tooth.	**Parti [Quebrei] um dente.**	perrtee [kaybray] oong dayngter
I have a toothache.	**Tenho dor de dentes.**	taynyoo doar der dayngtish
I have an abscess.	**Tenho um abcesso.**	taynyoo oong erbssehssoo
This tooth hurts.	**Dói-me este dente.**	doy mer ayshter dayngter
at the top	**em cima**	ahng^{y} seemer
at the bottom	**em baixo**	ahng^{y} bighshoo
in the front	**à frente**	ah frayngter
at the back	**atrás**	ertrahsh
Can you fix it temporarily?	**Pode tratá-lo provisoriamente?**	podder trertah loo proovizzorryermayngter
I don't want it taken out.	**Não quero arrancá-lo.**	nahng^{w} kehroo errahngkah loo
Could you give me an anaesthetic?	**Pode fazer-me uma anestesia?**	podder ferzayr mer oomer ernershterzeeer
I've lost a filling.	**Perdi um chumbo.**	perrdee oong shoongboo
The gum ...	**A gengiva ...**	er zhayngzheever
is very sore	**está muito inflamada**	ishtah moong^{y}too eengflermahder
is bleeding	**sangra**	sahnggrer
I've broken this denture.	**Parti [Quebrei] a dentadura.**	perrtee [kaybray] er dayngterdoorer
Can you repair this denture?	**Pode consertar esta dentadura?**	podder kawngserrtahr ehshter dayngterdoorer
When will it be ready?	**Quando estará pronta?**	kwahngdoo ishterrah prawngter

Reference section

Where do you come from? *Donde é?*

Africa	**a África**	er ahfrikker
Asia	**a Ásia**	er ahzyer
Australia	**a Austrália**	er owshtrahlyer
Europe	**a Europa**	er ehooropper
North America	**a América do Norte**	er ermehrikker doo norrter
South America	**a América do Sul**	er ermehrikker doo sool
Algeria	**a Argélia**	er errzhehlyer
Azores	**os Açores**	oosh erssoarersh
Bolivia	**a Bolívia**	er booleevyer
Brazil	**o Brasil**	oo brerzeel
Canada	**o Canadá**	oo kernerdah
China	**a China**	er sheener
Colombia	**a Colômbia**	er koolawngbyer
England	**a Inglaterra**	er eengglertehrrer
France	**a França**	er frahngser
Germany	**a Alemanha**	er erlermernyer
Great Britain	**a Grã-Bretanha**	er grahng brerternyer
Greece	**a Grécia**	er grehssyer
India	**a Índia**	er eengdyer
Ireland	**a Irlanda**	er irlahngder
Israel	**Israel**	izhrerehl
Italy	**a Itália**	er ittahlyer
Japan	**o Japão**	oo zherpahng^{w}
Madeira	**a Madeira**	er merdayrer
Morocco	**Marrocos**	merrokkoosh
New Zealand	**a Nova Zelândia**	er novver zerlahngdyer
Paraguay	**o Paraguai**	oo perrergwigh
Peru	**o Peru**	oo perroo
Portugal	**Portugal**	poortoogahl
Scotland	**a Escócia**	er ishkossyer
South Africa	**a África do Sul**	er ahfrikker doo sool
Soviet Union	**a União Soviética**	er oonyahng^{w} soovyehtikke
Spain	**a Espanha**	er ishpernyer
Switzerland	**a Suíça**	er sweesser
Tunisia	**a Tunísia**	er tooneezyer
United States	**os Estados Unidos**	oosh ishtahdoosh ooneedoosh
Uruguay	**o Uruguai**	oo ooroogwigh
Venezuela	**a Venezuela**	er vernerzwehler
Wales	**o País de Gales**	oo pereesh der gahlersh

Numbers *Números*

0	**zero**	zehroo
1	**um, uma**	oong oomer
2	**dois, duas**	doysh dooersh
3	**três**	traysh
4	**quatro**	kwahtroo
5	**cinco**	seengkoo
6	**seis**	saysh
7	**sete**	sehter
8	**oito**	oytoo
9	**nove**	novver
10	**dez**	dehsh
11	**onze**	awngzer
12	**doze**	doazer
13	**treze**	trayzer
14	**catorze**	kertoarzer
15	**quinze**	keengzer
16	**dezasseis**	derzerssaysh
17	**dezassete**	derzerssehter
18	**dezoito**	derzoytoo
19	**dezanove**	derzernovver
20	**vinte**	veengter
21	**vinte e um**	veengter ee oong
22	**vinte e dois**	veengter ee doysh
23	**vinte e três**	veengter ee traysh
24	**vinte e quatro**	veengter ee kwahtroo
25	**vinte e cinco**	veengter ee seengkoo
26	**vinte e seis**	veengter ee saysh
27	**vinte e sete**	veengter ee sehter
28	**vinte e oito**	veengter ee oytoo
29	**vinte e nove**	veengter ee novver
30	**trinta**	treengter
31	**trinta e um**	treengter ee oong
32	**trinta e dois**	treengter ee doysh
33	**trinta e três**	treengter ee traysh
40	**quarenta**	kwerrayngter
41	**quarenta e um**	kwerrayngter ee oong
42	**quarenta e dois**	kwerrayngter ee doysh
43	**quarenta e três**	kwerrayngter ee traysh
50	**cinquenta**	seengkwayngter
51	**cinquenta e um**	seengkwayngter ee oong
52	**cinquenta e dois**	seengkwayngter ee doysh
53	**cinquenta e três**	seengkwayngter ee traysh
60	**sessenta**	serssayngter
61	**sessenta e um**	serssayngter ee oong
62	**sessenta e dois**	serssayngter ee doysh

63	**sessenta e três**	ser**ssayng**ter ee traysh
70	**setenta**	ser**tayng**ter
71	**setenta e um**	ser**tayng**ter ee oong
72	**setenta e dois**	ser**tayng**ter ee doysh
73	**setenta e três**	ser**tayng**ter ee traysh
80	**oitenta**	oy**tayng**ter
81	**oitenta e um**	oy**tayng**ter ee oong
82	**oitenta e dois**	oy**tayng**ter ee doysh
83	**oitenta e três**	oy**tayng**ter ee traysh
90	**noventa**	noo**vayng**ter
91	**noventa e um**	noo**vayng**ter ee oong
92	**noventa e dois**	noo**vayng**ter ee doysh
93	**noventa e três**	noo**vayng**ter ee traysh
100	**cem/cento***	sahng^{y}/**sahng^{y}**too
101	**cento e um**	**sayng**too ee oong
102	**cento e dois**	**sayng**too ee doysh
110	**cento e dez**	**sayng**too ee dehsh
120	**cento e vinte**	**sayng**too ee **veeng**ter
130	**cento e trinta**	**sayng**too ee **treeng**ter
140	**cento e quarenta**	**sayng**too ee kwer**rayng**ter
150	**cento e cinquenta**	**sayng**too ee seeng**kwayng**ter
160	**cento e sessenta**	**sayng**too ee ser**ssayng**ter
170	**cento e setenta**	**sayng**too ee ser**tayng**ter
180	**cento e oitenta**	**sayng**too ee oy**tayng**ter
190	**cento e noventa**	**sayng**too ee noo**vayng**ter
200	**duzentos**	doo**zayng**toosh
300	**trezentos**	trer**zayng**toosh
400	**quatrocentos**	kwahtroo**ssayng**toosh
500	**quinhentos**	kinn**yayng**toosh
600	**seiscentos**	saysh**sayng**toosh
700	**setecentos**	sehter**ssayng**toosh
800	**oitocentos**	oytoo**ssayng**toosh
900	**novecentos**	novver**ssayng**toosh
1000	**mil**	meel
1100	**mil e cem**	meel ee sahng^{y}
1200	**mil e duzentos**	meel ee doo**zayng**toosh
2000	**dois mil**	doysh meel
5000	**cinco mil**	**seeng**koo meel
10,000	**dez mil**	dehsh meel
50,000	**cinquenta mil**	seeng**kwayng**ter meel
100,000	**cem mil**	sahng^{y} meel
1,000,000	**um milhão**	oong mill**yahng^{w}**
1,000,000,000	**um bilhão**	oong bill**yahng^{w}**

* *cem* is used before nouns and adjectives.

first	primeiro	primmayroo
second	segundo	sergoongdoo
third	terceiro	terrsayroo
fourth	quarto	kwahrtoo
fifth	quinto	keengtoo
sixth	sexto	sayshtoo
seventh	sétimo	sehtimmoo
eighth	oitavo	oytahvoo
ninth	nono	noanoo
tenth	décimo	dehssimmoo
once	uma vez	oomer vaysh
twice	duas vezes	dooersh vayzersh
three times	três vezes	traysh vayzersh
a half	uma metade	oomer mertahder
half a ...	meio ...	mayoo
half of ...	metade de ...	mertahder der
half (adj.)	meio	mayoo
a quarter/one third	um quarto/um terço	oong kwahrtoo/oong tayrsoo
a pair of	um par de	oong pahr der
a dozen	uma dúzia	oomer doozyer
one per cent	um por cento	oong poor sayngtoo
3.4%	3,4%	traysh veergooler kwahtroo poor sayngtoo
1981	mil novecentos e oitenta e um	meel novverssayngtoosh ee oytayngter ee oong
1992	mil novecentos e noventa e dois	meel novverssayngtoosh ee noovayngter ee doysh
2003	dois mil e três	doysh meel ee traysh

Year and age *Ano e idade*

year	o ano	oo ernoo
leap year	o ano bissexto	oo ernoo bissayshtoo
decade	a década	er dehkerder
century	o século	oo sehkooloo
this year	este ano	ayshter ernoo
last year	o ano passado	oo ernoo perssahdoo
next year	o próximo ano	oo prossimmoo ernoo
each year	cada ano	kerder ernoo
2 years ago	há 2 anos	ah 2 ernoosh
in one year	dentro de um ano	dayngtroo der oong ernoo
in the eighties	nos anos oitenta	noosh ernoosh oytayngter
the 16th century	o século dezasseis	oo sehkooloo derzerssaysh
in the 20th century	no século vinte	noo sehkooloo veengter

How old are you?	**Que idade tem?**	ker **iddah**der tahng^y
I'm 30 years old.	**Tenho trinta anos.**	**tay**nyoo **treeng**ter **er**noosh
He/She was born in 1960.	**Ele/Ela nasceu em mil novecentos e sessenta.**	**ay**ler/**eh**ler nersh**se**hoo ahng^y meel novverss**sayng**toosh ee ser**ssayng**ter
What is his/her age?	**Que idade tem ele/ela?**	ker **iddah**der tahng^y **ay**ler/**eh**ler
Children under 16 are not admitted.	**Não se admitem crianças menores de dezasseis anos.**	nahng^w ser erd**mee**tahng^y kry**ahng**sersh mer**no**rrersh der derzer**ssaysh** **er**noosh

Seasons *Estações do ano*

spring/summer	**a Primavera/o Verão**	er primmer**veh**rer/oo verr**ahng**^{w}
autumn/winter	**o Outono/o Inverno**	oo oat**oa**noo/oo eeng**vehr**noo
in spring	**na Primavera**	ner primmer**veh**rer
during the summer	**durante o Verão**	door**ahng**ter oo verr**ahng**^{w}
in autumn	**no Outono**	noo oat**oa**noo
during the winter	**durante o Inverno**	door**ahng**ter oo eeng**vehr**noo
high/low season	**a época alta/baixa**	er **eh**pooker **ahl**ter/**bigh**sher

Months *Meses*

January	**Janeiro**	zher**nay**roo
February	**Fevereiro**	ferver**ray**roo
March	**Março**	**mahr**soo
April	**Abril**	er**breel**
May	**Maio**	**migh**oo
June	**Junho**	**zhoo**nyoo
July	**Julho**	**zhoo**lyoo
August	**Agosto**	er**goash**too
September	**Setembro**	ser**tayng**broo
October	**Outubro**	oa**too**broo
November	**Novembro**	noo**vayng**broo
December	**Dezembro**	der**zayng**broo
in September	**em Setembro**	ahng^y ser**tayng**broo
since October	**desde Outubro**	**dayzh**der oa**too**broo
the beginning of ...	**o princípio de ...**	oo preeng**see**pyoo der
the middle of ...	**os meados de ...**	oosh **myah**doosh der
the end of ...	**o fim de ...**	oo **feeng** der

Days and date *Dias e data*

What day is it today?	**Que dia é hoje?**	ker deeer eh oazher
Sunday	**domingo***	doomeenggoo
Monday	**segunda-feira**	sergoongder fayrer
Tuesday	**terça-feira**	tayrser fayrer
Wednesday	**quarta-feira**	kwahrter fayrer
Thursday	**quinta-feira**	keengter fayrer
Friday	**sexta-feira**	sayshter fayrer
Saturday	**sábado**	sahberdoo
It's ...	**Estamos ...**	ishtermoosh
July 1	**no dia 1 [no 1º] de Julho**	noo deeer oong [noo primmayroa] der zhoolyoo
March 10	**no dia 10 de Março**	noo deeer dehsh der mahrsoo
in the morning	**de manhã**	der mernyahng
during the day	**durante o dia**	doorahngter oo deeer
in the afternoon	**à tarde**	ah tahrder
in the evening	**à noite**	ah noyter
at night	**à noite**	ah noyter
the day before yesterday	**anteontem**	ahngtyawngtahng^y
yesterday	**ontem**	awngtahng^y
today	**hoje**	oazher
tomorrow	**amanhã**	ahmernyahng
the day before	**a véspera**	er vehshperrer
the next day	**o dia seguinte**	oo deeer sergheengter
two days ago	**há dois dias**	ah doysh deeersh
in three days' time	**daqui a três dias**	derkee er traysh deeersh
last week	**a semana passada**	er sermerner perssahder
next week	**a próxima semana**	er prossimmer sermerner
for a fortnight (two weeks)	**durante duas semanas**	doorahngter dooersh sermernersh
birthday	**o dia de anos**	oo deeer der ernosh
day off	**o dia de folga**	oo deeer der follger
holiday	**o feriado**	oo ferryahdoo
holidays/vacation	**as férias**	ersh fehryersh
week	**a semana**	er sermerner
weekday	**o dia de semana**	oo deeer der sermerner
weekend	**o fim-de-semana**	oo feeng der sermerner
working day	**o dia útil**	oo deeer ootill

* The names of days aren't capitalized in Portuguese.

Public holidays *Feriados*

Listed below are the main public holidays in Portugal (P) and Brazil (B), when banks, offices and shops are closed. In addition, there are various regional holidays.

January 1	**Ano Novo**	New Year's Day	P	B
April 21	**Tiradentes**	Tiradentes' Day		B
April 25	**Dia de Portugal**	National Day	P	
May 1	**Dia do Trabalho**	Labour Day	P	B
June 10	**Dia de Camões**	Camoens' Day	P	
August 15	**Assunção**	Assumption	P	
September 7	**Independência**	Independence Day		B
October 5	**Dia da República**	Republic Day	P	
November 1	**Todos-os-Santos**	All Saints' Day	P	
November 2	**Finados**	All Souls' Day		B
November 15	**Proclamação da República**	Republic Day		B
December 1	**Restauração**	Restoration Day	P	
December 8	**Imaculada Conceição**	Immaculate Conception	P	B*
December 25	**Natal**	Christmas Day	P	B
Movable dates:	**Terça-feira de Carnaval**	Shrove Tuesday	P	B
	Sexta-feira Santa	Good Friday	P	B
	Corpo de Deus	Corpus Christi	P	B*

* Religious holiday not necessarily affecting business life.

Merry Christmas!	**Feliz Natal!**	ferleesh nertahl
Happy New Year!	**Próspero Ano Novo!**	proshperroo ernoo noavoo
Happy Easter!	**Páscoa feliz!**	pahshkwer ferleesh
Happy birthday!	**Parabéns!/Feliz aniversário!**	perrerbahng^{y}sh/ferleesh ernivversahryoo
Best wishes!	**Felicidades!**	ferlissiddahdish
Congratulations!	**Parabéns!**	perrerbahng^{y}sh
Good luck/ All the best!	**Boa sorte!**	boaer sorrter
Have a good trip!	**Boa viagem!**	boaer vyahzhahng^{y}
Have a good holiday!	**Boas férias!**	boaersh fehryersh
Best regards from ...	**Cumprimentos de ...**	koongprimmayngtoosh der
My regards to ...	**Cumprimentos a ...**	koongprimmayngtoosh er

What time is it? *Que horas são?*

Excuse me. Can you tell me the time?	**Desculpe. Pode dizer-me as horas?**	dish**kool**per. **po**dder diz-**zayr** mer ersh **o**rrersh
It's one o'clock.	**É uma hora*.**	eh **oo**mer **o**rrer
It's two o'clock.	**São duas horas.**	sahng^w **doo**ersh **o**rrersh
five past ...	**... e cinco**	... ee **seeng**koo
ten past ...	**... e dez**	... ee dehsh
a quarter past ...	**... e um quarto**	... ee oong **kwahr**too
twenty past ...	**... e vinte**	... ee **veeng**ter
twenty-five past ...	**... e vinte e cinco**	... ee **veeng**ter ee **seeng**koo
half past ...	**... e meia**	... ee **ma**yer
twenty-five to ...	**vinte e cinco para as ...**	**veeng**ter ee **seeng**koo **pe**rrer ersh ...
twenty to ...	**vinte para as ...**	**veeng**ter **pe**rrer ersh
a quarter to ...	**um quarto para as ...**	oong **kwahr**too **pe**rrer ersh
ten to ...	**dez para as ...**	dehsh **pe**rrer ersh ...
five to ...	**cinco para as ...**	**seeng**koo **pe**rrer ersh ...
in the morning/ afternoon/evening	**da manhã/da tarde/da noite**	der mer**nyahng**/der **tahr**der/der **noy**ter
noon/midnight	**meio-dia/meia-noite**	**ma**yoo **dee**er/**ma**yer **noy**ter
The train leaves at ...	**O comboio [trem] parte às ...**	oo kawng**boy**oo [trahng^y] **pahr**ter ahsh
13.04 (1.04 p.m.)	**treze horas e quatro minutos**	**tray**zer **o**rrersh ee **kwah**troo mi**nnoo**toosh
0.40 (0.40 a.m.)	**zero horas e quarenta minutos**	**zeh**roo **o**rrersh ee kwer**rayng**ter mi**nnoo**toosh
in five minutes	**daqui a cinco minutos**	der**kee** er **seeng**koo mi**nnoo**toosh
in a quarter of an hour	**daqui a um quarto de hora**	der**kee** er oong **kwahr**too der **o**rrer
half an hour ago	**há meia-hora**	ah **ma**yer **o**rrer
about two hours	**cerca de duas horas**	**sayr**ker der **doo**ersh **o**rrersh
more than 10 minutes	**mais de dez minutos**	mighsh de dehsh mi**nnoo**toosh
less than 30 seconds	**menos de trinta segundos**	**may**noosh der **treeng**ter ser**goong**doosh
The clock is fast/ slow.	**O relógio está adiantado/atrasado.**	oo rer**lo**zhyoo ish**tah** er-dyahng**tah**doo/ertrer**zah**doo

* In ordinary conversation, time is expressed as shown here. However, in official time the 24-hour clock is used, which means that after noon hours are counted from 13 to 24.

NUMBERS, see page 147

Common abbreviations *Abreviaturas usuais*

(a)	assinado	signed
a/c	ao cuidado de	c/o
A.C.B.	Automóvel Clube do Brasil	Brazilian Automobile Association
A.C.P.	Automóvel Clube de Portugal	Portuguese Automobile Association
apart., ap.	apartamento	flat (apartment)
Calç.	calçada	paved street
c/c	conta corrente	current account
c/v	cave	basement; cellar
Cia., C.^{ia}	companhia	company
CEE	Comunidade Económica Europeia	EEC, Common Market
CP	Caminhos de Ferro Portugueses	Portuguese Railways
D.	Dona	Mrs. (title of courtesy)
d., dto.	direito	on the right (in addresses)
e., esq.	esquerdo	on the left (in addresses)
ENATUR	Empresa Nacional de Turismo	Portuguese National Tourist Office
E.U.A.	Estados Unidos da América	U.S.A.
Exma., Exma	Excelentíssima	title of courtesy (followed by Mrs. or Mr.)
Exmo., Exmo	Excelentíssimo	
G.N.R.	Guarda Nacional Republicana	National Republican Guard (police)
h	hora	o'clock
IVA	Imposto sobre o Valor Acrescentado	VAT, value-added tax
L., L.^{o}	Largo	square
Lx.^{a}	Lisboa	Lisbon
Men.^{a}	Menina	Miss (Portugal)
P.	Praça	square
r/c	rés-do-chão	ground floor
Rem., Rem.^{te}	remetente	sender
R.N.	Rodoviária Nacional	Portuguese Transport Company
R.P.	Rádio-Patrulha	Police Patrol
RTP	Rádio e Televisão Portuguesa	Portuguese Broadcasting Company
R.	rua	street
s.f.f.	se faz favor	please
Sr., Sra., Srta.	Senhor, Senhora Senhorita	Mr., Mrs., Miss (Brazil)

Signs and notices *Sinais e letreiros*

Aberto	Open
Alfândega	Customs
Aluga-se	For hire/To let (for rent)
Atenção	Caution
Avariado	Out of order
Aviso	Notice
Caixa	Cash desk
Cavalheiros	Gentlemen
Completo	Full/No vacancies
Correio	Post office
Cuidado com o cão	Beware of the dog
É favor não incomodar	Do not disturb
É favor não mexer	Do not touch
Elevador	Lift (elevator)
Empurre	Push
Encerrado	Closed
Entrada	Entrance
Entrada livre	Free entrance
Entre (sem bater)	Enter (without knocking)
Espere, s.f.f.	Please wait
Fechado	Closed
Frio	Cold
Fumadores	Smoking allowed
Homens	Gentlemen
Informações	Information
Leilão	Auction
Livre	Vacant/Free
Lotação esgotada	Sold out (Theatre)
Ocupado	Occupied
Perigo (de morte)	Danger (of death)
Pintado de fresco	Wet paint
Privado	Private
Proibido ...	... forbidden
Proibido a cães	Dogs not allowed
Proibido fumar	No smoking
Puxe	Pull
Quente	Hot
Reservado	Reserved
Saída	Exit
Saída de emergência	Emergency exit
Saldos	Sale
Senhoras	Ladies
Toque à campainha, s.f.f.	Please ring
Vende-se	For sale
Veneno	Poison

Emergency *Urgências*

Call the police	**Chame a polícia**	**sher**mer er poo**lee**ssyer
Consulate	**Consulado**	kawngsoo**lah**doo
DANGER	**PERIGO**	per**ree**goo
Embassy	**Embaixada**	ayngbigh**shah**der
FIRE	**FOGO**	**foa**goo
Gas	**Gás**	gash
Get a doctor	**Chame um médico**	**sher**mer oong **meh**dikkoo
Go away	**Vá-se embora**	vah ser ayng**bor**rer
HELP	**SOCORRO**	soo**koar**roo
Get help	**Vá buscar ajuda**	vah boosh**kahr** er**zhoo**der
I'm ill	**Estou doente**	ish**toa dwayng**ter
I'm lost	**Perdi-me**	perr**dee** mer
Leave me alone	**Deixe-me em paz**	**day**sher mer ahng^{w} pash
LOOK OUT	**ATENCÃO**	ertayng**sahng**^{w}
POLICE	**POLÍCIA**	poo**lee**ssyer
Quick	**Depressa**	der**preh**sser
STOP	**ALTO**	**ahl**too
Stop that man/ woman	**Prenda aquele homem/aquela mulher**	**prayng**der er**kay**ler **om**mahng^{y}/er**keh**ler moo**lyehr**
STOP THIEF	**AGARRA QUE É LADRÃO**	er**gahr**rer ker eh ler**drahng**^{w}

Lost property—Theft *Perda—Roubo*

Where's the ...?	**Onde é ...?**	**awng**der eh
lost property (lost and found) office	**a secção dos perdidos e achados**	er sehk**sahng**^{w} doosh perr**dee**doosh ee er**shah**doosh
police station	**o posto da polícia**	oo **poash**too der poo**lee**ssyer
I want to report a theft.	**Quero dar parte de um roubo.**	**keh**roo dahr **pahr**ter der oong **roa**boo
My ... has been stolen.	**Roubaram-me ...**	roa**bah**rahng^{w} mer
handbag	**a mala de mão [bolsa]**	er **mah**ler der mahng^{w} [**boal**sah]
passport	**o passaporte**	o persser**porr**ter
I've lost my ...	**Perdi ...**	perr**dee**
ticket	**o meu bilhete**	oo **meh**oo bi**llyay**ter
wallet	**a minha carteira**	er **mee**nyer kerr**tay**rer
I lost it in ...	**Perdi-o(a) em ...**	perr**dee** oo(er) ahng^{y}

CAR ACCIDENTS, see page 78

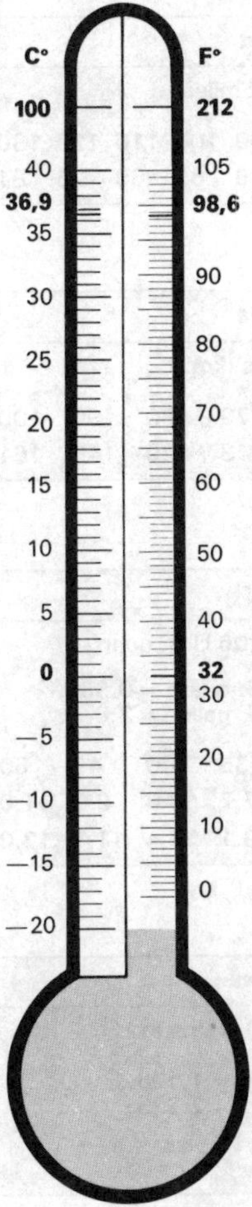

Conversion tables

Centimetres and inches

To change centimetres into inches, multiply by .39.

To change inches into centimetres, multiply by 2.54.

	in.	feet	yards
1 mm.	0.039	0.003	0.001
1 cm.	0.39	0.03	0.01
1 dm.	3.94	0.32	0.10
1 m.	39.40	3.28	1.09

	mm.	cm.	m.
1 in.	25.4	2.54	0.025
1 ft.	304.8	30.48	0.305
1 yd.	914.4	91.44	0.914

(32 metres = 35 yards)

Temperature

To convert centigrade into degrees Fahrenheit, multiply centigrade by 1.8 and add 32.

To convert degrees Fahrenheit into centigrade, subtract 32 from Fahrenheit and divide by 1.8.

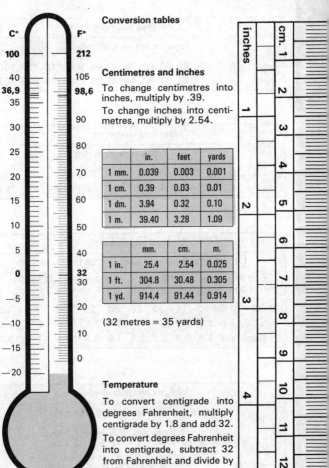

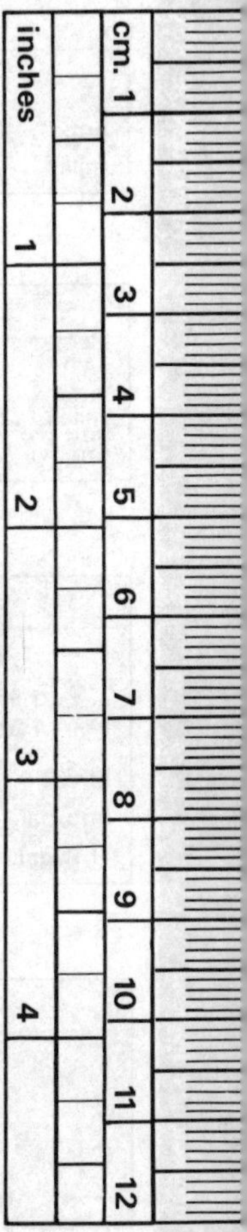

Kilometres into miles

1 kilometre (km.) = 0.62 miles

km.	10	20	30	40	50	60	70	80	90	100	110	120	130
miles	6	12	19	25	31	37	44	50	56	62	68	75	81

Miles into kilometres

1 mile = 1.609 kilometres (km.)

miles	10	20	30	40	50	60	70	80	90	100
km.	16	32	48	64	80	97	113	129	145	161

Fluid measures

1 litre (l.) = 0.88 imp. quart or 1.06 U.S. quart

1 imp. quart = 1.14 l.
1 imp. gallon = 4.55 l.

1 U.S. quart = 0.95 l.
1 U.S. gallon = 3.8 l.

litres	5	10	15	20	25	30	35	40	45	50
imp. gal.	1.1	2.2	3.3	4.4	5.5	6.6	7.7	8.8	9.9	11.0
U.S. gal.	1.3	2.6	3.9	5.2	6.5	7.8	9.1	10.4	11.7	13.0

Weights and measures

1 kilogram or kilo (kg.) = 1000 grams (g.)

100 g. = 3.5 oz.
200 g. = 7.0 oz.

½ kg. = 1.1 lb.
1 kg. = 2.2 lb.

1 oz. = 28.35 g.
1 lb. = 453.60 g.

CLOTHING SIZES, see page 115/YARDS AND INCHES, see page 112

Basic Grammar

Here's the briefest possible outline of some essential features of Portuguese grammar.

Articles

Articles agree with the noun in gender and number.

Definite article (the):

	masculine	feminine
singular	**o**	**a**
plural	**os**	**as**

Indefinite article (a/an):

	masculine	feminine
singular	**um**	**uma**
plural	**uns**	**umas**

Note: The plural corresponds to the English "some" or "a few".

To show possession, the preposition **de** (of) + the article is contracted to **do, da, dos** or **das.**

o princípio do mês	the beginning of the month
o fim da semana	the end of the week

Nouns

All nouns in Portuguese are either masculine or feminine. Normally, those ending in **o** are masculine and those ending in **a** are feminine. Generally, nouns which end in a vowel add **-s** to form the plural:

a menina	the little girl
as meninas	the little girls
o pato	the duck
os patos	the ducks

Words ending in **r, s** or **z** form the plural by adding **-es:**

a mulher	the woman
as mulheres	the women
o país	the country
os países	the countries
a luz	the light
as luzes	the lights

Words ending in a nasal sound **(em, im, om, um)** change their endings to **ens, ins, ons, uns** in the plural.

Adjectives

These agree with the nouns they modify in gender and number.

o belo livro	the nice book
a bela estátua	the fine statue
os homens altos	the tall men
as mulheres altas	the tall women

From these examples you can see that adjectives can come before or after the noun. This is a matter of sound and idiom.

Demonstrative adjectives

this	**este** (masc.)/**esta** (fem.)
that	**esse, aquele** (masc.)/ **essa, aquela** (fem.)
these	**estes** (masc.)/**estas** (fem.)
those	**esses, aqueles** (masc.)/ **essas, aquelas** (fem.)

The difference between the three forms is that **este** means within reach, **esse** a bit farther and **aquele** means out of reach. There are also three invariable demonstrative adjectives in Portuguese: **isto, isso** and **aquilo.**

Tome isto.	Take this.
Deixe isso, por favor.	Leave that, please.
Dê-me aquilo, ali.	Give me that, over there.

Possessive adjectives

These agree in number and gender with the noun they modify, i.e., with the thing possessed and not the possessor.

	masculine	feminine
my	**meu**	**minha**
your	**teu**	**tua**
his/her/its	**seu**	**sua**
our	**nosso**	**nossa**
your	**vosso**	**vossa**
their	**seu**	**sua**

All these forms add an **s** to form the plural.

Note: The form of the third person can be used instead of the second, as a form of politeness:

Meu amigo, o seu livro deixou-me óptima impressão.	My friend, your book made a very good impression on me.

Personal pronouns

	subject	direct object	indirect object
I	**eu**	**me**	**mim**
you	**tu**	**te**	**ti**
he/it	**ele**	**o**	**lhe**
she/it	**ela**	**a**	**lhe**
we	**nós**	**nos**	**nos**
you	**vós**	**vos**	**vos**
they (masc.)	**eles**	**os**	**lhes**
they (fem.)	**elas**	**as**	**lhes**

There are two forms for "you" (singular) in Portuguese: the intimate **tu** when talking to relatives, friends and children and **você,** which is used in all other cases between people who don't know each other very well. But when addressing someone you normally use the third person of the singular or of the plural (this is the polite form used throughout this book):

Como está (estão)?	How are you?

Verbs

There are four auxiliary verbs in Portuguese:

ter/haver	to have
ser/estar	to be

Ter indicates possession or a condition:

Tenho uma casa.	I have a house.
Tenho febre.	I have a fever.

Haver in the meaning of "to exist" is only used in the third person of the singular (there is/there are):

Há muitas pessoas aqui.	There are too many people here.

Ser indicates a permanent state:

Sou inglês.	I am English.

Estar indicates movement or a non-permanent state:

Estou a passear [Estou passeando].	I am walking.
Está doente.	He is ill.

	ter (to have)	**ser** (to be)	**estar** (to be)
eu	**tenho**	**sou**	**estou**
tu	**tens**	**és**	**estás**
ele/ela	**tem**	**é**	**está**
nós	**temos**	**somos**	**estamos**
vós	**tendes**	**sois**	**estais**
eles	**têm**	**são**	**estão**

Normally, the Portuguese do not use personal pronouns since the form of the verb and the sense of the phrase indicate the person:

Tens sede?	Are you thirsty?
Do que está a falar?	What is he/she talking about?

The three conjugations for regular verbs are distinguished by the ending of the infinitive.

	falar (to speak)	**viver** (to live)	**partir** (to leave)
eu	**falo**	**vivo**	**parto**
tu	**falas**	**vives**	**partes**
ele/ela	**fala**	**vive**	**parte**
nós	**falamos**	**vivemos**	**partimos**
vós	**falais**	**viveis**	**partis**
eles	**falam**	**vivem**	**partem**

As in all languages, the irregular verbs have to be learned. Here are four you'll find useful:

	poder (to be able)	**dizer** (to say)	**ir** (to go)	**pedir** (to ask)
eu	**posso**	**digo**	**vou**	**peço**
tu	**podes**	**dizes**	**vais**	**pedes**
ele/ela	**pode**	**diz**	**vai**	**pede**
nós	**podemos**	**dizemos**	**vamos**	**pedimos**
vós	**podeis**	**dizeis**	**ides**	**pedis**
eles	**podem**	**dizem**	**vão**	**pedem**

The **negative** is formed by placing **não** before the verb.

Falo português.	I speak Portuguese.
Não falo português.	I don't speak Portuguese.

In Portuguese, **questions** are often formed by changing the intonation of your voice. Very often the personal pronoun is left out both in affirmative sentences and in questions.

Está bem.	It's all right.
Está bem?	Is it all right?
Falo inglês.	I speak English.
Fala inglês?	Do you speak English?

DICTIONARY

Dictionary
and alphabetical index

English–Portuguese

f feminine *m* masculine *pl* plural

Brazilian alternatives are given in brackets [ ].

a um,uma 159
abbreviation abreviatura *f* 154
able, to be poder 163
about *(approximately)* cerca de 153
above acima (de) 16; por cima 63
abscess abcesso *m* 145
absorbent cotton algodão hidrófilo *m* 109
accept, to aceitar 62, 102
accessories acessórios *m/pl* 116, 125
accident acidente *m* 78, 139
accommodation alojamento *m* 22
account conta *f* 131
ache dor *f* 141
adaptor adaptador *m* 119
address endereço *m* 21, 31, 76, 79, 102
address book livrinho de endereços *m* 104
adhesive autocolante 105
admission entrada *f* 82
admission charge entrada *f* [ingresso *m*] 90
admit, to admitir 150
Africa África *f* 146
after depois (de) 16, 77
afternoon tarde *f* 151, 153
after-shave lotion loção para depois da barba *f* 110
against contra 140
age idade *f* 149, 150
ago há 149, 151
air conditioner ar condicionado *m* 23, 28
airmail por avião 133
airplane avião *m* 65
airport aeroporto *m* 17, 21, 65
alarm clock despertador *m* 121
alcohol álcool *m* 107; bebidas alcoólicas *f/pl* 37
alcoholic alcoólico(a) 58
all tudo 103
allergic alérgico(a) 141, 143
allow, to permitir 79
almond amêndoa *f* 52
alphabet alfabeto *m* 10, 135
also também 16
alter, to *(garment)* modificar 115
amazing espantoso(a) 84
amber âmbar *m* 122
ambulance ambulância *f* 79
American americano(a) 93, 105, 126
American plan pensão completa *f* 24
amethyst ametista *f* 122
amount importância *f* 62, 131
amplifier amplificador *m* 119
anaesthesia anestesia *f* 144, 145
analgesic analgésico *m* 109
anchovy anchova *f* 41
and e 16
animal animal *m* 85
aniseed erva-doce *f* 51
ankle tornozelo *m* 139
another outro(a) 55, 58, 123
answer, to *(phone)* atender 136
antibiotic antibiótico *m* 143
antidepressant antidepressivo *m* 143
antiques antiguidades *f/pl* 83
antique shop antiquário *m* 98
antiseptic anti-séptico(a) 109
antiseptic anti-séptico *m* 140
anyone alguém 13
anything alguma coisa 18, 25, 113
apartment *(flat)* apartamento *m* 22
aperitif aperitivo *m* 55
appendicitis apendicite *f* 142
appendix apêndice *m* 138
appetizer acepipe [salgadinho] *m* 41
apple maçã *f* 52, 64

Dicionário

appliance aparelho *m* 119
appointment marcação *f* 30; encontro marcado *m* 131; *(doctor)* consulta *f* 137, 145
apricot alperce [damasco] *m* 52
April Abril *m* 150
aquarium aquário *m* 81
archaeology arqueologia *f* 83
architect arquitecto *m* 83
area code indicativo *m* 134
arm braço *m* 138, 139
arrival chegada *f* 17, 65
arrive, to chegar 65, 68, 130
art arte *f* 83
art gallery galeria de arte *f* 81, 98
artichoke alcachofra *f* 49
article artigo *m* 101, 159
artificial artificial 37, 124
artist artista *m/f* 81,83
ashtray cinzeiro *m* 27, 36
Asia Ásia *f* 146
ask, to perguntar 76; *(for)* pedir 25, 61, 136,163
asparagus espargo [aspargo] *m* 41, 42, 49
aspirin aspirina *f* 109
assistance assistência *f* 78
assorted variado(a) 41
asthma asma *f* 142
at a, em 16
at least pelo menos 24
at once já 31
aubergine berinjela *f* 49
August Agosto *m* 150
aunt tia *f* 93
Australia Austrália *f* 146
automatic automático(a) 20, 122, 124
autumn Outono *m* 150
awful horroroso(a) 84; horrível 94
Azores Açores *m/pl* 146

B

baby bebé [nenê] *m* 24, 111
baby food comida para bebé [nenê] *f* 111
babysitter babysitter *f* 27
back atrás 30, 87, 145
back *(body)* costas *f/pl* 138
backache dor nas costas *f* 141
backpack mochila *f* 106
bacon toucinho *m* 38, 46
bad mau, má 15, 95
bag saco *m* 18, 103
baggage bagagem *f* 18, 26, 31, 71
baggage cart carrinho da bagagem *m* 18, 71
baggage check depósito da bagagem *m* 67, 71
baked no forno 45, 47
baker's padaria *f* 98
balance *(account)* balanço m 131
balcony varanda f 23
ball *(inflated)* bola *f* 128
ballet ballet *m* 88
ball-point pen esferográfica *f* 104
banana banana *f* 52, 64
bandage ligadura [atadura] *f* 109
Band-Aid penso rápido [bandaid] *m* 109
bangle bracelete *m* 121
bangs franja *f* 30
bank *(finance)* banco *m* 98, 129, 130
banknote nota *f* 130
barber's barbeiro *m* 30, 98
basilica basílica *f* 81
basketball basquetebol *m* 90
bath *(hotel)* banho *m* 23, 25
bathing cap touca de banho *f* 116
bathing hut barraca (de praia) *f* 91
bathing suit fato [maiô] de banho *m* 116
bathroom casa de banho *f* [banheiro *m*] 27
bath towel toalha de banho *f* 27
battery pilha *f* 119, 121, 125; *(car)* bateria *f* 75, 76
bay baía *f* 74
bay leaf louro *m* 51
be, to ser, estar 162; ficar 12
beach praia *f* 91
beach ball balão *m* 128
bean feijão *m* 49
beard barba *f* 31
beautiful lindo(a) 15, 84
beauty salon instituto de beleza *m* 30, 98
bed cama *f* 24, 144
bed and breakfast dormida e pequeno almoço [pernoite e café da manhã] *f* 24
bedpan bacia de cama *f* 144
beef carne de vaca *f* 46
beer cerveja *f* 55, 64
beet(root) beterraba *f* 49
before (*place*) em frente (de) 16; (*time*) antes (de) 16
begin, to começar 80, 87, 88
beginning princípio *m* 150

behind atrás (de) 16, 77
bell *(electric)* campainha *f* 144
bellboy paquete, groom [boy de hotel] *m* 26
below abaixo (de) 16; por baixo 63
belt cinto *m* 117
bend *(road) f* 79
berth beliche *m* 69, 70, 71
better melhor 15, 25, 101, 113
between entre 16
beverage bebida *f* 60
bicycle bicicleta *f* 74
big grande 15, 101
bill conta *f* 31, 62, 102; *(banknote)* nota *f* 130
billion *(Am.)* bilhão *m* 148
binoculars binõculos *m/pl* 123
bird pássaro *m* 85
birth nascimento *m* 25
birthday dia de anos *m* 151; aniversário *m* 152
biscuit *(Br.)* bolacha *f* 64
bitter amargo(a) 61
black preto(a) 113
bladder bexiga *f* 138
blade lâmina *f* 111
blanket cobertor *m* 27
bleach descoloração *f* 30
bleed, to sangrar 139, 145
blind *(window)* estore *m* 29
blister bolha *f* 139
block, to entupir 28
blood sangue *m* 142
blood pressure tensão arterial *f* 141
blood transfusion transfusão de sangue *f* 144
blouse blusa *f* 116
blow-dry brushing *m* 30
blue azul 113
boarding house pensão *f* 22
boat barco *m* 74
bobby pin gancho [grampo] de cabelo *m* 111
body corpo *m* 138
boil furúnculo *m* 139
boiled cozido(a) 47
boiled egg ovo cozido *m* 38
bond obrigação *f* 131
bone osso *m* 138
book livro *m* 13, 104
booking office marcação de lugares *f* 19, 67
booklet *(of tickets)* caderneta *f* 72
bookshop livraria *f* 98, 104
boot bota *f* 118
born, to be nascer 150
botanical gardens jardim botânico *m* 81
botany botânica *f* 83
bottle garrafa *f* 17, 55, 58
bottle-opener abre-garrafas [abridor de garrafas] *m* 106
bottom baixo *m* 145
bowel intestino *m* 138
box caixa *f* 120
boxing boxe *m* 90
boy menino *m* 112, 128
boyfriend namorado *m* 93
bra soutien *m* 116
bracelet pulseira *f* 121
braces *(suspenders)* suspensórios *m/pl* 116
brake travão [freio] *m* 78
brake fluid líquido dos travões [freios] *m* 75
brandy aguardente velha *f* 59
Brazil Brasil *m* 146
Brazilian brasileiro(a) 114, 127
bread pão *m* 36, 38, 64
break, to partir [quebrar] 123, 139, 145
break down, to avariar-se 78
breakdown avaria *f* 78
breakdown van pronto-socorro *m* 78
breakfast pequeno almoço [café da manhã] *m* 24, 34, 38
breast seio *m* 138
breathe, to respirar 141, 142
bricks *(toy)* jogo de construções *m* 128
bridge ponte *f* 85
briefs calças [calcinhas] *f/pl* 116
bring, to trazer 14
British britânico(a) 93
broiled grelhado(a) 45,47
broken partido(a) [quebrado(a)] 29, 140
brooch broche *m* 121
brother irmão *m* 93
brown castanho(a) [marrom] 113
bruise contusão *f* 139
brush escova *f* 111
bubble bath banho de espuma *m* 110
bucket balde *m* 128
buckle fivela *f* 117
build, to construir 83
building edifício *m* 81, 83
building blocks jogo de construções *m* 128

bulb lâmpada *f* 28,75, 119
bullfight tourada *f* 89
bullring praça de touros *f* 81
burn queimadura *f* 139
burn out, to *(bulb)* fundir 28
bus autocarro [ônibus] *m* 18, 19, 65, 72, 73
business negócios *m/pl* 16
business district centro de negócios *m* 81
business trip viagem de negócios *f* 93
bus stop paragem do autocarro [parada de ônibus] *f* 72, 73
busy, to be ter que fazer 96
but mas 16
butane gas gás butano *m* 32, 106
butcher's talho [açougue] *m* 98
butter manteiga *f* 36, 38, 64
button botão *m* 29, 117
buy, to comprar 68, 82, 104

C

cabana barraca (de praia) *f* 91
cabbage couve *f* 49
cabin *(ship)* cabine f 74
cable telegrama *f* 133
cable car teleférico *m* 74
cable release disparador *m* 125
cake bolo *m* 54, 64
cake shop pastelaria *f* 98
calculator calculadora *f* 105
calendar calendário *m* 104
call *(phone)* comunicação *f* 135; chamada *f* 136
call, to *(give name)* chamar 12; *(summon)* 78, 79, 156; *(phone)* telefonar 136
calm calmo(a) 91
cambric cambraia *f* 114
camel-hair pêlo de camelo *m* 114
camera máquina fotográfica *f* 124, 125
camera case capa de máquina fotográfica *f* 125
camera shop loja de artigos fotográficos *f* 98
camp, to acampar 32
campbed cama de campismo *f* 106
camping campismo *m* 32
camping equipment equipamento de campismo *m* 106
camp site parque de campismo *m* 32
can *(of peaches)* lata *f* 120
can *(to be able)* poder 13, 163
Canada Canadá *m* 146
Canadian canadiano(a) 93
cancel, to anular 65
candle vela *f*
candy rebuçado *m* [bala *f*] 126
can opener abre-latas [abridor de latas] *m* 106
cap boné *m*
caper alcaparra *f* 50
capital *(finance)* capital *m* 131
car automóvel *m*, carro *m* 19, 20, 75, 76, 78
carafe jarro *m* 58
carat quilate *m* 121
caravan rulote *f* 32
caraway cominho *m* 51
carbonated com gãs 59
carburettor carburdor *m* 78
card carta *f* 93; cartão *m* 131
card game baralho de cartas *m* 128
cardigan casaco de malha *m* 116
car hire aluguer de automóveis *m* 20
car park parque de automóveis *m* 77
car racing corridas de automóveis *f/pl* 90
car rental aluguer de automóveis *m* 20
carrot cenoura *f* 49
carry, to levar 21
cart carrinho *m* 18
carton *(of cigarettes)* pacote (de cigarros) *m* 17, 126
cartridge *(camera)* chargeur *m* 124
case *(glasses)* caixa *f* 123; *(camera)* capa *f* 125
cash, to levantar 130, 133
cash desk caixa *f* 103, 155
cassette cassete *f* 119, 127
castle castelo *m* 81
catalogue catálogo *m* 82
cathedral sé *f*, catedral *f* 81
Catholic católico(a) 84
cauliflower couve-flor *f* 49
caution cuidado *m* 79; atenção *f* 155
celery aipo *m* 49
cellophane tape fita adesiva *f* 104
cemetery cemitério *m* 81
centimetre centímetro *m* 112
centre centro *m* 19, 21, 76, 81
century século *m* 149
ceramics cerâmica *f* 83
cereal cereais *m/pl* 38
certificate certificado *m* 144
chain *(jewellery)* corrente *f* 121

chain bracelet corrente de pulso *f* 121
chair cadeira *f* 106
change *(money)* troco *m* 62; dinheiro trocado *m* 77, 130
change, to mudar 65, 68, 69, 73, 75, 123; *(money)* trocar 18, 19, 130
chapel capela *f* 81
charcoal carvão de lenha *m* 106
charge preço *m* 20, 32, 77, 89; taxa *f* 136
charge, to *(commission)* cobrar 130
charm *(trinket)* berloque *m* 121
charm bracelet pulseira de berloques *f* 121
cheap barato(a) 15, 24, 25, 101
check cheque *m* 130; *(restaurant)* conta *f* 62
check, to verificar 75; *(luggage)* despachar 71
check book livro de cheques *m* 131
check in, to *(airport)* apresentar-se 65
check out, to partir 31
cheese queijo *m* 51, 64
chemist's farmácia *f* 98, 108
cheque cheque *m* 130
cheque book livro de cheques *m* 131
cherry cereja *f* 52
chess xadrez *m* 93
chess set jogo de xadrez *m* 128
chest peito *m* 138, 141
chestnut castanha *f* 52
chewing gum pastilha elástica [chiclete] *f* 126
chewing tobacco tabaco [fumo] de mascar *m* 126
chicken frango *m* 48, 63; galinha *f* 48
chiffon chiffon *m* 114
child criança *f* 24, 61, 82, 150
children filhos *m/pl* 93
children's doctor pediatra *m/f* 137
china porcelana *f* 127
China China *f* 146
chips *(Br.)* batatas fritas *f/pl* 51, 63; *(Am.)* batatas fritas *f/pl* 64
chocolate chocolate *m* 120, 126; *(hot)* chocolate quente *m* 38, 60
chocolate bar tablete de chocolate *f* 64
choice escolha *f* 40
chop costeleta *f* 46
Christmas Natal *m* 152
chromium cromo *m* 122
church igreja *f* 81, 84
cigar charuto *m* 126
cigarette cigarro *m* 17, 95, 126
cigarette case cigarreira *f* 121, 126
cigarette holder boquilha [piteira] *f* 126
cigarette lighter isqueiro *m* 121
cine camera máquina de filmar *f* 124
cinema cinema *m* 86, 96
cinnamon canela *f* 50
circle *(theatre)* balcão *m* 87
city cidade *f* 81
clam amêijoa *f* 41, 44
classical clássico(a) 128
clean limpo(a) 61
clean, to limpar 29, 76
cleansing cream creme de limpeza *m* 110
cliff falésia *f* 85
clip broche de mola *m* 121
cloakroom vestiário *m* 87
clock relógio *m* 121, 153
clock-radio rádio-despertador *m* 119
close, to fechar 11, 82, 108, 132
closed fechado(a), encerrado(a) 155
cloth tela *f* 118
clothes roupa *f* 29, 116
clothes peg mola da roupa *f* 106
clothing vestuário *m* 112
cloud nuvem *f* 94
clove cravinho *m* 51
coach *(bus)* camioneta *f* [ônibus *m*] 72
coast costa *f* 85
coat casaco comprido *m* 116
coconut coco *m* 52, 54, 59, 60
cod bacalhau *m* 44, 45
coffee café *m* 38, 60, 64
cognac conhaque *m* 58
coin moeda *f* 130
cold frio(a) 15, 25, 38, 61, 94
cold *(illness)* constipação *f* [resfriado *m*] 108, 141
collect call comunicação pagável no destino *f* 135
colour cor *f* 103, 112, 124, 125
colour chart mostruário de cores *m* 30
colourfast de cor fixa 113
colour rinse rinsage *f* 30
colour slide slide *m* 124
comb pente *m* 111
come, to vir 35, 94, 95, 137,

comedy comédia *f* 86
commission commissão *f* 130
common *(frequent)* usual 154
compact disc disco compacto *m* 127
compartment compartimento *m* 70
compass bússola *f* 106
complaint reclamação *f* 61
concert concerto *m* 88
confirm, to confirmar 65
confirmation confirmação *f* 23
congratulation parabéns *m/pl* 152
connection *(train)* correspondência [conexão] *f* 65, 68
constipated com prisão de ventre [constipado(a)] 140
consulate consulado *m* 156
contact lens lente de contacto *f* 123
contain, to conter 37
contraceptive contraceptivo *m* 109
contract contrato *m* 131
control controle *m* 17
conversion conversão *f* 157
cookie bolacha *f* 64
cool box mala frigorífica *f* 106
copper cobre *m* 122
corduroy bombazina *f* 114
cork rolha *f* 61
corkscrew saca-rolhas *m* 106
corn *(Am.)* milho *m* 49; *(foot)* calo *m* 109
corner canto *m* 36; *(street)* esquina *f* 21, 77
corn plaster penso para os calos *m* 109
cosmetic cosmético *m* 110
cost custo *m* 131; preço *m* 136
cost, to custar 12, 80, 133
cotton algodão *m* 113, 114
cotton wool algodão hidrófilo *m* 109
cough tosse *f* 108, 141
cough, to tossir 142
cough drops pastilhas para a tosse *f/pl* 109
counter guiché *m* 133
country país *m* 92
countryside campo *m* 85
court house palácio de justiça *m* 81
cousin primo(a) *m/f* 93
crab caranguejo *m* 44
cramp cãibra *f* 141
crayon lápis de cor *m* 104
cream nata *f* 54; *(toiletry)* creme *m* 110; *(pharmaceutical)* pomada *f* 109
credit crédito *m* 130
credit card cartão de crédito *m* 20, 31, 62, 102, 130
crisps batatas fritas *f/pl* 64
crockery louça *f* 107
crossroads cruzamento *m* 77
cruise cruzeiro *m* 74
crystal cristal *m* 122
cucumber pepino *m* 49
cuff link botão de punho *m* [abotoadura *f*] 121
cup chávena [xícara] *f* 36, 60, 107
currency moeda corrente *f* 129
currency exchange office agência de câmbio *f*, câmbio *m* 18, 67, 129
current corrente *f* 91
curtain cortinado *m* 28
curve *(road)* curva *f* 79
customs alfândega *f* 16, 102
cut *(wound)* corte *m* 139
cut, to cortar 30, 136
cuticle remover produto para tirar as cutículas *m* 110
cutlery talheres *m/pl* 107, 121
cutlet costeleta *f* 46
cycling ciclismo *m* 89
cystitis cistite *f* 142

D

dairy leitaria *f* 98
dance, to dançar 88, 96
danger perigo *m* 155, 156
dangerous perigoso(a) 90
dark escuro(a) 25, 101, 112, 113
date *(day)* data *f* 25, 151; *(fruit)* tâmara *f* 52; *(appointment)* encontro *m* 95
daughter filha *f* 93
day dia *m* 16, 20, 24, 32, 80, 151
daylight luz do dia *m* 124
day off dia de folga *m* 124
death morte *f* 155
decade década *f* 149
decaffeinated sem cafeína 38, 60
December Dezembro *m* 150
decision decisão *f* 25, 102
deck *(ship)* convés *m* 74
deck chair cadeira de encosto *f* 91, 106
declare, to declarar 17, 18
deep fundo(a) 142
define, to descrever 101
delay atraso *m* 69
delicatessen salsicharia *f* 98
delicious delicioso(a) 62

deliver, to entregar 102
delivery entrega *f* 102
denim sarja *f* 114
dentist dentista *m/f* 98, 145
denture dentadura *f* 145
deodorant desodorizante [desodorante] *m* 110
department secção *f* 83, 100
department store grande armazém *m* 98
departure partida *f* 65, 80
deposit *(car hire)* sinal *m* 20; *(bank)* depósito *m* 130
deposit, to *(bank)* depositar 131
dessert sobremesa *f* 37, 53
detour *(traffic)* desvio *m* 79
develop, to revelar 124
diabetic diabético(a) 141
diabetic diabético(a) *m/f* 37
dialling code indicativo *m* 134
diamond diamante *m* 122
diaper fralda *f* 111
diarrhoea diarreia *f* 140
dictionary dicionário *m* 104
diesel gasóleo *m* 75
diet dieta *f* 37
difficult difícil 15
difficulty dificuldade *f* 28, 102, 141
digital digital 122
dine, to jantar 94
dining car carruagem-restaurante *f* 71
dining room sala de jantar *f* 27
dinner jantar *m* 34, 94
direct directo(a) 65
direct, to indicar a direcção 14
direction direcção *f* 76
director *(theatre)* realizador *m* 86
directory *(phone)* lista telefónica *f* 134
disabled deficiente físico(a) *m/f* 82
disc disco *m* 127
discotheque discoteca *f* 88, 89, 96
discount desconto *m* 131
disease doença *f* 142
dish prato *m* 36, 40
dishwashing detergent detergente para a louça *m* 106
disinfectant desinfectante *m* 109
dislocate, to deslocar 140
display case banca *f* 100
dissatisfied insatisfeito(a) 103
disturb, to incomodar 155
diversion *(traffic)* desvio *m* 79
dizziness vertigem *f* 140
doctor médico(a) *m/f* 79, 137, 144, 156; doutor(a) *m/f* 145
doctor's office consultório *m* 137
dog cão *m* 155
doll boneca *f* 128
dollar dólar *m* 18, 130
door porta *f* 28
double duplo(a) 58, 60
double bed cama de casal *f* 23
double room quarto duplo *m* 19, 23
down para baixo 16
downstairs em baixo 16
downtown centro da cidade *m*
dozen dúzia *f* 149
drawing paper papel de desenho *m* 104
drawing pin pionés *m* [tacha *f*] 104
dress vestido *m* 116
drink bebida *f* 58, 59, 61, 94, 95
drink, to beber 35, 36, 37
drinking water água potável *f* 32
drip, to *(tap)* verter 28
drive, to conduzir 21
driving licence carta de condução [carteira de motorista] *f* 20, 79
drop *(liquid)* gota *f* 109
drugstore farmácia *f* 98, 108
dry seco(a) 30, 58, 111
dry cleaner's lavandaria a seco *f* 29, 98
duck pato *m* 48
dummy chupeta *f* 111
during durante 16, 150, 151
duty *(customs)* direitos *m/pl* 18
duty-free shop free shop *f* 19
dye pintura do cabelo *f* 30

E

each cada 149
ear orelha *f* 138
earache dor de ouvidos *f* 141
early cedo 15
earring brinco *m* 121
east (l)este *m* 77
Easter Páscoa *f* 152
easy fácil 15
eat, to comer 36, 37, 144
eel enguia *f* 44
egg ovo *m* 38, 42, 64
eggplant berinjela *f* 49
eight oito 147
eighteen dezoito 147
eighth oitavo(a) 149
eighty oitenta 148
elastic elástico(a) 109

elastic bandage ligadura [atadura] elástica *f* 109
Elastoplast pensos rápidos [bandaids] *m/pl* 109
electric(al) eléctrico(a) 119
electrical appliance aparelho eléctrico *m* 119
electrician electricista *m* 98
electricity electricidade *f* 32
electronic electrónico(a) 125, 128
elevator elevador *m* 27, 74, 100
eleven onze 147
embarkation embarque *m* 74
embassy embaixada *f* 156
embroidery bordados *m/pl* 127
emerald esmeralda *f* 122
emergency urgência *f* 156
emergency exit saída de emergência *f* 27, 99, 155
emery board lima [lixa] de unhas *f* 110
empty vazio(a) 15
end fim *m* 150
engagement ring anel de noivado *m* 122
engine *(car)* motor *m* 78
England Inglaterra *f* 146
English inglês(esa) 13, 80, 82, 84, 104, 126
enjoy, to gostar 62, 92
enjoyable agradável 31
enjoy oneself, to divertir-se 96
enlarge, to ampliar 125
enough bastante 15
enquiry informação *f* 68
entrance entrada *f* 67, 99, 155
entrance fee entrada *f* [ingresso *m*] 82
envelope envelope *m* 27, 104
equipment equipamento *m* 91, 106
eraser borracha *f* 104
escalator escada rolante *f* 100
estimate estimação *f* 131
Europe Europa *f* 146
evening noite *f* 87, 94, 95, 96, 151, 153
evening dress traje de noite *m* 88; *(woman)* vestido de noite *m* 116
everything tudo 31
exchange, to trocar 103
exchange rate câmbio *m* 19, 130
excursion excursão *f* 80
excuse,to desculpar 12, 78, 153
exercise book caderno *m* 104
exhaust pipe tubo de escape *m* 78
exhibition exposição *f* 81
exit saída *f* 67, 79, 99, 155
expect, to estar à espera 130
expenses despesas *f/pl* 131
expensive caro(a) 15, 19, 24, 101
exposure counter contador *m* 125
express por expresso 133
expression expressão *f* 11
expressway auto-estrada *f* 76
extension cord/lead extensão *f* 119
external externo(a) 109
extra mais 24, 27
eye olho *m* 138, 139
eyebrow pencil lápis para os olhos *m* 110
eye drops gotas para os olhos *f/pl* 109
eye shadow sombra para os olhos *f* 110
eyesight vista *f* 123
eye specialist oftalmologista *m/f* 137

F

fabric *(cloth)* tecido *m* 113
face rosto *m* 138
face-pack máscara de beleza *f* 30
face powder pó de arroz *m* 110
factory fábrica *f* 81
fair feira *f* 81
fall queda *f* 139; *(autumn)* Outono *m* 150
family família *f* 93
fan ventoinha *f* 28
fan belt correia da ventoinha *f* 75
far longe 14, 100
fare preço *m* 21, 68, 73
farm quinta [fazenda] *f* 85
fat *(meat)* gordura *f* 37
father pai *m* 93
faucet torneira *f* 28
February Fevereiro *m* 150
fee *(doctor)* honorários *m/pl* 144
feeding bottle biberon *m* 111
feel, to *(physical state)* sentir-se 140, 142
felt feltro *m* 114
felt-tip pen caneta feltro *f* 104
ferry ferry-boat *m* 74
fever febre *f* 140
few poucos(as) 15; *(a)* alguns, algumas 15
field campo *m* 85
fifteen quinze 147
fifth quinto(a) 149

fifty cinquenta 147
fig figo *m* 52
file *(tool)* lima [lixa] *f* 110
fill in, to preencher 26, 144
filling *(tooth)* chumbo *m* 145
filling station estação de serviço *f* 75
film filme *m* 86; *(photography)* rolo [filme] *m* 124, 125
film winder botão de bobinagem *m* 125
filter filtro *m* 125
filter-tipped com filtro 126
find, to encontrar 12, 100, 137
fine *(OK)* (está) bem 12, 25
fine arts belas-artes *f/pl* 83
finger dedo *m* 138
finish, to acabar 87
fire fogo *m* 156
first primeiro(a) 68, 73, 149
first-aid kit estojo de primeiros-socorros *m* 106
first class primeira classe *f* 69
first course primeiro prato *m* 40
first name nome próprio [nome] *m* 25
fish peixe *m* 44
fish, to pescar 90
fishing tackle apetrechos de pesca *m/pl* 106
fishmonger's peixaria *f* 98
fit, to ficar bem 115
fitting room cabine de provas *f* 114
five cinco 147
fix, to consertar 75
fizzy *(mineral water)* com gás 59
flannel flanela *f* 114
flash *(photography)* flash m 125
flash attachment encaixe do flash *m* 125
flashlight lanterna de bolso *f* 106
flat raso(a) 118
flat *(apartment)* apartamento *m* 22
flat tyre furo *m* 75; pneu vazio *m* 78
flea market feira da ladra *f* 81
flight voo *m* 65
flippers barbatanas *f/pl* 128
floor andar *m* 27
florist's florista *m/f* 98
flour farinha *f* 37
flower flor *f* 85
flu gripe *f* 142
fluid líquido *m* 75, 123
fog nevoeiro *m* 94
folding chair cadeira de fechar *f* 106
folding table mesa de fechar *f* 107
folk dancing dança folclórica *f* 89
folk music música folclórica *f* 128
follow, to seguir 77
food alimentos *m/pl* 37; comida *f* 61, 111
food box caixa para alimentos *f* 106
food poisoning intoxicação alimentar *f* 142
foot pé *m* 138
football futebol *m* 89, 90
foot cream creme para os pés *m* 110
footpath caminho pedestre *m* 85
for por, para 16; durante 143, 151
forbid, to proibir 155
forecast previsão *f* 94
forest floresta *f* 85
forget, to esquecer-se 61
fork garfo *m* 36, 61, 107
form *(document)* formulário *m* 133; ficha *f* 25, 26
fortnight duas semanas *f/pl* 151
fortress fortaleza *f* 81
forty quarenta 147
foundation cream creme de base *m* 110
fountain fonte *f* 81
fountain pen caneta de tinta permanente [caneta-tinteiro] *f* 104
four quatro 147
fourteen catorze 147
fourth quarto(a) 149
frame *(glasses)* armação *f* 123
France França *f* 146
free livre 15, 70, 95, 155
french fries batatas fritas *f/pl* 50, 63
fresh fresco(a) 52, 61
Friday sexta-feira *f* 151
fried frito(a) 45, 47
fried egg ovo estrelado *m* 38, 42
friend amigo(a) *m/f* 95
fringe franja *f* 30
from de 16
front frente *f* 23, 75
fruit fruta *f* 52
fruit juice sumo [suco] de fruta *m* 37, 38, 59
frying-pan frigideira *f* 106
full cheio(a) 15; inteiro(a) 80; completo(a) 155
full board pensão completa *f* 24
full insurance seguro contra todos os riscos *m* 20
funicular elevador *m* 74
furniture mobiliário *m* 83
furrier's casa de peles *f* 98

G
gabardine gabardine f 114
gallery galeria *f* 81
game jogo *m* 128; *(food)* caça *f* 48
garage garagem *f* 26, 78
garden jardim *m* 81, 85
garlic alho *m* 50
gas gás *m* 156
gasoline gasolina *f* 75, 78
gastritis gastrite f 142
gauze gaze f 109
gem pedra preciosa *f* 121
general geral 27, 100
general delivery posta restante *f* 133
general practitioner médico(a) de clínica geral *m/f* 137
genitals órgãos genitais *m/pl* 138
gentleman cavalheiro *m* 155
genuine autêntico(a) 118
geology geologia *f* 83
Germany Alemanha *f* 146
get, to *(find)* arranjar [arrumar] 12, 32, 90; *(take)* apanhar [pegar] 19, 21, 69; *(call)* chamar 21, 31, 137, 156; *(obtain)* obter 134; *(go)* ir 76, 100
get off, to descer 73
get to, to ir para 19; chegar a 70
get up, to levantar-se 144
gherkin pepino de conserva *m* 49
gift presente *m* 127
gin gim *m* 60
gin and tonic gim tónico *m* 60
ginger gengibre *m* 51
girdle cinta *f* 116
girl menina *f* 112, 128
girlfriend namorada *f* 93; amiga *f* 95
give, to dar 14, 123, 135
gland glândula *f* 138
glass vidro *m* 122; *(drinking)* copo *m* 36, 55, 58, 61, 143
glasses óculos *m/pl* 123
gloomy lúgubre 84
glove luva *f* 116
glue cola *f* 104
go, to ir 96, 163
gold ouro *m* 121, 122
golden dourado(a) 113
gold-plated banhado a ouro 122
golf golfe *m* 90
golf club clube de golfe *m* 90
golf course campo de golfe *m* 90
good bom, boa 15, 101
good-bye adeus 10
Good Friday Sexta-feira Santa *f* 152
goods artigos *m/pl* 17
goose ganso *m* 48
go out, to sair 95
gram grama *f* 120
grammar book gramática *f* 104
grandfather avô *m* 93
grandmother avó *f* 93
grape uva *f* 52, 64
grapefruit toranja *f* 52
grapefruit juice sumo [suco] de toranja *m* 38
gray cinzento(a) 113
graze esfoladela *f* 139
greasy oleoso(a) 30, 111
great *(excellent)* óptimo(a) 95
Great Britain Grã-Bretanha *f* 146
Greece Grécia *f* 146
green verde 113
green bean feijão verde *m* [vagem *f*] 49
greengrocer's lugar de frutas e legumes *m* [quitanda *f*] 98
green salad salada de alface *f* 42
greeting saudação *f* 11
grey cinzento(a) 113
grilled grelhado(a) 45, 47
grocery mercearia *f* 98, 120
groundsheet tapete *m* 106
group grupo *m* 82
guide guia *m/f* 80
guidebook guia turístico *m* 82, 105
gum *(teeth)* gengiva *f* 145
gynaecologist ginecologista *m/f* 137

H
hair cabelo *m* 30, 111
hairbrush escova de cabelo *f* 111
haircut corte de cabelo *m* 30
hairdresser's cabeleireiro(a) *m/f* 27, 30, 98
hair dryer secador de cabelo *m* 119
hairgrip gancho [grampo] de cabelo *m* 111
hair lotion loção capilar *f* 111
hair slide travessão [clipe] *m* 111
hairspray laca [laquê] *f* 30, 111
half meio(a) 149
half metade *f* 149
half an hour meia-hora *f* 153
half board meia-pensão *f* 24
half price *(ticket)* meio-bilhete *m* 69
hall *(large room)* sala *f* 81, 88
hall porter porteiro *m* 26
ham presunto *m* 38, 41, 46; fiambre *m* 63, 64

hammer martelo *m* 106
hammock cama de rede [rede] *f* 106
hand mão *f* 138
handbag mala de mão [bolsa] *f* 116, 156
hand cream creme para as mãos *m* 110
handicrafts artesanato *m* 83
handkerchief lenço de bolso *m* 127
handmade feito(a) à mão 113
hanger cabide *m* 27
happy feliz 152
harbour porto *m* 81
hardware shop loja de ferragens *f* 98
hare lebre *f* 48
hat chapéu *m* 116
have, to ter 162
hayfever febre dos fenos *f* 108
hazelnut avelã *f* 52
he ele 161
head cabeça *f* 138, 139
headache dor de cabeça *f* 141
headphone auscultador [fone] *m* 119
headscarf lenço de pescoço *m* 127
head waiter chefe de mesa *m* 61
health saúde *f* 55
health food shop loja de produtos dietéticos *f* 98
health insurance seguro de doença *m* 144
health insurance form folha de seguro *f* 144
heart coração *m* 138
heart attack ataque cardíaco *m* 141
heat, to aquecer 91
heating aquecimento *m* 23, 28
heavy pesado(a) 14, 101
heel salto *m* 118
helicopter helicóptero *m* 74
hello! *(phone)* está [alô]? 135
help ajuda *f* 156
help! socorro! 156
help, to ajudar 13, 14, 21, 71, 100, 134; *(oneself)* servir-se 120
her seu, sua 161
here aqui 14
high alto(a) 91, 141
high season época alta *f* 150
high tide maré alta *f* 91
hill colina *f* 85
hire aluguer *m* 20
hire, to alugar 19, 20, 90, 91, 155
his seu, sua 161
history história *f* 83
hitchhike, to pedir boleia [carona] 7
hold on! *(phone)* não desligue! 136
hole buraco *m* 29
holiday feriado *m* 151
holidays férias *f/pl* 17, 151
home address morada *f* 25, 31
home-made caseiro(a) 40
honey mel *m* 38
hope, to esperar 96
horseback riding equitação *f* 90
horse racing corridas de cavalos *f/p* 90
hospital hospital *m* 98, 144
hot quente 15, 25, 38, 61
hotel hotel *m* 19, 21, 22, 80
hot dog cachorro (quente) *m* 63
hotel guide guia de hotéis *m* 19
hotel reservation reserva de hotel *f* 19
hot water água quente *f* 23, 28
hot-water bottle saco de água quente *m* 27
hour hora *f* 153
house casa *f* 83, 85
hovercraft hovercraft *m* 74
how como 12
how far a que distância 12, 76, 85
how long quanto tempo 12, 24
how many quantos(as) 12
how much quanto 12, 24
hundred cem, cento 148
hungry, to be ter fome 14, 35
hunt, to caçar 90
hurry *(to be in a)* estar com pressa 21
hurt, to doer 139, 145; *(oneself)* ferir-se 139
husband marido *m* 93
hydrofoil hidroplano [aerobarco] *m* 74

I

I eu 161
ice gelo *m* 94
ice-cream gelado [sorvete] *m* 53, 6
ice cube cubo de gelo *m* 27
ice pack placa frigorífica *f* 106
ill doente 140, 156
illness doença *f* 140
important importante 14
imported importado(a) 113
impressive impressionante 84
in em 16
include, to incluir 24

included incluído(a) 20, 31, 32, 62, 80
indigestion indigestão *f* 141
indoor *(swimming pool)* coberto(a) 91
inexpensive barato(a) 35, 124
infect, to infectar 140
infection infecção *f* 141
inflammation inflamação *f* 142
inflation inflação *f* 131
inflation rate índice de inflação *m* 131
influenza gripe *f* 142
information informação *f* 67, 155
injection injecção *f* 142, 144
injure, to ferir 139
injured ferido(a) 79, 139
injury ferimento *m* 139
ink tinta *f* 105
inn pousada *f* 22, 33; estalagem *f* 22, 23
inquiry informação *f* 68
insect bite picada de insecto *f* 108
insect repellent produto insectífugo *m* 109
insect spray spray insecticida *m* 109
inside dentro 16
instead of em vez de 37
insurance seguro *m* 20, 79, 144
insurance company companhia de seguros *f* 79
interest interesse *m* 80; *(bank)* juro *m* 131
interested, to be estar interessado(a) 83, 96
interesting interessante 84
international internacional 133, 134
interpreter intérprete *m/f* 131
intersection cruzamento *m* 77
introduce, to apresentar 92
introduction apresentação *f* 92, 130
investment investimento *m* 131
invitation convite *m* 94
invite, to convidar 94
invoice factura *f* 131
iodine tintura de iodo *f* 109
Ireland Irlanda *f* 146
Irish irlandês(esa) 93
iron *(laundry)* ferro de engomar *m* 119
iron, to passar a ferro 29
ironmonger's loja de ferragens *f* 98
Italy Itália *f* 146
its seu, sua 161
ivory marfim *m* 122

J

jacket casaco *m* 116
jade jade *m* 122
jam doce de fruta *m* [geléia *f*] 38, 63
jam, to empenar 28; encravar 125
January Janeiro *m* 150
Japan Japão *m* 146
jar frasco *m* 120
jaundice icterícia *f* 142
jaw maxila *f* 138
jeans jeans *m/pl* 116
jewel jóia *f* 121
jewel box cofre de jóias *m* 121
jeweller's ourivesaria *f* 99, 121
joint articulação *f* 138
journey viagem *f* 72, 152
juice sumo [suco] *m* 38, 59, 60
July Julho *m* 150
June Junho *m* 150
just *(only)* só 37, 100

K

keep, to guardar 62
kerosene petróleo *m* 106
key chave *f* 27
kidney rim *m* 46, 138
kilo(gram) quilo(grama) *m* 120
kilometre quilómetro *m* 20
kind amável 95
kind *(type)* espécie *f* 44; género *m* 140
knee joelho *m* 138
knife faca *f* 36, 61, 107
knock, to bater 155
know, to saber 16, 24; conhecer 96, 114

L

label etiqueta *f* 105
lace renda *f* 114, 127
lady senhora *f* 155
lake lago *m* 85
lamb borrego *m* 46
lamp candeeiro [abajur] *m* 29, 119
landmark ponto de referência *m* 85
landscape paisagem *f* 92
lantern lanterna *f* 106
large grande 20, 101, 118
last último(a) 15, 68, 73; passado(a) 149, 151
last name apelido [sobrenome] *m* 25
late tarde 15
later mais tarde 135
laugh, to rir 95

launderette lavandaria automática *f* 99
laundry *(place)* lavandaria *f* 29, 99; *(clothes)* roupa *f* 29
laundry service serviço de lavandaria *m* 23
laxative laxativo *m* 109
lead *(metal)* chumbo *m* 75
leap year ano bissexto *m* 149
leather cabedal [couro] *m* 114, 118
leatherwork artigos de couro *m/pl* 127
leave, to partir 31, 68, 163; sair 69, 74; deixar 26, 96, 156
leek alho porro *m*
left esquerda 21, 63, 69, 77
left-luggage office depósito da bagagem *m* 67, 71
leg perna *f* 48, 138
lemon limão *m* 36, 38, 52, 60, 64
lemonade gasosa *f* 59
lens *(glasses)* lente *f* 123; *(camera)* objectiva *f* 125
lens cap tampa para a objectiva *f* 125
lentil lentilha *f* 49
less menos 15
let, to *(hire out)* alugar 155
letter carta *f* 132
letter box caixa do correio *f* 132
letter of credit carta de crédito *f* 132
lettuce alface *f* 49
level crossing passagem de nível *f* 79
library biblioteca *f* 81, 99
lie down, to deitar-se 142
life belt cinto de salvação *m* 74
life boat bote salva-vidas *m* 74
lifeguard banheiro [salva-vidas] *m* 74
lift elevador *m* 27, 74, 100
light leve 15, 53, 101; ligeiro(a) 128; *(colour)* claro(a) 101, 112, 113
light luz *f* 28, 124; *(cigarette)* lume *m* 95
lighter isqueiro *m* 126
lighter fluid gasolina para isqueiro *f* 126
lighter gas gás para isqueiro *m* 126
light meter fotómetro *m* 125
lightning relâmpago *m* 94
like, to gostar 25, 92, 102, 112; *(want, wish)* querer 14, 23, 103; desejar 35, 103
line linha *f* 73, 136
linen *(cloth)* linho *m* 114
lip lábio *m* 138
lipsalve bâton para o cieiro *m* 110
lipstick bâton *m* 110
liqueur licor *m* 58
listen, to ouvir 128
litre litro *m* 58, 75, 120
little *(a)* um pouco 15
live, to viver 83, 163
liver fígado *m* 46, 138
lobster lavagante *m* 44
London Londres *f* 130
long comprido(a) 15, 115, 116
long-sighted presbita 123
look, to ver 100, 123
look for, to procurar 14
look out! atenção! 156
loose *(clothes)* largo(a) 115
lorry camião [caminhão] *m* 79
lose, to perder 123, 156; *(one's way)* perder-se 14, 156
loss perda *f* 131
lost and found office secção dos perdidos e achados *f* 67, 156
lost property office secção dos perdidos e achados *f* 67, 156
lot *(a)* muito 15
lotion loção *f* 110
loud *(voice)* alto(a) 135
lovely lindo(a) 94
low baixo(a) 91, 141
lower inferior 69, 71
low season época baixa *f* 150
low tide maré baixa *f* 91
luck sorte *f* 135, 152
luggage bagagem *f* 26, 31, 71
luggage locker depósito da bagagem automático *m* 18, 67, 71
luggage trolley carrinho da bagagem *m* 18, 71
lump *(bump)* galo, alto *m* 139
lunch almoço *m* 34, 80
lunch, to almoçar 94
lung pulmão *m* 138

M

machine máquina *f* 113
mackerel cavala *f* 44
Madeira wine vinho da Madeira *m* 55, 58
magazine revista *f* 105
magnificent magnífico(a) 84
maid criada de quarto [arrumadeira] *f* 26

ail, to pôr no correio 28
ail correio *m* 28, 133
ailbox caixa do correio *f* 132
ain principal 40
ake, to fazer 131
ake-up remover pad disco de algodão *m* 110
an homem *m* 115, 155
anager gerente *m* 26
anicure manicura *f* 30
any muitos(as) 15
ap mapa *m* 76, 105; planta *f* 105
arch Março *m* 150
arinated marinado(a) 45
arket mercado *m* 81, 99
armalade doce *m* [geléia *f*] de laranja 38
arried casado(a) 93
ass *(church)* missa *f* 84
atch fósforo *m* 106, 126; *(sport)* jogo *m* 89; combate *m* 90
atch, to *(colour)* condizer 112
atinée matinée f 87
attress colchão *m* 106
auve lilás 113
ay Maio *m* 150
ay *(can)* poder 13, 162
eadow prado *m* 85
eal refeição *f* 24, 62, 143
ean, to querer dizer 11, 25
eans meio *m* 74
easles sarampo *m* 142
easure, to tirar as medidas 114
eat carne *f* 46, 61
echanic mecânico *m* 78
echanical pencil lapiseira *f* 105
edical médico(a) 144
edical certificate certificado médico *m* 144
edicine medicina *f* 83; *(drug)* medicamento, remédio *m* 143
edium *(meat)* meio passado(a) 47
edium-sized de tamanho médio 20
eet, to encontrar 96
elon melão *m* 41, 52
emorial monumento comemorativo *m* 81
end, to consertar 75; *(clothes)* arranjar [consertar] 29
enthol *(cigarettes)* mentolado(a) 126
enu ementa *f* [cardápio *m*] 36, 37, 39, 40
essage recado *m* 28, 136
methylated spirits álcool desnaturado *m* 106
metre metro *m* 112
mezzanine *(theatre)* balcão *m* 87
middle meio *m* 69, 87
midnight meia-noite *f* 153
mild suave 126
mileage quilometragem *f* 20
milk leite *m* 38, 60, 64
milkshake batido [milkshake] *m* 59, 60
milliard bilhão *m* 148
million milhão *m* 148
mineral water água mineral *f* 59
minister *(religion)* pastor *m* 84
mint hortelã *f* 51
minute minuto *m* 153
mirror espelho *m* 114, 123
Miss Menina [Senhorita] *f* 11
miss, to faltar 18, 29, 61
mistake engano *m* 61; *(to make a mistake)* enganar-se 31, 62, 102
mixed salad salada mista *f* 42
modified American plan meia-pensão *f* 24
moisturizing cream creme hidratante *m* 110
moment momento *m* 136
monastery mosteiro *m* 81
Monday segunda-feira *f* 151
money dinheiro *m* 129, 130
money order vale de correio *m* 133
month mês *m* 16, 150
monument monumento *m* 81
moon lua *f* 94
moped bicicleta motorizada *f* 74
more mais 16
morning manhã *f* 151, 153
Morocco Marrocos *m* 146
mortgage hipoteca *f* 131
mosque mesquita *f* 84
mosquito net mosquiteiro *m* 106
mother mãe *f* 93
motorbike motocicleta *f* 74
motorboat barco a motor *m* 91
motorway auto-estrada *f* 76
mountain montanha *f* 85
mountain range serra *f* 85
moustache bigode *m* 31
mouth boca *f* 138
mouthwash gargarejo *m* 109
move, to mexer 139
movie filme *m* 86
movie camera máquina de filmar *f* 124

movies cinema *f* 86, 96
Mr. Senhor *m* 11
Mrs. Senhora *f* 11
much muito 15
mug caneca *f* 55, 107
muscle músculo *m* 138
museum museu *m* 81
mushroom cogumelo *m* 49
music música *f* 83, 128
musical comédia musical *f* 86
mussel mexilhão *m* 44
must, to ter de 23, 31; dever 37, 61
mustard mostarda *f* 36, 51, 64
mutton carneiro *m* 46
my meu, minha 161

N

nail *(human)* unha *f* 110
nail brush escova de unhas *f* 110
nail clippers corta-unhas *m* 110
nail file lima [lixa] de unhas *f* 110
nail polish verniz [esmalte] de unhas *m* 110
nail polish remover dissolvente de verniz [esmalte] *m* 110
nail scissors tesoura de unhas *f* 110
name nome *m* 23, 25, 79, 85
napkin guardanapo *m* 36, 105, 107
nappy fralda *f* 111
narrow apertado(a) 118
nationality nacionalidade *f* 25, 92
natural natural 83
natural history ciências naturais *f/pl* 83
nausea náusea *f* 140
near perto (de) 15, 16
nearby aqui perto 77, 84
nearest mais próximo(a) 78, 98
neat *(drink)* puro(a) 56
neck pescoço *m* 138; *(nape)* nuca *f* 30
necklace colar *m* 121
need, to precisar 29, 118, 137
needle agulha *f* 27
negative negativo *m* 124, 125
nephew sobrinho *m* 93
nerve nervo *m* 138
nervous nervoso(a) 138
nervous system sistema nervoso *m* 138
never nunca 16
new novo(a) 15
newspaper jornal *m* 104, 105
newsstand quiosque *m* [banca *f*] de jornais 19, 67, 99, 104
New Year Ano Novo *m* 152
New York Nova Iorque *f* 130
New Zealand Nova Zelândia *f* 146
next próximo(a) 15, 65, 68, 73, 76, 149, 151; seguinte 151
next to ao lado de 16, 77
niece sobrinha *f* 93
night noite *f* 24, 151
nightclub boîte *f* 88
night cream creme de noite *m* 110
nightdress camisa de dormir [camisola] *f* 116
nine nove 147
nineteen dezanove 147
ninety noventa 148
ninth nono(a) 149
no não 11
noisy barulhento(a) 25
nonalcoholic não alcoólico(a) 59
none nenhum(a) 16
nonsmoker não-fumador *m* 36, 70
noon meio-dia *m* 31, 153
normal normal 30
north norte *m* 77
North America América do Norte *f* 146
nose nariz *m* 138
nosebleed hemorragia nasal *f* 141
nose drops gotas para o nariz *f/pl* 109
not não 16, 163
note *(banknote)* nota *f* 130
notebook bloco de apontamentos *m* 105
note paper papel de carta *m* 105
nothing nada 16, 17
notice *(sign)* letreiro *m* 155
notify, to avisar 144
November Novembro *m* 150
now agora 16
number número *m* 25, 26, 65, 135, 136, 147
nurse enfermeira *f* 144
nutmeg noz-moscada *f* 51

O

occupied ocupado(a) 14, 155
o'clock hora(s) 153
October Outubro *m* 150
octopus polvo *m* 44
offer, to oferecer 95
office secção *f* 67, 156; estação *f* 99, 132; agência *f* 129
oil óleo *m* 75, 111
oily *(greasy)* oleoso(a) 111

old velho(a), idoso(a) 15
old town cidade velha *f* 81
olive azeitona *f* 41
olive oil azeite *m* 36, 50
omelet omelete *f* 42
on sobre 16
on and off intermitente 140
once uma vez 149
one um, uma 147
one-way *(ticket)* ida 65, 69; *(street)* de sentido único 77
onion cebola *f* 49
only só 16, 24, 80
onyx ónix *m* 122
open aberto(a) 15, 82, 155
open, to abrir 12, 18, 108, 130, 132, 142
open-air ao ar livre 91
opening hours horas de abertura *f/pl* 82
opera ópera *f* 88
opera house teatro da ópera *m* 81, 88
operation operação *f* 144
operator telefonista *m/f* 134
operetta opereta *f* 88
opposite en frente (de) 77
optician oculista *m/f* 99, 123
or ou 16
orange cor-de-laranja 113
orange laranja *f* 52, 64
orange juice sumo [suco] de laranja *m* 38, 59
orangeade laranjada *f* 59
orchestra orquestra *f* 88; *(seats)* plateia *f* 87
order *(goods, meal)* encomenda *f* 40, 102
order, to *(goods, meal)* encomendar 61, 102, 103
oregano orégão *m* 51
ornithology ornitologia *f* 83
other outro(a) 58
our nosso(a) 161
out of order avariado(a) 155
out of stock esgotado(a) 103
outlet *(electric)* tomada *f* 27
outside (lá) fora 16, 36
oval oval 101
overdone passado(a) demais 61
overheat, to *(engine)* aquecer demais 78
overnight *(stay)* por uma noite 24
owe, to dever 144
oyster ostra *f* 41, 44

P

pacifier chupeta *f* 111
packet pacote *m* 120; *(cigarettes)* maço *m* 126
page *(hotel)* paquete, groom [boy de hotel] *m* 26
pail balde *m* 128
pain dor *f* 140, 141, 144
painkiller analgésico *m* 140
paint, to pintar 83
paintbox caixa de tintas *f* 105
painter pintor *m* 83
painting pintura *f* 83
pair par *m* 116, 118, 149
pajamas pijama *m* 117
palace palácio *m* 81
palpitation palpitação *f* 141
pancake crepe *m* [panqueca *f*] 63
panties calças [calcinhas] *f/pl* 116
pants *(trousers)* calças compridas *f/pl* 116
panty girdle cinta-calça *f* 116
panty hose collant *m* 116
paper papel *m* 105
paperback livro de bolso *m* 105
paperclip clipe *m* 105
paper napkin guardanapo de papel *m* 105
paraffin *(fuel)* petróleo *m* 107
parcel encomenda *f* [pacote *m*] 132
pardon? como disse? 12
parents pais *m/pl* 93
park parque *m* 81
park, to estacionar 26, 77
parking estacionamento *m* 77, 79
parking meter parcómetro *m* 77
parliament assembleia nacional *f* 81
parsley salsa *f* 51
part parte *f* 138
partridge perdiz *f* 48
party *(social gathering)* festa *f* 94
passport passaporte *m* 17, 18, 25, 26, 156
passport photo fotografia de passaporte *f* 124
pass through, to estar de passagem 17
paste *(glue)* cola *f* 105
pastry bolo *m* 64
pastry shop pastelaria *f* 99
patch, to *(clothes)* remendar 29
path caminho *m* 85
patient paciente *m/f* 144
pattern padrão *m* 112
pay, to pagar 31, 62, 68, 102

payment pagamento *m* 102, 131
pea ervilha *f* 49
peach pêssego *m* 54
peak pico *m*, cume *m* 85
peanut amendoim *m* 55
pear pêra *f* 52
pearl pérola *f* 122
pedestrian peão [pedestre] *m* 79
pen caneta *f* 105
pencil lápis *m* 105
pencil sharpener apara-lápis [apontador] *m* 105
pendant pingente *m* 121
penicilline penicilina *f* 143
penknife canivete *m* 107
pensioner reformado(a) [aposentado(a)] *m/f* 82
people pessoas *f/pl* 93
pepper pimenta *f* 36, 51, 64
per cent por cento 149
percentage percentagem *f* 131
per day por dia 20, 32, 90
perform, to *(theatre)* representar 86
perfume perfume *m* 110
perfume shop perfumaria *f* 108
perhaps talvez 16
per hour à hora 77
period *(monthly)* menstruação *f* 141
period pains dores menstruais *f/pl* 141
permanent wave permanente *f* 30
permit licença *f* 90
per night por noite 24
person pessoa *f* 32
personal pessoal 17
personal/person-to-person call comunicação com pré-aviso *f* 135
per week por semana 20, 24
petrol gasolina *f* 75, 78
pewter estanho *m* 122
pheasant faisão *m* 48
photo fotografia *f* 124
photocopy fotocópia *f* 131
photograph, to tirar fotografias 82
photographer fotógrafo *m/f* 99
photography fotografia *f* 124
phrase expressão *f* 13
pick up, to *(person)* buscar 80, 96
picnic piquenique *m* 63
picnic basket cesto de piquenique *m* 107
picture quadro *m* 83; *(photo)* fotografia *f* 82
piece pedaço *m* 120
pigeon pombo *m* 48
pill comprimido *m* 143; *(contraceptive)* pílula *f* 141
pillow almofada *f* [travesseiro *m*] 27
pimiento piri-piri *m* 51
pin alfinete *m* 111, 121; *(hair)* gancho [grampo] *m* 111
pineapple ananás [abacaxi] *m* 52, 59
pink cor-de-rosa 113
pipe cachimbo *m* 126
pipe cleaner limpa-cachimbos *m* 126
pipe tobacco tabaco [fumo] para cachimbo *m* 126
pipe tool esgaravatador de cachimbos *m* 126
place lugar *m* 25, 76
place of birth lugar de nascimento *m* 25
plane avião *m* 65
planetarium planetário *m* 81
plaster *(cast)* gesso *m* 140
plastic plástico *m* 107
plastic bag saco de plástico *m* 107
plate prato *m* 36, 61, 107
platform *(station)* cais *m* [plataforma *f*] 67, 68, 69, 70
platinum platina *f* 122
play *(theatre)* peça *f* 86
play, to *(theatre)* desempenhar 86; *(music)* tocar 88; *(game)* jogar 89, 93
playground campo de jogos *m* 32
playing card carta de jogar *f* 105
please por favor, se faz favor 11
plimsolls ténis *m/pl* 118
plug *(electric)* ficha *f* 29, 119
plum ameixa *f* 52
pneumonia pneumonia *f* 142
poached escaldado(a) 45; *(eggs)* escalfado(a) 42
pocket bolso *m* 117
pocket calculator calculadora de bolso *f* 105
pocket watch relógio de bolso *m* 121
point, to *(show)* mostrar 13
poison veneno *m* 109, 155
poisoning intoxicação *f* 142
police polícia *f* 78, 156
police station posto da polícia *m* 99, 156
polish *(nails)* verniz [esmalte] *m* 110
pop music música pop *f* 128
poplin popelina *f* 114
porcelain porcelana *f* 127

pork porco *m* 46
port porto *m* 74; *(wine)* vinho do Porto *m* 58
portable portátil 119
porter carregador *m* 18, 71; *(hotel)* bagageiro *m* 26
portion bocado *m* 37, 53; dose *f* 61
Portugal Portugal *m* 146
Portuguese português(esa) 12, 13, 104, 114, 127
possible possível 137
post *(letters)* correio *m* 28, 133
post, to pôr no correio 28
postage franquia *f* 132
postage stamp selo *m* 28, 126, 132
postcard bilhete postal *m* 105, 126, 132
poste restante posta restante *f* 133
post office estação de correios *f* 99, 132
potato batata *f* 49, 50
pottery olaria *f* 83; loiça de barro *f* 127
poultry criação *f* 48
pound *(money)* libra *f* 18, 130
powder pó *m* 110
powder compact caixinha de pó de arroz *f* 121
prawn gamba *f* [camarão grande *m*] 44
preference preferência *f* 101
pregnant grávida 141
premium *(gasoline)* super *f* 75
prescribe, to receitar 143
prescription receita (médica) *f* 108, 143
press, to *(iron)* passar a ferro ao vapor 29
press stud botão de mola [de pressão] *m* 117
pressure pressão *f* 75
pretty bonito(a) 84
price preço *m* 24
priest padre *m* 84
print *(photo)* cópia *f* 125
private particular 23, 80; privado(a) 80, 91, 155
processing *(photo)* revelação *f* 124
profession profissão *f* 25
profit lucro *m* 131
programme programa *m* 87
prohibit, to proibir 79
pronunciation pronúncia *f* 6, 10, 95
propelling pencil lapiseira *f* 105
Protestant protestante 84
provide, to arranjar [arrumar] 131
prune ameixa seca *f* 52
public holiday feriado *m* 152
pull, to puxar 155
pullover camisola de malha *f* [pulôver *m*] 116
pumpkin abóbora *f* 49
puncture furo *m* 75
purchase compra *f* 131
pure puro(a) 113
purple roxo(a) 113
push, to empurrar 155
put, to pôr 24
pyjamas pijama *m* 116

Q

quality qualidade *f* 103, 113
quantity quantidade *f* 15, 103
quarter quarto *m* 149; *(part of town)* bairro *m* 81
quarter of an hour quarto de hora *m* 153
quartz quartzo *m* 122
question pergunta *f* 12
quick rápido(a) 15
quickly depressa 137, 156
quiet tranquilo(a) 23; sossegado(a) 25

R

rabbi rabino *m* 84
rabbit coelho *m* 48
race course/track hipódromo *m* 90
racket *(sport)* raquete *f* 90
radiator radiador *m* 78
radio *(set)* rádio *m* 23, 28, 119
radish rabanete *m* 49
railroad crossing passagem de nível *f* 79
railway caminho de ferro *m* [estrada de ferro *f*] 66, 154
railway station estação (dos caminhos de ferro) [estação (ferroviária)] *f* 21, 66, 67, 70
rain chuva *f* 94
rain, to chover 94
raincoat capa da chuva *f* 117
rain forest selva *f* 85
raisin passa (de uva) *f* 52
rangefinder telémetro *m* 125
rare *(meat)* mal passado(a) 47, 61
rash erupção *f* 139
raspberry framboesa *f* 52
rate tarifa *f* 20; *(inflation)* índice *m* 131

razor gilete *f* [barbeador *m*] 110
razor blade lâmina de barbear *f* 111
read, to ler 40
reading lamp candeeiro [abajur] *m* 27
ready pronto(a) 29, 118, 123, 125, 145
rear atrás 75
receipt recibo *m* 103, 144
reception recepção *f* 23
receptionist recepcionista *m/f* 26
recommend, to recomendar 22, 35, 36, 80, 86, 88, 137, 145
record *(disc)* disco *m* 127, 128
record player gira-discos [toca-discos] *m* 119
rectangular rectangular 101
red vermelho(a) 113; *(wine)* tinto 59
reduction desconto *m* 24, 82
refill carga *f* 105
refund reembolso *m* 103
regards cumprimentos *m/pl* 152
region região *f* 92
register, to *(luggage)* despachar 71
registered mail registado(a) 133
registration registo *m* 25
registration form ficha *f* 25, 26
regular *(petrol)* normal *f* 75
religion religião *f* 83
religious service serviço religioso *m*, culto *m* 84
rent, to alugar 20, 90, 91, 155
rental aluguer *m* 20
repair conserto *m* 25
repair, to consertar 29, 118, 119, 121, 123, 125, 145
repeat, to repetir 13
report, to *(a theft)* dar parte de 156
reservation reserva *f* 19, 23; *(seat)* marcação de lugares *f* 65, 69
reservations office marcação de lugares 19, 67
reserve, to reservar 19, 23, 35, 87; *(seat)* marcar 69
restaurant restaurante *m* 19, 32, 34, 35, 67
return *(ticket)* ida e volta 65, 69
return, to *(give back)* devolver 103
reverse the charges, to fazer uma comunicação pagável no destino 135
rheumatism reumatismo *m* 141
rib costela *f* 138
ribbon fita *f* 105
rice arroz *m* 50
right direita 21, 63, 69, 77, 79; *(correct)* certo(a) 15
ring *(on finger)* anel *m* 122
ring, to tocar 155; telefonar 134
river rio *m* 85
road estrada *f* 76, 77, 85
road assistance assistência na estrada *f* 78
road map mapa das estradas *m* 105
road sign sinal de trânsito *m* 79
roasted assado(a) 47
roll *(bread)* papo-seco [pãozinho] *m* 38, 64
roller skate patim de rodas *m* 128
roll film rolo (de fotografias) *m* 124
roll-neck de gola alta 116
room quarto *m* 19, 23, 24, 25, 28; *(space)* lugar *m* 32
room number número do quarto *m* 26
room service serviço de quartos *m* 23
rope corda *f* 107
rosary rosário *m* 122
rosé rosé 57, 58
rosemary rosmaninho *m* 51
round redondo(a) 101
round *(golf)* jogo *m* 90
round-neck de decote redondo 116
roundtrip *(ticket)* ida e volta 65, 69
route itinerário *m* 85
rowing boat barco a remos *m* 91
rubber borracha *f* 105, 118
ruby rubi *m* 122
rucksack mochila *f* 107
rug tapete *m* 127
ruin ruína *f* 81
ruler *(for measuring)* régua *f* 105
rum rum *m* 58
running water água corrente *f* 23

S

safe *(not dangerous)* sem perigo 91
safe cofre *m* 26
safety pin alfinete-de-ama *m* 111
saffron açafrão *m* 50
sailing boat barco à vela *m* 91
salad salada *f* 42
sale venda *f* 131; *(bargains)* saldos *m/pl* 100, 155
sales tax IVA *m* 24, 102, 154
salmon salmão *m* 44
salt sal *m* 37, 51, 64
salty salgado(a) 61
same mesmo(a) 118

sand areia *f* 91
sandal sandália *f* 118
sandwich sanduíche *f* [*m*] 63
sanitary towel/napkin penso higiénico [toalha higiénica *f*] 109
sapphire safira *f* 122
sardine sardinha *f* 41, 44
satin cetim *m* 114
Saturday sábado *m* 151
saucepan tacho *m* 107
saucer pires *m* 107
sausage salsicha *f* 46, 64
say, to dizer 163
scarf lenço de pescoço *m* 117
scarlet escarlate 113
scissors tesoura *f* 110
scooter scooter *f* 74
Scotland Escócia *f* 146
scrambled egg ovo mexido *m* 38, 42
sculptor escultor *m* 83
sculpture escultura *f* 83
sea mar *m* 23, 85, 91
sea bass robalo *m* 44
seafood mariscos *m/pl* 44
season época *f* 40, 150; estação do ano *f* 150
seasoning condimentos *m/pl* 51
seat lugar *m* 69, 70, 87
seat belt cinto de segurança *m* 75
second segundo(a) 149
second segundo *m* 153
second class segunda classe *f* 69
second hand ponteiro de segundos *m* 122
second-hand em segunda mão 104
second-hand shop loja de velharias *f* 99
secretary secretário(a) *m/f* 27
section sector *m* 141
see, to ver 89, 90
sell, to vender 100
send, to mandar 78, 102, 133; enviar 103, 133
sentence frase *f* 13
separately separadamente 62
September Setembro *m* 150
service serviço *m* 24, 62, 98, 100; *(religion)* culto *m* 84
serviette guardanapo *m* 36
set *(hair)* mise *f* 30
set menu refeição a preço fixo *f* 36
setting lotion fixador *m* 30, 111
seven sete 147
seventeen dezassete 147
seventh sétimo(a) 149
seventy setenta 148
sew, to *(button)* pregar 29
shade *(colour)* tom *m* 112
shampoo shampoo [xampu] *m* 30, 111
shape forma *f* 103
share *(finance)* acção *f* 131
sharp *(pain)* agudo(a) 140
shave, to fazer a barba 31
shaver máquina de barbear *f* [barbeador eléctrico *m*] 27, 119
shaving cream creme da barba *m* 111
she ela 161
shelf prateleira *f* 120
shellfish crustáceos *m/pl* 40
sherry Xerez *m* 58
ship navio *m* 74
shirt camisa *f* 117
shivers calafrios *m/pl* 140
shoe sapato *m* 118
shoelace atacador [cordão] de sapatos *m* 118
shoemaker's sapateiro *m* 99
shoe polish graxa *f* 118
shoe shop sapataria *f* 99
shop loja *f* 98
shopping compras *f/pl* 97
shopping area zona comercial *f* 82, 100
shopping centre centro comercial *m* 99
shop window vitrine *f* 100, 112
short curto(a) 15, 30, 115, 116
shorts calções *m/pl* 117
short-sighted míope 123
shoulder ombro *m* 138
shovel pá *f* 128
show espectáculo *m* 86, 87
show, to mostrar 13, 14, 76, 100, 101, 103, 119, 124
shower duche *m* 23, 32
shrimp camarão *m* 41, 44
shrink, to encolher 113
shut fechado(a) 15
shutter *(window)* janela de madeira *f* 29; *(camera)* obturador *m* 125
sick *(ill)* doente 140, 156
sickness *(illness)* doença *f* 140
side lado *m* 30
sideboards/burns suíças [costeletas] *f/pl* 31
sightseeing visita turística *f* 80
sightseeing tour circuito turístico *m* 80

sign *(notice)* letreiro *m* 155; *(road)* sinal *m* 79
sign, to assinar 26, 130
signature assinatura *f* 25
signet ring anel de sinete *m* 122
silence silêncio *m* 79
silk seda *f* 114
silver *(colour)* prateado(a) 113
silver prata *f* 121, 122
silver-plated banhado(a) a prata 122
silverware pratas *f/pl* 122
simple simples 124
since desde 15, 150
sing, to cantar 88
single *(not married)* solteiro(a) 93; *(ticket)* ida 65, 69
single room quarto individual *m* 19, 23
sister irmã *f* 93
sit down, to sentar-se 95
six seis 147
sixteen dezasseis 147
sixth sexto(a) 149
sixty sessenta 147
size tamanho *m* 124; *(clothes)* medida *f* 114, 115; *(shoes)* número *m* 118
ski esqui *m* 91
skin pele *f* 138
skin-diving pesca submarina *f* 91
skirt saia *f* 117
sky céu *m* 94
sleep, to dormir 144
sleeping bag saco-cama *m* 107
sleeping car carruagem-camas *f* [vagão-leitos *m*] 69, 70
sleeping pill sonífero *m* 143
sleeve manga *f* 116
slice *(ham)* fatia *f* 120
slide *(photo)* slide *m* 124
slip saia de baixo *f* 117
slipper chinelo *m* 118
slow lento(a) 15
slow down, to afrouxar 79
slowly devagar 13, 21, 135
small pequeno(a) 15, 20, 25, 101, 118
smoke, to fumar 95
smoked fumado(a) [defumado(a)] 45
smoker fumador *m* 70
snack refeição leve *f* 63
snack bar snack-bar *m* [lanchonete *f*] 33, 67
snail caracol *m* 41
snap fastener botão de mola [de pressão] *m* 117
sneakers ténis *m/pl* 118
snuff rapé *m* 126
soap sabonete *m* 27, 111
soccer futebol *m* 89, 90
sock peúga [meia curta] *f* 117
socket *(outlet)* tomada *f* 27
soft drink refrigerante *m* 40, 64
sold out *(theatre)* lotação esgotada 87, 155
sole sola *f* 118; *(fish)* linguado *m* 44
soloist solista *m/f* 68
someone alguém 95
something qualquer coisa 29, 108, 112, 113, 139
somewhere em qualquer lado 87
son filho *m* 93
song canção *f* 128
soon em breve 16
sore throat dor de garganta *f* 141
sorry desculpe, perdão 12; *(to be)* lamentar 87
sort *(kind)* género *m* 86, 120
soup sopa *f* 43
south sul *m* 77
South Africa África do Sul *f* 146
South America América do Sul *f* 146
souvenir lembrança *f* 127
souvenir shop loja de lembranças *f* 99
Soviet Union União Soviética *f* 146
spade pá *f* 128
Spain Espanha *f* 146
spare tyre pneu sobresselente *m* 75
sparking plug vela *f* 76
sparkling *(wine)* espumante 57, 58
spark plug vela *f* 76
speak, to falar 13, 135, 163
speaker *(loudspeaker)* alto-falante *m* 119
special especial 20, 37
special delivery por expresso 133
specialist especialista *m/f* 142
speciality especialidade *f* 40
specimen amostra *f* 142
spectacle case caixa de óculos *f* 123
spell, to soletrar 13
spend, to gastar 101
spinach espinafre *m* 49
spine coluna vertebral *f* 138
spiny lobster lagosta *f* 44
sponge esponja *f* 111
spoon colher *f* 36, 61, 107
sport desporto [esporte] *m* 89

DICTIONARY

Dicionário

sporting goods shop loja de artigos desportivos [esportivos] *f* 99
sprain, to torcer 140
spring *(season)* Primavera *f* 150; *(water)* nascente *f* 85
square quadrado(a) 101
square praça *f* 82; largo *m* 154
stadium estádio *m* 82
staff pessoal *m* 26
stain nódoa [mancha] *f* 29
stainless steel aço inoxidável *m* 107, 122
stalls *(theatre)* plateia *f* 87
stamp *(postage)* selo *m* 28, 126, 132
staple agrafo [grampo] *m* 105
star estrela *f* 94
start, to começar 80, 87; *(car)* pegar 78
starter *(appetizer)* acepipe [salgadinho] *m* 41
station *(railway)* estação *f* 21, 67, 70, 73
stationer's papelaria *f* 99, 104
statue estátua *f* 82
stay estadia *f* 31
stay, to ficar 17, 24, 26; *(reside)* estar hospedado(a) 93
steak bife [filé] *m*
steal, to roubar 156
steamed cozido(a) ao vapor 45
steamer vapor *m* 74
steering wheel volante *m* 78
stewed guisado(a) 47
stiff neck torcicolo *m* 141
still *(mineral water)* sem gás 59
sting picada *f* 139
sting, to picar 139
stitch, to coser [costurar] 29, 118
stock exchange bolsa *f* 82
stocking meia *f* 117
stomach estômago *m* 138
stomach ache dor de estômago *f* 141
stools fezes *f/pl* 142
stop *(bus)* paragem [parada] *f* 72, 73
stop! alto! 156
stop, to parar 21, 68, 72
stop thief! agarra que é ladrão! 156
store *(shop)* loja *f* 98
straight ahead sempre em frente 21, 77
strange estranho(a) 84
strawberry morango *m* 52
street rua *f* 25
streetcar eléctrico [bonde] *m* 72
street map planta da cidade *f* 19
string cordel [barbante] *m* 105
strong forte 126, 143
student estudante *m/f* 82, 93
study, to estudar 93
stuffed recheado(a) 41, 42, 47
sturdy resistente 101
subway *(railway)* metro(politano) *m* 73
suede camurça *f* 114, 118
sugar açúcar *m* 37, 63, 64
suit *(man)* fato [terno] *m* 117; *(woman)* fato [terno] de saia e casaco *m* 117
suitcase mala *f* 18
summer Verão *m* 150
sun sol *m* 94
sunburn queimadura do sol *f* 108
Sunday domingo *m* 151
sunglasses óculos de sol *m/pl* 123
sunshade *(beach)* chapéu de sol *m* 91
sunstroke insolação *f* 141
sun-tan cream creme para bronzear *m* 111
sun-tan oil óleo para bronzear *m* 111
super *(petrol)* super *f* 75
superb estupendo(a) 84
supermarket supermercado *m* 99
suppository supositório *m* 109
surcharge suplemento *m* 68, 69
surfboard prancha de surf *f* 91
surgery *(consulting room)* consultório *m* 137
surname apelido [sobrenome] *m* 25
suspenders *(Am.)* suspensórios *m/pl* 117
swallow, to engolir 143
sweatshirt camisola *f* [suéter *m*] de algodão 117
sweet doce 59, 61
sweet *(candy)* rebuçado *m* [bala *f*] 126
sweet corn milho *m* 49
sweetener edulcorante *m* 37
swell, to inchar 139
swelling inchaço *m* 139
swim, to nadar, tomar banho 91
swimming natação *f* 90
swimming pool piscina *f* 32, 90
swimming trunks fato [maiô] de banho *m* 117
swimsuit fato [maiô] de banho *m* 117

switch interruptor *m* 29
switchboard operator telefonista *m/f* 26
Switzerland Suíça *f* 146
swollen inchado(a) 139
swordfish espadarte *m* 44
synagogue sinagoga *f* 84
synthetic sintético(a) 113
system sistema *m* 138

T

table mesa *f* 35, 36, 107; *(list)* tábua *f* 157
tablet comprimido *m* 109
take, to levar 18, 21, 63, 73
talcum powder pó de talco *m* 111
tampon tampão higiénico *m* 109
tangerine tangerina *f* 52
tap *(water)* torneira *f* 28
tape recorder gravador *m* 119
tart tarte *f* 54
tax taxa *f* 32; IVA *m* 24, 102
taxi táxi *m* 19, 21, 31
tea chá *m* 38, 60, 64
team equipa *f* 89
tear, to rasgar 140
tearoom salão de chá *m* 34
teaspoon colher de chá *f* 107, 143
telegram telegrama *m* 133
telegraph office estação telegráfica *f* 99
telephone telefone *m* 28, 79, 134
telephone, to telefonar 134
telephone booth cabine telefónica *f* 134
telephone call comunicação *f* 135; chamada *f* 136
telephone directory lista telefónica *f* 134
telephone number número de telefone *m* 134, 135
telephoto lens teleobjectiva *f* 125
television *(set)* televisão *f* 23, 28, 119
telex telex *m* 133
telex, to mandar um telex 130
tell, to dizer 13, 76, 136; indicar 76
temperature temperatura *f* 91, 142; *(fever)* febre *f* 140
temporary provisório(a) 145
ten dez 147
tendon tendão *m* 138
tennis ténis *m* 90
tennis court campo de ténis *m* 90
tennis racket raquete de ténis *f* 90
tent tenda *f* 32, 107
tenth décimo(a) 149
tent peg estaca de tenda *f* 107
tent pole mastro de tenda *m* 107
term *(word)* termo *m* 131
terminal *(transport)* terminal *m* 72
terrace esplanada *f* 36
terrifying pavoroso(a) 84
terrycloth pano turco [tecido felpudo] *m* 114
tetanus tétano *m* 140
than (do) que 16
thank you obrigado(a) 11
that esse(a), aquele(a) 160; isso, aquilo 11, 100
the o, a 159
theatre teatro *m* 82, 86
theft roubo *m* 156
their seu, sua 161
then então 16
there aí 14, 15
thermometer termómetro *m* 109, 144
these estes(as) 160
they eles(as) 161
thief ladrão *m* 156
thigh coxa *f* 138
thin fino(a) 113
think, to *(believe)* crer 31, 62
third terceiro(a) 149
third terço *m* 149
thirsty, to be ter sede 13, 35
thirteen treze 147
thirty trinta 147
this este(a) 160; isto 12, 100
those esses(as), aqueles(as) 160
thousand mil 148
thread linha *f* 27
three três 147
throat garganta *f* 138, 141
throat lozenge pastilha para a garganta *f* 109
through através (de) 16
through train comboio [trem] directo *m* 68, 69
thumb polegar *m* 138
thumbtack pionés *m* [tacha *f*] 105
thunder trovão *m* 94
thunderstorm trovoada *f* 94
Thursday quinta-feira *f* 151
thyme tomilho *m* 51
ticket bilhete *m* 65, 69, 72, 87, 89, 156
ticket office bilheteira [bilheteria] *f* 67

tide maré *f* 91
tie gravata *f* 117
tie clip mola de gravata *f* 122
tie pin alfinete de gravata *m* 122
tight *(clothes)* apertado(a) 115
tights collant *m* 117
time tempo *m* 80; *(clock)* hora *f* 80, 137, 153; *(occasion)* vez *f* 143
timetable horário *m* 68
tin *(can)* lata *f* 120
tinfoil papel de alumínio *m* 107
tin opener abre-latas [abridor de latas] *m* 107
tint produto colorante *m* 111
tinted de cor 123
tire pneu *m* 75, 76
tired cansado(a) 14
tissue *(handkerchief)* lenço de papel *m* 111
to a 16
toast torrada *f* 38, 63
tobacco tabaco [fumo] *m* 126
tobacconist's tabacaria *f* 99, 126
today hoje 29, 151
toe dedo do pé *m* 138
toilet casa de banho *f* [banheiro *m*] 32, 37, 67
toilet paper papel higiénico *m* 111
toiletry produtos de higiene e cosméticos *m/pl* 110
toilet water água-de-colónia *f* 111
token *(phone)* ficha *f* 134
toll portagem *f* [pedágio *m*] 75, 79
tomato tomate *m* 49
tomb túmulo *m* 82
tomorrow amanhã 29, 151
tongue língua *f* 46, 138
tonic water água tónica *f* 59
tonight hoje à noite 86, 87, 88, 95
tonsil amígdala *f* 138
too demasiado(a) 15; demais 24; *(also)* também 16
tooth dente *m* 145
toothache dor de dentes *f* 145
toothbrush escova de dentes *f* 111, 119
toothpaste pasta de dentes *f* 111
top cima *f* 30, 145
topaz topázio *m* 122
torch *(flashlight)* lanterna de bolso *f* 107
touch, to mexer 155
tough *(meat)* duro(a) 61
tour circuito *m* 80
tourist office turismo *m* 22, 80
tourist tax taxa de turismo *f* 32
towards para, cerca de 16
towel toalha *f* 27, 111
tower torre *f* 82
town cidade *f* 19, 21, 76, 105
town hall câmara municipal *f* 82
tow truck pronto-socorro *m* 78
toy brinquedo *m* 128
toy shop loja de brinquedos *f* 99
track *(station)* linha *f* 68, 69; *(race course)* hipódromo *m* 90
tracksuit fato de treino [training] *m* 117
traffic trânsito *m* 76
traffic light semáforo *m* 77, 79
trailer rulote *f* 32
train comboio [trem] *m* 66, 67, 68, 69, 70
tram eléctrico [bonde] *m* 72
tranquillizer calmante *m* 143
transfer *(bank)* transferência *f* 131
transformer transformador *m* 119
translate, to traduzir 13
transport transporte *m* 74
travel, to viajar 93
travel agency agência de viagens *f* 99
travel guide guia turístico *m* 105
traveller's cheque cheque de viagem *m* 18, 62, 102, 130
travel sickness enjoo (da viagem) *m* 108
treatment tratamento *m* 143
tree árvore *f* 85
tremendous tremendo(a) 84
trim, to *(beard)* aparar 31
trip viagem *f* 72, 93, 152
trolley carrinho *m* 18, 71
trousers calças compridas *f/pl* 117
trout truta *f* 45
truck camião [caminhão] *m* 79
try, to provar 58, 114
T-shirt camiseta *f* 117
tube tubo *m* 120
Tuesday terça-feira *f* 151
tumbler copo *m* 107
tuna atum *m* 44
tunny atum *m* 44
turkey peru *m* 48
turn, to *(change direction)* virar 21, 77
turnip nabo *m* 49
turquoise azul-turquesa 113
turquoise turquesa *f* 122
turtleneck de gola alta 116

DICTIONARY

tweezers pinça para depilar *f* 111
twelve doze 147
twenty vinte 147
twice duas vezes 149
twin beds duas camas *f/pl* 23
two dois, duas 147
typewriter máquina de escrever *f* 27, 105
typewriter ribbon fita para máquina de escrever *f* 105
typical típico(a) 127
typing paper papel para máquina de escrever *m* 105
tyre pneu *m* 75, 76

U

ugly feio(a) 15, 84
umbrella guarda-chuva *m* 117; *(beach)* chapéu de sol *m* 91
uncle tio *m* 93
unconscious sem sentidos 139
under debaixo (de) 16
underdone *(meat)* mal passado(a) 47, 61
underground *(railway)* metro(politano) *m* 73
underpants cuecas *f/pl* 117
undershirt camisola interior [camiseta] *f* 117
understand, to compreender [entender] 13
undress, to despir(-se) 142
United States Estados Unidos *m/pl* 146
university universidade *f* 82
unleaded sem chumbo 75
until até 16
up para cima 16
upper superior(a) 69, 7l
upset stomach indigestão *f* 108
upstairs em cima 16
urgent urgente 14, 145
urine urina *f* 142
use uso *m* 17, 109
use, to utilizar 134
useful útil 16
usual habitual 143

V

vacancy quarto vago *m* 23
vacant livre 14,155
vacation férias *f/pl* 151
vaccinate, to vacinar 140
vacuum flask termo *m* [garrafa térmica *f*] 107
vaginal vaginal 141
vaginal infection infecção vaginal *f* 141
valley vale *m* 85
value valor *m* 131
value-added tax IVA *m* 24, 102, 154
vanilla baunilha *f* 50
VAT *(sales tax)* IVA *m* 24, 102, 154
veal vitela *f* 46
vegetable legume *m* 49
vegetable store lugar de frutas e legumes *m* [quitanda *f*] 99
vegetarian vegetariano(a) 37
velvet veludo *m* 114
velveteen veludo de algodão *m* 114
venereal disease doença venérea *f* 142
venison veado *m* 48
vermouth vermute *m* 55,58
very muito 16
vest camisola interior [camiseta] *f* 117; *(Am.)* colete *m* 117
veterinarian veterinário(a) *m/f* 99
video cassette videocassete *f* 119, 124, 127
video recorder gravador vídeo *m* 119
view vista *f* 23, 25
village aldeia *f* 85; povoação *f* 76
vinegar vinagre *m* 37, 51
vineyard vinha *f* 85
visit, to visitar 84
visiting hours horas de visita *f/pl* 144
vitamin pills vitaminas *f/pl* 144
V-neck de decote em bico 116
volleyball voleibol *m* 90
voltage voltagem *f* 27, 119
vomit, to vomitar 140

W

waistcoat colete *m* 117
wait, to esperar 21, 108
waiter criado de mesa [garçom] *m* 26
waiting room sala de espera *f* 67
waitress criada de mesa [garçonete] *f* 26
wake, to acordar 27, 7l
Wales País de Gales *m* 146
walk, to andar a pé 74; ir a pé 85
wall muro *m* 85
wallet carteira *f* 156
walnut noz *f* 52

Dicionário

want, to *(wish)* querer, desejar 14
wash, to lavar 29, 113
wash basin lavatório *m* [pia *f*] 28
washing powder detergente para a roupa *m* 107
watch relógio *m* 121, 122
watchband correia de relógio *f* 122
watchmaker's relojoaria *f* 99, 121
watchstrap correia de relógio *f* 122
water água *f* 23, 28, 32, 38, 75, 91
waterfall cascada *f* 85
water flask cantil *m* 107
watermelon melancia *f* 52
waterproof à prova de água 122
water-ski esqui aquático *m* 91
wave onda *f* 91
way caminho *m* 76
we nós 161
weather tempo *m* 94
weather forecast previsões do tempo *f/pl* 94
wedding ring aliança *f* 122
Wednesday quarta-feira *f* 151
week semana *f* 17, 20, 24, 80, 151
weekday dia de semana *m* 151
weekend fim-de-semana *m* 20, 151
well *(healthy)* bem 11, 140
well-done *(meat)* bem passado(a) 47
west oeste *m* 77
what o quê 12; o que 12, 14; que 151, 153; qual 20, 21; como 12
wheel roda *f* 78
when quando 12
where onde 12
which qual 12
whisky uísque *m* 58
white branco(a) 58, 113
whiting pescada *f* 44
who quem 12
why porquê 12
wick torcida *f* 126
wickerware artigos de verga *m/pl* 127
wide largo(a) 118
wide-angle lens objectiva grande angular *f* 125
wife mulher *f* 93
wig peruca *f* 111
wind vento *m* 94
windmill moinho *m* 85
window janela *f* 28, 36, 69; *(shop)* vitrine *f* 100, 112
windscreen/shield pára-brisas *m* 76
windsurfer prancha à vela *f* 91
wine vinho *m* 56, 58, 61
wine list lista dos vinhos *f* 58
wine merchant's comerciante de vinhos *m* 99
winter Inverno *m* 150
wiper limpa-vidros *m* 76
with com 16
withdraw, to *(bank)* levantar 130
without sem 16
woman mulher *f* 141; senhora *f* 115
wonderful maravilhoso(a) 96
wood madeira *f* 127; *(forest)* mata *f* 85
wood alcohol álcool desnaturado *m* 107
woodwork artigos de madeira *m/pl* 127
wool lã *f* 113, 114
word palavra *f* 13, 16, 133
work, to *(function)* funcionar 28, 119
working day dia útil *m* 151
worse pior 15
worsted lã cardada *f* 114
wound ferida *f* 139
wrap, to embrulhar 103
wristwatch relógio de pulso *m* 122
write, to escrever 13, 101
writing pad bloco de papel *m* 105
writing paper papel de carta *m* 27
wrong errado(a) 15, 135

X

X-ray *(photo)* radiografia *f* 140

Y

year ano *m* 149
yellow amarelo(a) 113
yes sim 11
yesterday ontem 151
yet ainda 16
yoghurt iogurte *m* 64
you tu, você 161
young jovem 15
your teu, tua, seu, sua, vosso(a) 161
youth hostel pousada de juventude *f* 22, 32

Z

zero zero *m* 147
zip(per) fecho éclair *m* 117
zoo jardim zoológico m 82
zoology zoologia *f* 83

Índice português

VENEZUELA
GUYANA
FRENCH GUIANA
SURINAM
Bogotá
COLOMBIA
Quito
ECUADOR
Macapá
Manaus
Amazonas
Belém
Fortaleza
Pôrto Velho
Tapajós
BRAZIL
Recife
Lima
Salvador
PERU
BOLIVIA
Cuiabá
La Paz
Brasília
PACIFIC OCEAN
Belo Horizonte
Vitória
PARAGUAY
São Paulo
CHILE
Rio de Janeiro
Asunción
Pôrto Alegre
ARGENTINA
URUGUAY
Santiago
Montevideo
Buenos Aires
Negro
2000 km
1500 miles
SOUTH ATLANTIC OCEAN
Tierra del Fuego
Cabo de Hornos

La Coruña
Braga
Porto
Douro
Aveiro
Coimbra
Madrid
PORTUGAL
Tejo
SPAIN
Sintra
Lisboa
Estoril
Evora
Guadiana
Setúbal
Córdoba
Guadal quivir
Lagos
Faro
Sevilla
Málaga
300 km
Cádiz
200 miles
MEDITERRANEAN
ATLANTIC OCEAN
MOROCCO

RANCE	Brittany France (256 pages) French Riviera Loire Valley Normandy* Paris
ERMANY	Berlin Munich The Rhine Valley
USTRIA d WITZER- AND	Tyrol Vienna Switzerland (192 pages)
REECE, YPRUS & URKEY	Athens Corfu Crete Rhodes Greek Islands of the Aegean Peloponnese Salonica and Northern Greece Cyprus Istanbul/Aegean Coast
ALY and ALTA	Florence Italian Adriatic Italian Riviera Italy (256 pages)* Rome Sicily Venice Malta
ETHER- ANDS and CANDI- AVIA	Amsterdam Copenhagen Helsinki Oslo and Bergen Stockholm
ORTUGAL	Algarve Lisbon Madeira
PAIN	Barcelona and Costa Dorada Canary Islands Costa Blanca Costa Brava Costa del Sol and Andalusia Ibiza and Formentera Madrid Majorca and Minorca
EASTERN EUROPE	Budapest Dubrovnik and Southern Dalmatia Hungary (192 pages) Istria and Croatian Coast Moscow & Leningrad Split and Dalmatia
NORTH AMERICA	U.S.A. (256 pages) California Florida Hawaii New York Toronto Montreal
CARIBBEAN, LATIN AMERICA	Puerto Rico Virgin Islands Bahamas Bermuda French West Indies Jamaica Southern Caribbean Mexico City Rio de Janeiro
EUROPE	Business Travel Guide – Europe (368 pages) Pocket guide to Europe (480 pages) Cities of Europe (504 pages)
CRUISE GUIDES	Caribbean cruise guide (368 pages) Alaska cruise guide (168 pages) Handbook to Cruising (240 pages)

* n preparation

Most titles with British and U.S. destinations are available in French, German, Spanish and as many as 7 other languages.

DICTIONARIES

Bilingual with 12,500 concepts each way. Highly practical for travellers, with pronunciation shown plus menu reader, basic expressions and useful information. Over 330 pages.

Danish	Finnish	German	Norwegian	Spanish
Dutch	French	Italian	Portuguese	Swedish

Berlitz Books, a world of information in your pocket! At all leading bookshops and airport newsstands.

Finally... a fast, fun, and affordable way to learn a foreign language...

INTRODUCING THE BERLITZ EXPRESS PROGRAMS

Self-study programs for beginners

Available in:
- Spanish
- French
- German
- Italian